MW01087200

PROSPEROUS
PET BUSINESS

Interviews with the Experts:
Volume One

KRISTIN MORRISON

OTHER BOOKS BY KRISTIN MORRISON:

Six-Figure Pet Sitting:
Catapult Your Pet Sitting Business
to Unlimited Success

Six-Figure Pet Business:
Unleash the Potential in Your Dog Training,
Pet Grooming and Doggy Day Care Business

Prosperous Pet Business:
Interviews with the Experts: Volume Two

WHAT PET BUSINESS OWNERS HAVE TO SAY ABOUT

PROSPEROUS PET BUSINESS
INTERVIEWS WITH THE EXPERTS: VOLUME ONE:

"I ravenously began reading this book and tore through several chapters at once! Much of the buzz from owners just like us all over the country is that they are talking about and implementing every single one of the subjects covered right here in this book. A must read if you are thinking about getting into the pet sitting or dog walking industry or are already immersed in the trenches of it. I could not get enough of **Prosperous Pet Business** *and just wanted to keep reading more!"*

Heather Branch
Best Friends Forever Pet Services, LLC ™
Business of the Year winner for the National Association
of Professional Pet Sitters

"This book is highly recommended for those considering starting a pet business or those who have been in the business for a while. Each interview that Kristin conducts is packed with takeaways, several that are great reminders and refreshers but several that are new and insightful ways to enrich and strengthen a business. This is a wonderful reference that contains best practices from some of the best leaders in the industry."

Linda Crist
Owner, Odds & Ends
Cartersville, Georgia

"I find the written word to be so powerful. Having something in written form enables me to make a concrete connection: to revisit the speakers' words of wisdom and to read their thoughts over and over to capture all their insight. Your conferences are brilliant and putting the content into written form enhances its comprehension. This book rocks!"

Joan E. Caradonna
Fuzzy Friends Pet Care
Swampscott, Massachusetts

"Thank you Kristin for putting your pet conference recording into print! I found new and enlightening points in print that I had missed when listening to all the fabulous interviews originally. You have really covered a great many topics with people who have been there and done that. I've never believed in reinventing the wheel. Your book will help me to be sure I follow some sound and savvy advice from the experts!"

Teri Thomas, CPDT-KA
Angels in the Making, LLC
Grand Junction, Colorado

"This book is practical, enriching and encouraging!
So much of what I needed to read in order to move my business forward. I will refer to Kristin's conversations in this book for years to come."

Tomika Bruen
Out For a Walk Pet Sitting & Dog Walking
Los Angeles, California

"This is the book I wish I had access to in the beginning. Highly recommended!! It's not just a great reference for operating a successful pet business while avoiding all the pitfalls, but also an outstanding resource on living an all-around successful and blessed life while running any growing business. So many of us forget to take care of ourselves on this journey, and Kristin is an extremely talented motivator in this regard, bringing us back to what really matters. Remember why you founded your pet business to begin with? It's SO easy to lose sight of that! The business information in here definitely packs a punch, and learning why you cannot serve others in your greatest capacity until you've journeyed down the often daunting path of caring for yourself first... now that's priceless!! Thanks, Kristin!"

Sandra Ward
The Strut'N Mutt
Haverhill, Massachusetts

"This book was just what I needed! Although I had tuned into the pet business conference, having the written word to read (and re-read in some instances), I was really able to learn the lesson. It was an easy read, and I found myself laughing at times, pondering ideas at others and getting emotionally connected. Thanks for bringing the Prosperous Pet Business Online Conference to life with the written word!"

Eleanor McCoy
East Paws Pet Services
Fort Lauderdale, Florida

"While reading **Prosperous Pet Business**, I felt like I was attending a pet business conference in the comfort of my home. I found the experts to be very interesting and their information very valuable. If you own a pet business, I highly recommend this book."

Lorie Bryngelson
Peace of Mind Professional Pet Care
Nederland, Colorado

"**Prosperous Pet Business: Interviews with the Experts** *is a MUST READ for ALL pet professionals. Kristin has interviewed over 20 experts in their own fields, encompassing the financial, emotional, and physical well-being of the human – as well as communication with and motivation of the canine. This book is a wonderful reference to their advice. I LOVE this holistic approach of dealing with all aspects of ourselves and our business.*"

Robin Donahey
Paws 4 Pet Sitting
Davenport, Florida

"*Kristin Morrison truly speaks from the heart with this amazing book. Her lineup of interviews is top notch. This book addresses the entire picture from dog training, finances, having fun, diet and health, social media, public relations and more. If you have a pet business, this book will rock your world.*"

June Collins
President Max-well's Pet Services, LLC
Jupiter, Florida

"**Prosperous Pet Business: Interviews with the Experts** *is truly a wealth of information. Kristin interviewed so many wonderful people. They provided so much useful advice for pet business owners. The book really helped me look at my business with new eyes. After nine years in business, it is great to see new areas in which I can improve that had not even occurred to me. It has given me a new spark to better my business instead of just keeping the status quo.*"

Nicole Halbur
TLC Pet Sitting, LLC
Lake Havasu City, Arizona

This book, like everything else Kristin does, is an invaluable read. Kristin presents information in a way that keeps me enthralled throughout the entire process. I read her book **Six-Figure Pet Sitting** *when I started my business, have attended classes, listened to podcasts, and watched the conference series she put together. Even though I did all of those things, I still very much benefitted from this book. It presents the information in a new medium that really hammers home the thoughts and ideas that make one successful. Don't think twice – just read it. You won't regret it.*

Melissa Hammond
Backyards to Barnyards Pet Care Services
Sterling, Connecticut

No part of this book may be reproduced in any form or by any electronic or mechanical means including information storage and retrieval systems, or be sold or resold, without permission in writing from the author. The only exception is that a reviewer may quote short excerpts in a review.

Limit of Liability / Disclaimer of Warranty: While the publisher and author have used their best efforts in preparing this book, they make no representations or warranties, express or implied, with respect to the accuracy or completeness of the contents of this book or otherwise, and specifically disclaim any implied warranties, including any implied warranties of merchantability or fitness for a particular purpose. There are no warranties which extend beyond the descriptions contained in this paragraph. No warranties may be created or extended by sales representatives or written sales materials. The information provided herein and the opinions stated herein are not guaranteed or warranted to produce any particular results, and the advice and strategies contained herein are not suitable for every individual and may not be suitable for your situation. You should consult with a professional where appropriate. By providing information or links to other companies or websites, the publisher and the author do not guarantee, approve, or endorse the information or products available at any linked websites or mentioned companies or persons. This publication is designed to provide information with regard to the subject matter covered. It is sold or provided with the understanding that neither the publisher nor the author is engaged in rendering legal, accounting or other professional service. If legal advice or other expert assistance is required, the services of a competent professional should be sought. Neither the publisher nor the author shall be liable for any loss or loss of profit or any other commercial damages, including but not limited to special, incidental, consequential, or other damages.

Prosperous Pet Business: Interviews with the Experts: Volume One

Copyright © 2016 by Kristin Morrison

All rights reserved.

ISBN-13: 978-0-692-75569-3

ISBN-10: 0-692-75569-1

This book is dedicated to all the speakers interviewed for the Prosperous Pet Business Online Conference.

Thank you for saying "Yes!" and for generously sharing your time, wisdom, and energy to help the thousands of pet business owners who attended the conference.

A NOTE ABOUT THIS BOOK BEFORE YOU BEGIN:

I wanted this book to be as easily readable as possible,
so my name and the interviewee name are listed only beside
the initial paragraph for each of us.
You'll notice that my words are in ***bold italics***
and the person I'm speaking with is in regular font, with the
exception of Chapter Ten when I'm being interviewed.

~ Kristin Morrison

Table of Contents

Chapter One: Patti Moran
How to Create a Profitable and Empowered Pet Business . . . 25

Chapter Two: Arden Moore
Purr-fecting the Art of Work Reinvention 41

Chapter Three: Veronica Boutelle
*Simple Ways Pet Business Owners Can Save Time (Ahhh!)
and Make More Money* 59

Chapter Four: Thom Somes
*How to Recover from (and Move Beyond!) Pet Business
Burnout.* 75

Chapter Five: Alicia Dattner
*Using Improv and Play to Lighten the (BLEEP!) Up in
Your Business and Your Life* 89

Chapter Six: Trish King
*How Pet Professionals Can Skillfully Handle Dogs (and the
Dogs' Human Parents!)* 103

Chapter Seven: Jerrod Sessler
The Art of Making More Money in Your Pet Business 119

Chapter Eight: Chess Edwards
*Using Healthy Living and Eating to Create Energy
for Optimal Living (and Running Your Business)* 135

Chapter Nine: Therese Kopiwoda & Danielle Lambert
*How to Develop a Powerful Online Presence
with Social Media* 153

Chapter Ten: Kristin Morrison
*How to Create More Freedom in Your Pet Business
and Your Life* 167

Chapter Eleven: Paul Mann
*All About Franchising: How to Turn Your Pet Business into
a Franchise and What's Involved in Buying a Franchise* . . . 185

Chapter Twelve: Caroline Golon
*Branding and PR: How to Brand Your Pet Business to Gain
Clients and Get on TV* 203

Chapter Thirteen: Dr. Ian Dunbar
*How to Train and Motivate Dogs and Humans (Including
Your Clients and Staff!)* 219

Chapter Fourteen: Susan Briggs
*How to Keep Track of Your Numbers in Your Pet Business
(Yes, It Can Be Fun, Easy, and Illuminating!)* 237

Chapter Fifteen: Dee Hoult
Navigating Pet Business Challenges with Ease and Grace . 257

Chapter Sixteen: Rita Reimers & Tiffany Reynolds
*Running Your Pet Business Remotely: How to Set Up Your
Pet Business in Multiple Locations* 275

Chapter Seventeen: Lisa Maria
*Using Yoga and Mindfulness to Relieve Stress in
Your Pet Business.* 293

Chapter Eighteen: Lisa Taron

How to Make Your Business Blog Profitable,

Easy, and Fun to Write. 305

Chapter Nineteen: Andrea Arden

Secrets for Pet Business Success. 323

Programs to Help You Achieve Success 339

Prosperous Pet Business Recommended Reading 345

About the Author 350

Prologue

A few years ago, I had an idea.

The idea was this: I wanted to create a pet business conference that pet business owners from around the world could attend. And not just *attend* the conference but attend with ease… without leaving their homes or offices. I wanted them to be able to attend in their pajamas if they wanted or while they comfortably ate their lunch or sipped tea. If they were away from their homes or offices, I wanted them to be able to easily listen and learn on their smartphones or tablets while driving to a dog training client or while out walking dogs or feeding a cat.

Thanks to the amazing pet business owners, dog trainers, animal educators, and mind/body/spirit speakers who participated as interviewees in the first annual Prosperous Pet Business Online Conference (deep bow to you all), that idea and vision became reality.

This book contains the interviews from the first conference.

Prosperous Pet Business: Interviews with the Experts: Volume One is for you regardless of whether you are thinking of starting a pet business or whether you are already a dog trainer, pet sitter, dog walker, pet groomer, or doggy day care owner. And if I haven't mentioned your particular pet business, don't worry. Any service-based pet business owner will find value in this book.

Spoiler alert: This book is going to rock your world (and your pet business)!

I say that with confidence because we received hundreds of emails and Facebook comments from pet business owners from all over the world who attended the conference and who were blown away by the information that you now hold in your hands.

Attendees included many thousands of pet business owners, as well as those who were exploring the idea of pet business ownership from all 50 of the United States. That was exciting but not a surprise. We expected a lot of U.S. conference attendees. But what was a surprise was the number and varied locations of our international attendees: India, Pakistan, Africa, Jakarta, Singapore, Australia, UK, Finland, France, Spain, and many others.

As I mentioned, I received many heartfelt emails from pet business owners from all over the world. The emails were so moving. One international attendee wrote:

> *"Thanks a lot for helping me access the conference. It's amazing and very useful. Thanks a lot for doing this. Great effort. I'm in India."*

And another wrote:

> *"Thank you for this opportunity to listen to these great speakers. Especially here in Finland, where pet business is very small and not considered a 'real business,' this gives me hope and trust to follow my own path."*

When I first started my pet care business years ago, it was not considered by many to be a "real business," but I was determined to make it one. I wanted to grow the business as fast as I could. And grow it did… but not without many growing pains. In the beginning, I made a lot of mistakes (often falling flat on my face; it was embarrassing and humbling). I learned a lot through those falls, which is the gift of mistakes. Through persistence and hard work, I got a lot of clients very quickly.

As I was growing the business, I learned what worked and what didn't when it came to running and growing a pet business. It was often a painful, not-at-all-fun process because the more "successful" my business became, the less successful I felt: I had little to no time and energy for the "me" that I was before I had started my pet business. It seemed that I was making a lot of money, but my expenses were high and my bank account was low month after month. I woke up one day and realized that I was working all the time, making a decent amount of revenue but somehow not having much to show for it. Even more importantly, I had little to no time to spend with the people I love and the activities I enjoy. I realized if this was "success," I wasn't interested. Something had to change.

I looked at the business owners around me, and I didn't see anyone who had both time and money. They had either one or the other, but not both. And I wanted both. (You can hear me talk about that in more detail in episode #7 of the Prosperous Pet Business podcast on iTunes and on the Prosperous Pet Business website.)

So here's what I did: I gave myself 365 days to change the way I ran my pet business. I decided that if I didn't have more time and money at the end of that year, I didn't want to keep running my business.

The race was on and even though I was exhausted, I dove headfirst into business practices that were creative, unusual, and different from what I had been doing. If I wanted a different result, I realized I would have to run my business in a completely different way than I had been running it.

Within a few months, I knew I was on to something because my net profit started to rise and the time I spent working in the business started to decrease. By the end of that year, I had hired a manager to help me run my business, and I was working only three days a week and making a lot more money than I had previously. It felt like a miracle, but it wasn't. Things had shifted because of a lot of the strategies you will read in this book. You hold many of the keys to that "miracle" in your hands.

In 2000, after I had created a totally different reality for myself and my business, I began coaching pet business owners and helping them create successful pet businesses with ease. I still coach pet business owners today through my one-on-one coaching sessions, monthly webinars, and four-week online pet business group programs. I am deeply inspired by my clients' willingness and openness to apply the combination of logical, traditional, and out-of-the-box methods we use to help them shape-shift and transform their pet businesses.

When I created the first online conference, I knew that, in addition to interviewing pet business owners on the nuts and bolts of running a business, I wanted to have mind/body/spirit speakers too. Incorporating mind/body/spirit approaches into my own business had been one of the missing keys when I was struggling with it many years ago.

So many pet business owners (and business owners in general) become so immersed in running their businesses that they forget to create a vibrant and rich life for themselves – and that's where the mind/body/spirit focus can help. Their lives get pushed to the side while their businesses take the forefront. They don't practice loving self-care (so important when running a business), and it affects their relationships with themselves, others, and their businesses. When we put at least some attention on our mind, spirit, and body, it lowers stress, relieves tension, and creates a sense of well-being and happiness. We need to put that metaphorical oxygen mask on ourselves before we serve our clients.

This book is a map to creating wholeness in your business and life… and a lot of other things that you'll discover as you dive in. These interviews contain holistic approaches to business. Through these interviews, you'll learn solid nuts and bolts of running a successful company, and you'll also learn an empowered, holistic approach to running your business. I'm so excited for you!

Here's a warning for you before you begin: Use this book at your own risk. Read it only if you want your pet business and your life to change… a lot.

Happy reading, learning, shape-shifting, and growing,

Kristin Morrison

Acknowledgements

It takes a village to write a book, and this one required a big, wonderful tribe!

I dedicated the book to those I interviewed for the Prosperous Pet Business Online Conference, and you all deserve another round of big, hearty thanks.

THANK YOU, dear speakers! Thank you to Patti Moran, Arden Moore, Veronica Boutelle, Thom Somes, Alicia Dattner, Trish King, Jerrod Sessler, Chess Edwards, Therese Kopiwoda, Danielle Lambert, Paul Mann, Caroline Golon, Ian Dunbar, Susan Briggs, Dee Hoult, Rita Reimers, Tiffany Reynolds, Lisa Maria, Lisa Taron, and Andrea Arden.

Sincere appreciation to my amazing coaching clients who inspire me with their openness, willingness, and commitment to transform their pet businesses and their lives. I am honored to assist you on your journey.

Thanks to the Jumpstart Program and Catapult Program participants. Your support of my work and of each other means a lot. It's beautiful to watch you rally for the other attendees on the private Facebook pages. Seeing you be support allies for one another warms my heart. I am especially grateful to those Catapult and Jumpstart Program attendees who read this book and gave me your feedback prior to publication. I know you all have full lives and businesses, and it means so much to me that you took time out of your schedules to make that happen. Thank you so much.

Deep bows of gratitude to my Thursday Business Group peeps (you know who you are). After a few years as a solopreneur, I discovered that having regular, ongoing support was crucial for my business and life success, and it made business and life much more fun! The support from my Thursday Business Group is one of the main reasons you are holding this book in your hands, dear readers. Before I had this support, I was a tulip bulb stuck in a brown paper bag. Lots of potential but no growth or bloom. Getting consistent support and love from my Thursday Business Group was the dirt, water, and nourishment I needed to sprout and thrive. I'm forever grateful. I like being a tulip rather than stuck in that dark bag. It's much more fun in the light.

I'm very grateful to my Monthly Coaching Group buddies. You have been there for me in all things book- and business-related… some of you for many years now. Thank you, dear Kathleena and Lisa P. Our monthly vision meeting is so powerful. Being with you two wise souls is zesty, fun, and real. Thank you so much to Robert and Suzanne. You both uplift me and give me wise, intuitive guidance. I come away clearer after we meet. You are rock-solid, spiritually minded business owners, and your guidance and deep listening is invaluable. Thank you oh-so-much to Cynthia and Sharon. I love the way we laugh and joke and then dig deep to expand and nudge (and sometimes push) each other to grow into our fullest Self.

Special thanks to my fabulous editor, Ann D. You have the gift of being able to make changes in the words without losing my "voice," and that is a rare gift indeed. Grateful for you and your speedy, professional, and solid editing. So glad we found each other years ago. My books would not be the same without you.

Tonie, wonderful web-mistress: Every business owner needs a great web person, and I scored the jackpot with you. I appreciate how you are always available for me and your work is professional and seamless. It's amazing that we've worked together now for (wow) over 10 years. Your brain knows me and my work so well that often you are one step ahead of me and on top of things before I've even asked. Thank you for being intuitive, smart, and so wonderful to work with.

The best virtual assistant in the world deserves a big shout out and here it is: Diana, thank you for helping make all my projects flow more easily. I love how you roll up your sleeves and "get 'er done." You assist me in so many big and small ways that I'd be lost without you. Very happy we found each other.

To my dear friend Alicia: I thanked you above in the speaker section and you deserve another love note here because of what a good and loving friend you are. I'm so grateful for your solid, fun, cherished presence in my life. You make me laugh. A lot. I'm blessed to have you as my dear, darling friend. Thank you for all your support and cheerleading. I love you.

Sweet Adva: You are there for me, rain or shine, and I appreciate our friendship so much. I'm grateful for the delicious, home-cooked meals you make for me and for our chats on your comfy sofa that have nothing to do with business.

Thanks to my 90-day Challenge group and especially to Pam, Lizbeth, Nancy, John, Lyn, and Linda. You help me exercise when I really don't want to, and your posts gave me inspiration to get out there and move, which in turn gave me energy and focus to work on this book.

To the allies on Coach who prop me with their raised thumbs and their loving comments. Thanks especially to Martha K., Haiku, Christine K., Bob, Bella Flower, Achim, Marina Kl, and Simon V.

Thank you to my favorite person in the world, my love, Spencer. I am grateful for you every moment of every day, Sweetie. You make life way more fun and delicious. Thanks for being my steadfast supporter in life and business. I am so lucky.

ONE

How to Create a Profitable and Empowered Pet Business

Interview with Patti Moran

There's one word that will set you FREE in your pet business, and Patti is here to share what that one word is. You'll also learn about the various big and little mistakes that business owners make, and (thank goodness) how to avoid making them. (We can all use some advice from someone who "gets it," right?) Well, after years of being at the forefront in the pet industry, Patti does! Pull up a chair, get comfortable, and let's show you how to make your business ultra-profitable and empowered!

In this chapter, you will learn:

- The one word that will set you free in your pet business
- Patti's top four tips for pet business success
- Mistakes pet sitters and other pet business owners make (and how to avoid them)
- The best business advice that Patti ever received (and the best advice she ever gave)
- How to avoid burnout in your business
- And much more!

Kristin's Musings:

Here's how I experienced Patti during our interview: She's incredibly sweet and wise. Great energy combined with a big heart. I was taken with her kind smile and intelligence. This woman essentially put professional pet sitting on the map, and that's no small feat. What a lady! And on behalf of all pet sitters out there: Thank you, Patti!

Patti Moran's Bio:

Patti Moran developed pet sitting as a profession after starting her own pet sitting business in North Carolina in 1983. After word of her business spread to other parts of the United States, Moran was prompted to put her how-to advice on paper; the premier reference, *Pet Sitting for Profit*, was published in 1987. As others joined her in the profession, Moran began the National Association of Pet Sitters in 1989 and also founded Pet Sitters International (PSI) in 1994. With 7,000 member businesses, PSI is the leading educational organization for professional pet sitters in the world. You can find out more about PSI at *www.PetSit.com.*

Interview with Patti Moran
Founder, Pet Sitters International

Kristin Morrison: *I am so excited to welcome Patti Moran here. She is the founder of Pet Sitters International. She is an author. She's a public speaker, and she's an amazing force in the pet sitting world. It brings me such delight to have you here, Patti. Thank you so much.*

Patti Moran: Well, thank you so much for letting me be a part of this. I think it's wonderful what you're doing.

Thank you. Having you here really adds to the wonderful energy of this conference, and I'm thrilled to have you here. So, how did you get into the pet sitting industry?

Well, Kristin, I got into it out of necessity because I needed a job but also quite by accident. I had just been terminated from my position of seven years in the corporate world, a place that I thought I would grow old and die. I found myself very disillusioned with the corporate world, and it just seemed to me that the only way to possibly ensure my job security and financial freedom would be to start my own business and be responsible for my future. But what kind of business was the problem.

Now this was back in 1982 or '83 when there was another recession that had taken place in this country. The company that I had worked for gave me a severance package, so I had a few months and I started researching business ideas. It was during that time that one of my best friends came back to the Winston-Salem area where we lived, and she was home for a friend's wedding. I asked her what she had done with her dog because we're both long-time dog lovers. She said, *"Oh, it's the neatest thing in my new neighborhood. There's a lady who… she's a pet sitter."* It was like, *"A what?"* Because this was 1983, and my friend and

I both looked at each other… and I realized that's me. That's what I need to do. But how do you do this?

That was August of 1983. Even though I'd been researching a small business, I hadn't come across professional pet sitting. There was a lot of good information that told you sort of how to start a small business, and I thought it was such a great idea, such a needed service for pet owners. I thought, "*Yeah, why hasn't somebody else done this in my city?*"

So, I just decided that I was going to do it, so I jumped in and with the help of her sister, who had also worked for the same company, and the two of us started our pet sitting business in December of 1983. And, as they say, the rest is history.

That's great. I started my own pet care business in 1995. I remember there was nothing out there for pet sitters at that time, except for your book and Pet Sitters International. I felt like, "Thank God there's something." I was so excited to discover you. So, how did Pet Sitters International come to be?

Well, I did write the book because I was getting so many calls in the first and second year of operating my pet sitting service from people who heard about what I was doing in other parts of the country, and I was sympathetic. There wasn't really any written word or directional guidebook for this profession. At first, I tried to help people with telephone consultations, but it was soon taking so much of my time that I wanted to be pet sitting and running my own business.

That's when I sat down and put everything into a written format. I thought once people had the information that then they would let me run my business. But instead, they kept calling me, and we sort of began an informal network of people who were doing this. As we continued to talk, we found that a common problem for the profession was that people couldn't find good business insurance. So that's where the idea for an association came from. I thought, *"Well, there's getting to be more of us and since insurance companies wouldn't take us seriously… that we were a credible, viable business risk… maybe if we bind together and get clout in numbers, that the insurance companies would take another look at us."*

So, I checked with some of them and said, *"Hey, if I start an association, does that interest you?"* They said yes, so I did.

That's great. Going back to your own pet sitting business, what were some of the challenges that arose in your own business and how did you deal with them?

Everything was a challenge, Kristin. It was like I was in uncharted territory, but I think it's Ralph Waldo Emerson who said, *"Don't take the path well-traveled. Instead take the path less known and blaze a trail."* So I learned a lot of things the hard way, such as always try the key to a person's house when they give it to you. Instead of when you return to make your first visit, and you find, oh, they gave you the back door key or it's their office key. You can't get in.

So that was a challenge. I didn't know to put policies and procedures in place until I started getting calls saying, *"Well, why won't you make a midnight visit to care for my dog?"* So I've learned that there were things like that which you needed as I went along.

Fortunately, I tried to learn from every mistake I made and not to make it again, but there were some hard-won lessons.

Anything that you think that pet sitters really need to know when they're starting out? I know you mentioned a few things, but is there anything else that you think, "Oh, new pet sitters really need to know this?"

Well, number one I think that when you're starting a business, you need to realize that it's your business. You are in control of it, and you need to maintain that control because if you don't, if you don't have your rules in place for how you're going to operate your business, then you are going to get clients who are going to try to tell you what your business is and you're not going to be in control anymore. And you're going to take the last-minute caller who calls. Your weekend is booked already and then here comes a call at 9:00 on Friday night, *"Can you please, please, please?"*

You're going to take the job. You're going to be overwhelmed for the weekend. You're going to hate yourself the whole weekend. So you need to know that you're in the driver's seat. You determine who you sit for, what kind of breed you sit for, how far you go in making your pet sitting rounds. And that's going to be a big thing.

And then also: Just know that there are so many resources available to pet sitters now. I think there's almost no excuse for failure anymore. Because there's so much available.

You don't have to reinvent the wheel. The territory is charted now.

It's true. And thank you for blazing the trail. I know that's a lot of work with a machete to get out there and hack the grass.

> CREATE YOUR POLICIES AND PROCEDURES AND STICK TO THEM TO AVOID PET BUSINESS BURNOUT AND KEEP YOU IN CHARGE OF RUNNING YOUR BUSINESS.

Fortunately, it's been a lot of fun, too, and a lot of wonderful opportunities and just a lot of great people and a lot of wonderful pets along the way.

You've helped many people and pets. Going back to what you said about business owners being in control, Patti, I just love that. One of the things that I learned in my business was "no" is not a four-letter word and really getting comfortable saying it. It was really uncomfortable in the beginning with my clients and my staff to set boundaries, to say "No." Yet the more I did it, the more comfortable I got with it. And that is an act of self esteem: to take care of ourselves and say no when we need to say no. But it's really uncomfortable in the beginning.

Unfortunately, I don't know why it is so hard, and I have wondered through the years because pet sitting is comprised primarily of females. Our membership here at Pet Sitters International is over 90 percent female. Also, people who get into this business, they love pets.

I think the two probably go hand in hand together, but when you love pets, you just sort of tend to be a nice person. So it's hard to say no to other people who love their pet, but it definitely is something that we, whether as females or just business owners, we do need to learn sooner versus later.

We take care of others. It's kind of this natural inclination. Even on the airplane, the flight attendants will instruct women to put their oxygen masks on themselves first before putting it on their child. I think they say that because we women tend to care for others first. We think about others, which is a beautiful thing, but when it comes to business, it's so important to think about it like a business. When I'm working with pet business owners, I often remind them, "Yes, you love your pet business and you're taking care of all these great pets, yet this is not a nonprofit." Owning a pet business is a for-profit venture, and it's really important to remember that.

If you don't take care of yourself, you're going to be no good to your business and to the people and the pets that are depending upon you.

As well as the people in our lives. I find what gives me the most satisfaction are my relationships with my partner, my friends, and family. That's what life is about for me. That's the meaning, and the business is right below that. I love all things business-related, but that doesn't get me flowing. It's not the prime motivator for me. So I think if business owners can really remember what IS their prime motivator for living life, not just running their business, but what truly motivates them, I think that can be a really powerful way to put priorities first and put ourselves first too.

Our businesses can be a means to the end. So it doesn't need to be the end of us.

Exactly. I work with a lot of pet business owners on creating more freedom in their business because a lot of people feel like it's a ball and chain. So how can we have a different relationship to our business, one where it doesn't rule us, but we rule it? There is some learning involved in that process. There is a learning curve involved there for most people. It doesn't happen naturally.

Well, I think, too, when you're first starting out and you so want to succeed, so when the first phone call comes in or the first email, it's like, *"Oh, well. Even if it is ten miles farther than I thought I would go."* It's just so easy to think, *"Well, I'll take it"* or *"I'll do this one"* or whatever, and then one day, it's spiraled out of control.

And then it's like whack-a-mole where you have to deal with all the business because it's spread all over the place. I know I had to deal with that in my business. In the beginning, everybody wants to take whatever is there. It's kind of a natural intuitive reaction. But that can come back to really bite you in the butt later on. So what are some keys for success for pet sitters?

I guess what I like to call the four L's, and that is that you need to listen because you can gain a lot from listening. I know we've had a lot of want-to-be pet sitters or new pet sitters starting out that come to our annual conferences. They say they're just considering pet sitting as a career or whatever, but they thought they would come to where the information was. And they really just spend their days listening to what people in the business are saying. Then they say, *"I learned so much just from people who are already doing this."*

Again, taking advantage of all the resources that are out there, which would be the second L: To learn as much as you can because like I say, so many of the things that can be a problem in pet sitting, so many of us have made them already, and we can tell you what you should not do. So learn.

Third, live by your principles, your ethics, your conscience, because whether you succeed or fail, when it's all said and done, it's a matter of did you do the best you could do and can you sleep at night?

Then the fourth L would be to love, and that's to love what you do because otherwise you're not going to be good at it and you're also not going to have any fun.

Oh, I just love the four L's. That's beautiful. I'm wondering, going back to loving what you do, we were talking earlier about saying no and that brings me to the question of burnout. A lot of pet sitters suffer from burnout. How can pet sitters avoid burnout so that they continuously love what they're doing?

REMEMBER THE FOUR L'S: LISTEN, LEARN, LIVE BY YOUR PRINCIPLES, LOVE WHAT YOU DO.

Well, I'm glad you brought that up because that is one of the biggest risks, biggest threats to being in this business. It's a position where you don't want to find yourself. But if you do, take the proper steps, as we said, starting out with policies and procedures in place that you actually will follow and stick to.

You have to think about your goals with the business: Do you just want to be a sole proprietor or do you see yourself expanding the business? And if you're just wanting to be a sole proprietor, you still have to think about, *"Well, what if I'm sick? How about the days I do need a day off? How about a weekend for me occasionally, a holiday I might want to celebrate with my family?"* Make sure that you do have a backup, and that can often be found by networking with another pet sitter in your area who also chooses to be a sole proprietor and getting a working relationship like that.

But again, it can be avoided. It's just that you have to make sure at the outset that you have used – you know how they say, *"Hindsight is always better than foresight?"*

You have to put the foresight in place. Like I say, talking with other pet sitters as far as how they do their schedules, how far they go when making their rounds, how many days they work, what kind of days they give, what kind of time they give themselves off. And as we discussed earlier, you have to make "me" time.

Yes. It's so important. I have really made it a practice in my own life to put myself and my schedule first before my clients and before anything else. So exercise. I meditate in the morning. I write in my journal. I do morning pages, which I heard about from Julia Cameron. She wrote **The Artist's Way,** *and she talks about the practice of morning pages and just writing three pages each day. Kind of stream of consciousness. And there's something about that. For me, it's like emptying the trash in the morning. And also getting business ideas. I write about the importance of that in my book.*

So, I really want to encourage pet sitters out there who are experiencing burnout to really put them (days off) as an appointment in your book.

That's one thing. The clients who call and request your services, just because your calendar is booked, they don't have to know if it's time for you to actually go and get a massage. If it's time for you to have lunch with a friend. That's just as important. And sometimes letting clients know that you can't sit for them because you're completely booked will make them have more respect for what you're doing. You will be a better pet sitter and around a lot longer to pet sit for people.

So thinking about the downsides of pet sitting, a lot of people go into it thinking, "Oh, I get to play with animals." And it's such a great profession, and yet what are some of the downsides that pet sitters have to face in being pet sitters?

Well, here we go back to being the nice people who love pets, and we're wearing the rose-colored glasses, and we think, *"Oh, my gosh. This would just be the best job, the best career on the earth."* Yes, it is and it can be, but that's what we want it to be.

But that's a part of the foresight that you want to look at and make sure that you know what you're getting yourself into. I think, to me, a downside is the emotional aspect of pet sitting that you don't necessarily have if you're working in an office environment and your computer goes down one day. I don't think you're going to sit there and cry. But we get very attached to the animals under our care. With animals being living creatures, it is possible that you will lose one to death or you may have an upset pet owner who calls you and breaks the news to you. There is an emotional component to pet sitting that you don't face in every career. You have to be aware. But it can also be a blessing because then you can be of help to the pet owner who needs you at that time. It's a way that we can give back in this career that a lot of other careers don't get to contribute like we do.

Depending on where you live and where you're based, the weather can be a problem. Now here in North Carolina, there were some mornings that I woke up and it was sleeting. Snow was forecast and my bed was awfully warm. But you've got to get up and go let those dogs out. And rainy days, walking dogs out in the bad weather. But for every rainy day, there's also a beautiful sunny day that you're getting your exercise and you're getting paid too. It's just that you've got to anticipate that with the good comes the bad. Again, if you're good at what you do and you don't set your parameters, you can end up working 365 days a year, holidays, weekends, and you're on your way to burnout.

It's true. Going back to what you said about losing the pets, I flashed on remembering this Rottweiler that I took care of, Jaeger (my doggy soul mate is what I called him). I would walk the neighbor dog, and he would look at me on the balcony and he would start barking like, "I want you to walk me too." Finally, his owner said, "He keeps barking at you. I'm going to hire you for dog walking." So I started walking him, and I'd never really connected with a Rottweiler before. They had been a little bit scary to me. The only connection I had had with them was in movies, Cujo. Was Cujo a German shepherd? I can't remember. Anyway, I remember scary movies with Rottweilers.

Jaeger died at five-and-a-half from a heart attack, and it was so sad. I just remember thinking, "Oh, my God. I don't know if I can do this job... keep opening my heart to these pets that are going to die at some point." And yet we do. We keep opening our hearts, and I think it just grows the heart too. Losing the pet, as painful as it is, really helps to expand our heart.

I agree totally with you. But again, you have to psychologically prepare yourself that it is a part of the job. I guess on the bright side that you had the experiences of knowing and loving that animal. As I mentioned earlier, that maybe you will be able to help the pet owner who needs you.

Kind of jumping into a different vein, what do you recommend for pet sitters who are kind of stuck in their business and they need and want to expand it, but they're having a hard time growing it?

> THERE WILL ALWAYS BE GOOD DAYS AND BAD DAYS AS WELL AS JOY AND SORROW IN YOUR PET SITTING CAREER.

I think the first thing that they need to do is to understand that it's possible. It's possible. You can let go. There can be life after just you as the pet sitter or just the business manager, that there are great people out there who would love to help you. I know some pet sitters think, *"Well, my client would never let another pet sitter come into their home."* But they've let you come into their home. They love the work you do. They trust what you do. And if this is a person who you are recommending and vouching for and you have made sure there's a clear criminal history and background check, they will trust this person… that it is possible.

The same is true with even a manager for your business because, a lot of times, we start out as the pet sitter. We're getting more calls than we can physically handle, so we see the need to add additional staff members because we're taking the calls and booking the jobs. You get to the point where you're in the office all the time and you need help with a manager coming in.

Again, others have gone before you. Others have had these same fears that nobody can do it as well as we do it or the clients won't like them as well as they like us. You just have to be open that it can be done and it can be done successfully.

Absolutely. I went from doing all the pet sitting myself the first two years of my business and then hiring pet sitters and dog walkers and then hiring a manager. Then I went from working seven days a week to working three days a week and then two days a week. And then I went to Bali.

I went to Bali for six months and then India, and my manager was running my business while I was gone, and I had never heard of a pet sitter doing that. So that was my version of blazing a trail. I thought, "Oh, my God. Can I really do this?" But they were amazing. I think when we get people who really love our business as much as we do, and it is possible to find those people, then we can have more freedom and really enjoy our life more. And also have that capacity to be able to really drive the ship instead of being in the belly of the ship. When we're in the belly of the ship, we can't see anything else. When we're the captain, we have the vision, and we're able to really create even more success.

Sometimes it's counterintuitive to pet sitters, I think. They think, "Well, I'm not going to be able to grow my business if somebody else is helping me." But, actually, you will be able to grow much more, I think, by having someone.

Well, that's one of the best pieces of... it might be the best business advice that I ever received. And it sort of came at me as a surprise. But the person told me, *"Sometimes the best thing you can do for your business is to get away from it."*

It was like that gave me permission to think, *"Yes, you can leave."* And it's so true because sometimes you can't see the forest for the trees. But when we do change our pace, change our scenery, sometimes you can find the answer or a different perspective or just a refreshed attitude to go back and be better than when you left.

Absolutely. It's powerful. Yes. You talked about the best advice you received. What's the best advice you've ever given?

Well, the *"just say no"* as you have been teaching pet sitters as well because that is something that we desperately need to learn in this industry: How to say no and that it's okay to say no.

And then the other would be, *"If it doesn't feel right, it probably isn't."* So trust your intuition. Because every day is different in this business. Every home is different. Every pet is varied. You can never know it all, but I think we do have an innate communication and that is something that we need to listen to.

Yes, well said. So anything else you'd like to share before we end?

Keep those keys on you at all times. Also, try that key. And pet sitting… it is a career, I think, in which we are making the world a better place because we're making it a better world for the pets that are able to stay at home under our care and for their people who are able to travel with peace of mind that their pets are in good hands. How many people at the end of their workday can say the same?

It's true. Thank you so much, Patti, for being here. I'm just so grateful.

And thank you, Kristin. It's been a pleasure. I think we're going to have to have you come to one of our Pet Sitters International conferences and talk to some of our members who are approaching burnout and get them some meditation tips and journaling. It's just fantastic what you're doing.

Thank you. I would be so delighted to. How can pet sitters get hold of Pet Sitters International?

Just go to our website: *www.petsit.com.*

TWO

Purr-fecting the Art of Work Reinvention

Interview with Arden Moore

You've bid bye-bye to the W-2 world of paid vacations and steady paychecks. Many of you are embarking on encore pet business careers or finally tapping into your entrepreneurial self. So, how can you convert fear into fearlessness? Turn passions into profits? Join Four Legged Life® Founder, Arden Moore, as she unleashes nine traits you need to thrive in today's ever-evolving pet business world.

In this chapter, you will learn:

- How to take the leap from working for someone else to working for yourself
- What skills are necessary to excel at being self-employed
- How to convert fear to fearlessness
- What's required to transition to self-employment in an emotionally and financially healthy way
- Nine traits that business owners need to have to thrive in the business world
- And more!

Kristin's Musings:

Arden Moore is a hoot! She's goofy, fun, and wise all at the same time. I had a great time doing this interview, and I think she did too. I love how she shares how she courageously made the leap from a nine-to-five job to business owner and how you can too.

Arden Moore's Bio:

Arden Moore – The Pawsitive Coach™ – happily wears many "collars" in the pet world: radio show host, author, professional speaker, editor, media consultant, dog/cat behavior consultant, and master pet first aid instructor.

Each week, more than 1 million people tune into her *Oh Behave* show on Pet Life Radio, the world's No. 1 pet radio network. Arden's guests include A-list celebrities such as Betty White and Jennifer Aniston, and "top dogs" in the pet industry, including Dr. Marty Becker and Victoria Stilwell.

Arden is the founder of Four Legged Life®, an online pet community, and creator of National Dog Party Day, an annual event that raises money for pet charities and brings out the playful party animal in people and their dogs.

As an in-demand pet safety, behavior, and lifestyle expert, Arden is on a mission: to bring out the best in pets and their people. She shares her home with two dogs, two cats, and an overworked vacuum cleaner. Visit Arden Moore's website to find out more: *www.FourLeggedLife.com.*

Interview with Arden Moore
Founder, Four Legged Life®

Kristin Morrison: *I am so, so happy to have Arden Moore here. She is an author. She's a public speaker. She's a media consultant. She's also a dog behavior consultant. And she is the host of the popular podcast show,* **Oh Behave.** *It's on Pet Life Radio. Welcome, Arden.*

Arden Moore: Hey, paws up, Kristin.

So happy to have you here. So, you have your pet posse here, which is great.

Oh, yes. Chipper, Cleo, Clinton, Zeki, and now a little kitten, an orange tabby named Casey.

Okay, let's get started. I want to check in with you about what we're talking about: How people can leave their jobs in order to really jump into their fulfilling businesses with pets. So, how can folks take the leap from working in their day job to starting their business?

Well, I think these days there's a lot of reinvention going on. To me, it's all about following your passion but following your passion smartly. I mean, you may love pets, but you may have a six-figure job, and you shouldn't just quit and hope and pray you're going to find a job in the pet industry. You do need to do a little homework. I'm living testament to that. For 15 years, I have been without a W-2 now. I was in the corporate world for 20 years. Now I'm in my own world – and it could be kind of crazy sometimes – for 15. So if I can do it, you guys can do it.

I agree. I know, for me, I started my pet sitting company in 1995, and I've been self-employed ever since then. It's been a number of years, and I would never want to go back. It's incredible, and it can be very challenging, too.

Yes, it can be. You know, you have to have a sense of humor and you have to know that everything is not going to go smoothly, true? Sometimes our mistakes are our best benefits. If everything went cruising along, you probably wouldn't be as successful as if you had some hiccups along the way.

It's true. I think with any big challenge there's always going to be hiccups. I mean, even Joseph Campbell – I don't know if you've ever heard about him – but he talks about the hero's journey. When we're really living a life that is something that we're trying to create beyond our wildest dreams, there's always going to be those mountains to climb over. And it requires perseverance and strength. So what skills do you think are needed for those who want to be self-employed?

Well, I think it starts with identifying and having a business plan. Nice to have good intentions, but you have to have a business plan. You have to have good solid mentors who give you constructive criticism. You don't need a bunch of cheerleaders and you don't need a bunch of downers. *"Oh, no. It's never going to work. That is not going to happen."*

I also encourage you to do some volunteering in certain areas that you might have an interest in to maybe team up with a mentor. There are a lot of great professional pet sitters, if that's your passion, who will be glad to take you along for the ride. There are a lot of animal behavior groups that you can team up with. I go to a lot of conferences. Today, I think the pet industry is finally getting to behave more like a business. It isn't just a bunch of people, *"Oh, I like cats. I like parrots."* No, we've actually got some smart people like you who are business minded and they are that to their passion.

Yes, I agree, Arden. That's really well said. When I started my business many years ago, I had no idea what was required. I had to learn the hard way because there weren't a lot of resources available at that time for people in the pet care industries. Now there are a lot of resources, and it's such a great time to start a business like that. When we talk about what skills are needed, I love what you said. I also had to create the ability to be able to work from home and not get distracted by "Oh, my gosh. I've got to clean my house. Or a friend is calling me; I've got to answer that." So working from home requires the ability to really focus on the project at hand, whether it be answering the phone for your business or whether it be billing clients. It's really helpful, I think, to have office hours, too, so that you have a business and a life.

In the corporate world, you're always tempted to take that longer break. You're always wanting to chat with a colleague, sometimes not about business. I found that you may be surprised, but you could be more efficient when you're running your own business if you don't have those office distractions.

I have an office in my home, and I also do a lot of traveling on the road, so it's *"have laptop, will go."* I have found that I like the ability to do certain things early in the morning and then later at night. But I am like you. The phone that I answer or the text that I answer, I do my best to keep it within a time constraint because you don't want to be always responding quickly all the time. Sometimes you need to let things marinate and then you can give a better answer. So don't be so quick to always reply all the time because in the business world, calling or emailing back too quickly can show a little desperation, I think.

I also think when you do respond right away it begins to train your clients that you will always respond instantly, and they grow to think that that's the way you're always going to handle all their communications... immediately.

It's like liking a boy or a girl and doing too much to try to win them over and they're backpedaling. In the pet industry, they're going to backpedal, so keep a loose leash is what I say. Keep a loose leash.

Thinking about how people can make that leap to self-employment, I know a lot of things came up for me emotionally to make that leap. It was a really big decision. How can people ease that transition emotionally for themselves and what comes up when people make that transition?

That's a really good point because your emotional health is going to make you or break you when you're self-employed. I think you have to have a sense of humor, and I think it's very, very important when you are getting feedback from others that you seek feedback from people who have already done it. You know, you can have your cousin who you really love or your sister or your brother who seems to have you in their corner, but if they've always been in the W-2 world, they don't know how to relate to what it's like to launch a business.

I have a sister who has been an auditor for 33 years in the corporate world. When I said I was going to be self-employed, she responded, *"Oh, no. You'll never make it work."* And I realized I needed to stop asking my sister, Deb, and start talking to people who have done it. I find in the pet industry, more so than others, there's a real spirit of collaboration. Find these people who are willing to help you succeed.

I think exercise is also really important. I have two dogs. I walk and run them all the time. I actually tried Zumba now, so now I don't quite have two left feet. Physical exercise when you're really stressed out... and water. Seriously, guys, water. Not the wine. Water.

I think those little things help, so those are a couple of things. Just don't give up. Take a small step. You don't have to take a big bite out of the whole project. I have some cards where people really appreciated what I've done for them. When I'm having that *"Oh, no, pity Arden"* day, I pull out – I have a stack – I just pull out one at random and I read it. You know, it makes a difference. It's better than a shrink.

You need to have any way to make joy and an emotional boost. And don't underestimate the allies you have right in your home that may have three or four legs.

I love that. I also really appreciate what you said about not listening to people and not engaging with people who aren't supportive of you because I think there are a lot of supporters out there if you really look. There will be a few who aren't supportive and their voices can be very loud. I had some of those in the beginning.

I love my sister, but I know she's not the person to turn to for advice on running my own business. Deb is the best, but Deb's never put her toe in that water.

Exactly. That's a question to ask yourself if somebody is really not behind you in something that you're attempting to launch or to create: Have they ever done it? And if they haven't, they're not a person to listen to because they have no idea.

The gentleman who I mentored with a long time ago, Steve Biller, who is a publisher of many magazines, gave me the best advice. He said, *"Arden, your biggest client today may not be your biggest client next year, may not even be on your radar. Can you stomach that? And if you can, then you're an entrepreneur."* And my stomach is okay.

I think it's important, too, not to think that you've got this great account and it's going to last forever because the world evolves, and you've got to be adaptive.

It's true. Clients move. Their pets die. And that's why it's good to have lots of clients and not depend on only a few steady clients. Really begin to get lots of clients so that you have a wide range of resources. Making the leap from working for somebody else to working for yourself requires financial commitment, too. How do people make that leap?

You've got to be smart. Before I made that leap, I was working at Rodale Press and *Prevention* magazine. I was a senior writer and writing books and magazines. I did save money. I would urge people, especially if you have mortgages like me and live in California, to remember that money doesn't grow on trees. You really need to have about four, ideally six months' savings before you make that complete leap off that pier into the waters of the W-9 world. I think it's important because it's for your own salvation. You're not freaking out whether you have to use this money to buy groceries or use this money to get a website designer.

So be smart. Actually, that's a good thing because if you can save four to six months' salary beyond your retirement money and all that other stuff, it's a statement to yourself that you can do it on your own. So you have to have a little fiscal strength.

It's true. I love that, the fiscal strength. When I'm working with pet business owners who are at whatever job they have and want to transition to creating a pet business, I always suggest that they have at least four to six months' savings before they make that leap. But also, if you can, start part time.

That's a great idea. Put your toe in the water. Yes, you're not going to get as many hours of sleep as you're used to or get to watch all those reality TV shows that you just have to see, but it's a good investment because you're investing in yourself.

In my opinion, if you are motivated, owning your own business is the best investment to make. It's an investment in yourself... in your present and your future. For a lot of people, taking that step really brings up a lot of fear. How can people convert that fear to fearlessness?

HAVING YOUR OWN BUSINESS IS INVESTING IN YOURSELF. BEFORE MAKING THE LEAP, HAVE FOUR TO SIX MONTHS OF SAVINGS AS A FINANCIAL CUSHION.

I do it every day. I mean, if I can do it – I'm five foot one and a half – you can do it. I think fear is more of an emotion of the unknown. When you say to yourself, *"You cannot control the future. You can do your best to get in the direction you want,"* then some of that fear isn't as possible.

I like it when I try something crazy. I was in the Cayman Islands on a vacation, and I did the 20-foot dive into the big pool of water. It was so cleansing. I'm not stupid. I'm not going to be riding a motorcycle without a helmet through rush hour or things like that. But sometimes when you're trying to start your own business, do something not related to pets that you've never done before. Like I'm trying Zumba. Seriously? They know I do the Snoopy dance. I'm not really the best dancer, but that's how I tackle my fears. I attempt something else and say, *"Hey, you did all right."* Are you going to be a Zumba teacher in the future? No. But can you at least keep up in class? Yes. So sometimes doing something totally different actually gets you to have the fortitude to take on fears in your industry.

It's so funny because they wear these little coin-like belts around their bodies in the class and they're like, *"Now do you want to wear the belt?"* I say, *"Hey, I've got two left feet and I'm trying to get the left and the left to harmonize. I can't do accessories right now. Give me a few weeks."* So maybe in a few weeks, I'll do a Zumba with the coins on my belly.

Oh, that's great. I think it's great to be able to laugh about fear, too, because I think we get very serious. Arden, I don't know if you've heard the acronym about fear? F.E.A.R.: False Evidence Appearing Real.

When I think about fear – because I've had to work through a lot of fear in my life, both physically and emotionally, taking risks in my life – I get how valuable that acronym has been for me. Taking risks on an emotional level leads to really growing as a human being. There's nothing like it on the planet. If you want to be fully alive, step into your fear.

The thing is, we talk about courage all the time. But to have courage really requires stepping through the fear. It's not like you can magically get courageous, right? Courage requires stepping through the fear.

It does. To all the folks out there who are thinking about reinventing themselves, just remind yourself of what you've already conquered. Some of you may have had a birth of a child, taken a pet through a really sick illness, figured out how to do really complicated math, learned Excel. I mean on and on and on and on. Remind yourself that you did it and you have the capabilities to do it in another way.

I think it's great. I would give that as an action step for everybody: Make a list of your successes. Things about which you've had a

> F.E.A.R. = FALSE EVIDENCE APPEARING REAL. REMEMBER: IT'S FALSE EVIDENCE. DIVE IN.

lot of fear, yet you've gone past that and even really surprised yourself by doing them. As we were talking about this, I was reminded about the cards that you create to boost yourself up by the kudos that you've received from others.

I also have a "Feel Good File," so I do it a little differently. I put emails that people send to me of their gratitude after having worked with me into my "Feel Good File." I'm looking at my file as we talk! I pull from that when I need a little bit of an esteem boost. It's so helpful.

That's a great thing to do. It's priceless, truly priceless and powerful. Your hormones in your head, the cortisol – the stress – you've really got to keep them in check. Things like your file, my letters, the art of just petting a kitten and hearing that Mack-truck purr is lowering your blood pressure. They are the little things we can do that literally don't cost anything.

Try to live in the now or, as my cats say, live in the *Me-NOW*. Because we're too busy fretting about what has already happened, wondering what's going to happen, that we forget to actually take a breath of air, let it out, and begin. I teach pet first aid. I'm a master instructor. I tell students that one of the biggest elements when you walk into a pet emergency – the very first thing you need to do – is take an inhale and an exhale. I know it sounds really California-ish, but it actually gets you focused on *now*. Then you can be more effective to help your pet.

The same thing applies to being an entrepreneur or reinventing yourself. Before you pick up that phone for that business call or step up behind a podium, take a big breath of air and let it out… and it does make a difference. It gets you ready to go.

It really does. I just want to encourage everybody right now to take a deep breath. A lot of us aren't breathing. I was talking with a yoga teacher who I recently interviewed for this conference, and we discussed shallow breath and breathing and how breath is life. We forget that. We forget to take big, deep breaths. We've got to breathe.

I can hold my breath a long time underwater, but that's not going to make me successful as an entrepreneur.

That's true. I meditate. Not every morning, but a lot of mornings, and I find that really helps me start my day in a powerful way. There may be people who are religious out there who don't believe in meditation. That's fine. Maybe it's prayer for you... where you just have some prayer time with your Higher Power.

Take your dogs out for a walk. A ten-minute, 20-minute walk. Turn off your phone and focus on your dog and focus on the sights, the sounds, the smells and actually walk *with* your dog... not walk your dog. There's a difference because then there's a bonding going on. I just love being able to have a dog on a six- or a four-foot lead. None of those long zip lines where the dog is way out in front of you because you're your dog's "B word" because you're behind the dog and there's no communication.

I think we have to really connect with our pets. Sometimes they see something like a butterfly. You wouldn't have seen that butterfly if you hadn't watched your dog. So it sounds corny, but it's powerful. That's exercising you and your pet, and you come back and you're ready to go.

That's gorgeous. I love the language you used, too. Language is so important. I love how you said instead of walking your dog, walking WITH your dog.

Yes, that's important. We take it for granted, but I'm the crazy lady in the neighborhood who does crazy things with Chipper and Cleo when we're walking fast. We call it the jackrabbit. Then we do slow like the molasses. We go in circles. I make them do puppy pushups. We go on different routes. We walk backward. I have people honking at me now. But they're laughing *WITH* me, and I'm in a good mood. My emotions are up. My pets think I'm wacky, but they're so glad they've got me. I'm so glad I've got them. And we come back, and I'm ready to go. That's why I'm called the *paw*sitive coach because I really want to bring out the best in pets and their people. Because too many people – and this is a good tip: Please, folks – don't say you're coming into the pet industry because you just like pets and you don't like people. Please don't use that negative phrase.

Love people. I love dogs. I love cats, all critters, all sentient beings. It'll come across if you do and are truly in it for all rather than just getting out of the human rat race to get into the four-legged rat race. It won't work. People will see that. So, please, be sincere. I hope you like people because that's how you're going to be successful.

It's true. You can also think about it like this: The people are the ones paying. They're the ones hiring you to care for their pet. You need to be able to connect with the human clients and the pet clients.

Yes, some people say they don't like people as a badge of honor. It's actually a really bad thing to display. I would never say, *"I just don't like people."* Well, you know what? If you don't like people, you might want to go to another planet… because there are lots of people on this one!

There are some butt heads out there, right? Two-legged butt heads. And there are some beautiful people out there. Sometimes when I get really irritated with somebody I have to step back and then I've got to say, *"Well, there is something I may be projecting or maybe that person just had the crappiest day in their life and you just happened to come into the view just then. Lucky you."* So, listen to their message but don't make a prejudgment.

Don't you find, Arden, that the people who are sometimes the hardest to love, who are really hard and they're angry, they are the most sensitive loving beings if you just…

You just have to crack that core. My sister, Deb, can be grumpy to most people. She is by far my best friend on the planet. I am so glad we had a womb shared that was only two years apart, but, you know, she got it all set up for me before I came. She's my best friend. She doesn't make friends easily, but I will tell you this: Every friend that Deb has is a genuine solid friend. She doesn't like to just do acquaintances. I think it's nice that I have someone like her in my life.

She doesn't know anything about the W-9 world. That's okay.

So, going back to pet business: What are some mistakes that pet business owners make when they're starting and running their business?

They're trying to do too much too fast. There are key things you need. You do need a website. You do need to have a social media presence. But build slowly. Don't try to open four stores at one time or write four books or create four products. Take it slow. Be patient because when you dilute yourself, you actually fool yourself into thinking you can do everything. You're not a super hero. Just take it slower than you want because each step needs to be done well. If you try to leap four steps above, you're not going to make it work.

Yes, that's great. Well said. So I know that you have nine traits that business owners really need to do to thrive in the business world. What are they?

Well, the first one is you do take risk. For example, when I started in the business in 1999, I had a website that was my name. Yay. But I'm not Cher. I'm not Madonna. I'm not this one-word name. Instead, everybody wonders who the heck Arden Moore is. So I took a risk about four years ago and I created a brand, Four Legged Life®. Arden Moore is in the background, but it's Four Legged Life® at the forefront. I took a risk for shifting into a whole new thing because I talked to people and I asked, "*What would you remember more? Arden Moore or Four Legged Life?*" The answer: "*Four Legged Life.*"

The other thing is if I ever become so hot and famous and rich and all that and I want to sell, I can sell my brand, which is Four Legged Life®, not Arden Moore. So take a risk.

Another thing is really surf the social media waters. I have two dogs that surf. I live in California, so I listen to them. Little things. Technology is getting easier and easier in time. We're doing a Google hangout. Little one-minute videos on Facebook help. Twitter: I've done Twitter parties. Team up with people who know how to do it. If you don't, it's okay.

Create positive partnerships. Learn and share. I'm a master in pet first aid, and I like the fact that you're never too old to learn something new. I never imagined that four years ago I would love, love, love teaching people how to keep their pets safe. Now I team up with my dog, Chipper, a golden retriever husky, and Zeki, the cool cat that has her own Facebook following. I teach hands-on, veterinary-approved pet first aid classes with a real dog and a real cat that will let you brush their teeth, check their little pulse, wrap them in a restraint muzzle, all for the low, low price of low-sodium deli turkey. So, that's important.

Be inventive. I got crazy. I created a new national dog holiday, National Dog Party Day. It's a party with your pet. It's a date night. And every year, we do it. We're growing it slowly, and we give the money to a hard-working, small- or medium-sized charity in that area.

Embrace play. Seriously. I like to have some fun. My dogs surf. I boogie board. I'm not the greatest. But do something fun like surf with your dog.

And dream big. The sky's the limit. Don't limit yourself.

Finally, embrace Lady Luck. Now I'm not telling you to put all your business savings into a wild card or anything, but every once in a while, some little good fortune smiles upon you. Your book royalty comes bigger than you expect or you get really a good contract. So just put the energy out there. You never know. You know, sometimes good things happen. They just happen. Embrace it. It's okay. Let's say you got something great and you didn't even work at it. Well, maybe it was your time in the little cosmic circle to win the little pet lottery. So, just embrace Lady Luck. So, I hope those tips help.

Those tips are great. I especially love how you talked about allowing the good to come to us.

You know what the other thing is? I'm not really driven by the dollar. And that probably irritates the people who are in the W-2 world because they've got their 401(k)s and they know when their vacations are and all that. But what really keeps me going, keeps me energetic, keeps me motivated is when I have somebody say, *"Wow, you made a difference in the life of my pet and me."* That's an asset. That's something that's priceless. I am very fortunate to be able to help people. I like to help people. Every day I want to learn something. Every day I want to share something. That's important as someone is putting their toe in the water. But don't be chasing the dollar. Make sure you're making a difference, and then the dollar will come. The dollar will come.

TRAITS THAT YOU NEED AS A BUSINESS OWNER: TAKE A RISK, SURF SOCIAL MEDIA AND TAP TECHNOLOGY, CREATE POSITIVE PARTNERSHIPS AND COLLABORATE, LEARN, SHARE, BE INVENTIVE, EMBRACE PLAY, DREAM BIG, EMBRACE LADY LUCK.

It's true. It's not about the money. It may seem like it is. Even with my business, Six-Figure Pet Business Academy, what comes first is the love of what you're doing. If that's not there and your heart isn't in it, that's not good. If money is your motivating factor for starting your pet business, you're probably not going to be successful. And if you are successful, you're not going to be content with what you have.

Yes. I *used* to say *"I'm poor and famous,"* but that's not a good thing to say. I find a lot of people who don't have as much money as someone else and they're happier. It's a silly, trite cliché, but really money – dollars – do not buy happiness. You make happiness. Our pets help us become happy, but it starts with us. It's how you feel about each day when you get up and you're ready to take on the day.

We can claim happiness. Right here. Right now. We keep thinking, "It's out there. If this happens or if this happens or if I get or buy this, I'll be happy."

Would have, could have, should have does not work as an entrepreneur. You can't always do the moves of others because they'll checkmate you. So just realize you can control certain things with yourself, but you can't control the moves of others. You can influence. You can encourage. But they're the ones who make their call. You don't know their circumstance. That's really important.

Thank you so much, Arden. You are incredibly delightful and wonderful.

Why, thank you. And thanks for what you're doing, Kristin. It's been a delight to be with you.

THREE

Simple Ways Pet Business Owners Can Save Time (Ahhh!) and Make More Money

Interview with Veronica Boutelle

Are your profits not as high as you'd like them to be? Do you find yourself challenged when you raise your rates and change your policies? Don't worry; there's hope! And if you need to let go of difficult clients, this chapter will surely help. Veronica will help you create more time and money in your business (and who doesn't want more of that?).

In this chapter, you will learn:

- How to increase your net worth in a surprising way
- Easy methods to feel empowered in running your business
- How to deal with client pushback about your policies
- Why letting go of difficult clients (and difficult pets) will bring you more money
- How to tap into what really motivates you when it comes to running your business
- And more!

Kristin's Musings:

What do you get when you combine years of pet business experience with a lot of heart and soulfulness? Veronica! She's warm, engaging, and a kindred spirit. I found myself wanting to interview her much longer than the 30 minutes we had set aside. I could have continued talking with her all afternoon!

Veronica Boutelle's Bio:

Veronica Boutelle, MA Ed., CTC, is the founder of dog*tec, through which she has been helping dog professionals create their dream businesses since 2003. Her books include *How to Run a Dog Business: Putting Your Career Where Your Heart Is, Minding Your Dog Business,* and *The Business of Dog Walking: How to Make a Living Doing What You Love.* dog*tec's Dog Walking Academy program has raised the bar for professional dog walkers and is available in five countries and counting. Veronica is a sought-after speaker internationally and writes for multiple industry journals. She is the former Director of Behavior and Training for the San Francisco SPCA. You can find out more about Veronica Boutelle and dog*tec at *www.Dog-tec.org*.

Interview with Veronica Boutelle
Founder, dog*tec

Kristin Morrison: *I am so excited to welcome Veronica Boutelle. She is the founder of dog*tec Dog Walking Academy. She is an author. She is a conference speaker. And it's just such a pleasure and an honor to have you share information. Thank you so much.*

Veronica Boutelle: Oh, Kristin, thank you so much. It's so fun to be part of this process. I'm so excited about the conference.

I have heard so many wonderful things about you, and it's just such a delight to finally get to connect with you. So how did you get into the dog walking business?

It feels like an entire lifetime ago and it was entirely by accident. I was in the middle of a career change and trying to decide what to do next. I was spending afternoons with my own dogs walking up in the hills and doing a lot of thinking and soul searching. I kept running into this wonderful dog walker, and we seemed to have the same schedule out there. At some point she said to me, *"You know, the only reason I'm all the way out here is that I have one client way out here. All my other clients are in the next town over. I've been thinking about letting this dog go. And you're here every day and you should take this client."* So I did, and I ended up building a dog walking business. So I sort of stumbled into it actually.

That reminds me of my story, which is a bit similar. I was on a bike path years ago, and I passed this woman who had a dog walking t-shirt with a phone number on it. We passed each other, and she had two dogs and I asked, "Do you have a dog walking business?" She replied, "Yes, I do. Do you want to work for me?" And I said, "Yes, I do." So I started walking dogs for her, and then I started my own business three months later. It sounds like a similar serendipitous happening. Where it found you. You didn't go searching for it. That's a powerful calling. When it finds you, it's beautiful.

What do you think are some traits of successful pet business owners? What would you say are some really good qualities that they have?

One of the things I think is the most important is to value yourself. I think that most of us come into this industry from a place of altruism because we love the dogs, and we want to do well by them and we want to take care of the clients as well. I think a lot of times dog business owners forget to value themselves. They forget to recognize the skill sets they have and the incredible work that they're doing for people. I see that a lot in people not charging what they're worth. And not using policies to protect themselves. I think sometimes we mistake good customer service for bending over backward to the point of breaking and not putting some safe, sustainable boundaries around us so that we can do this for the long haul.

It's very important to value ourselves as much as we value the dogs and people we care for.

Yes. I love how you say that because I found in my work with pet business owners that when people really begin to value themselves and their service, their rates begin to go up.

Yes, they do. And their business grows too.

I think pet business owners are often so afraid to charge well or to raise their rates. They're convinced that they're not going to get business, but the reality is that when you raise your rates, you tend to get more business because it signals a level of professionalism. People want the best for their animals, and we have a funny culture in which, fair or not, accurate or not, we tend to equate cost with value. We assume that more expensive services are more valuable services. I think it's often an erroneous assumption, but we do make it. I think we worry about pricing ourselves out of the market of really serious clients because we're afraid to say, *"Yes, I do have that value. I'm worth that and I know what I'm doing."*

I know I have that experience when I'm looking for a service business. If they're not charging very much, I wonder. There is this thought that goes into my head, "Are they very good? Is this a valuable company?" It can be counterintuitive for a lot of pet business owners because they think, "Well, if I don't charge very much then I'll probably get more clients." But it's often the opposite. Those clients who do go for the low-priced companies tend to be really challenging clients, right?

> PEOPLE TEND TO EQUATE VALUE WITH COST. BE SURE TO VALUE YOURSELF AND YOUR TIME AND CHARGE WHAT YOU ARE WORTH. UNDERCHARGING OFTEN LEADS TO CHALLENGING CLIENTS WHO DON'T VALUE YOU.

It's so true. When you raise your rates, you're drawing people who are drawn to you not because they're making decisions based on price but because they're making decisions based on value. Those are the clients who you tend to have the really wonderful long-term relationships with, the true brand loyalty.

That word you used: counterintuitive… I think that's perfect. It's funny when people come to us and say, *"Oh, I'm really having a hard time. I'm having a hard time getting clients."* One of the first things we look at is: What is your rate? But it's not to see if it's too high. It's always to see if it's too low.

I say, "Show me your rate list and we'll start there."

Right. And don't you find, too, there's incredible fear of charging more? It's amazing. I find it's such an incredible moment to see that dissipate for pet business owners, but they've been so frightened to do it. Then they do it, and all of a sudden, everything starts to turn around. It's so empowering.

The word that comes to mind is liberated. They feel liberated. They feel free. When I'm working with people who change their rates and raise them, there's this energy that gets released where they begin to really value themselves, not only in their business but in their life. They start setting boundaries with people.

That's right, and confidence really increases. That's such a big job for people. You know, we're all drawn to confidence. If we can do things in our businesses that engender that for ourselves, that leads to further success also. It becomes this wonderful snowball effect.

The self-worth equating net worth… that really does translate. In the raising of the rates, it's almost acting as if it's okay. They may think, I'm afraid, but I'm just going to go for it. I imagine you've experienced this, too, Veronica, when you work with somebody. You have them raise their rates, and they're terrified, right? They do it and then their clients often say, "I was wondering when you would raise your rates." Their clients often ask them why they didn't do it sooner.

I just had that experience yesterday. It's so, so common when they're so afraid and then the reality is that not only did they not lose clients, but they receive this flood of positive reinforcement: *"Oh, gosh, you know, it's about time,"* and *"You're so worth it,"* and *"I'm so glad you're doing this."* It's amazing that clients actually take that moment to say how grateful they are for the service. I love to see it.

That's beautiful. You talked earlier about policies, and I'd love to talk about that. I'm curious about what policies you think pet business owners should really be looking at in their business.

One of the things that we push the hardest for dog walkers – and this is another one of those counterintuitive pieces that we often get a little bit of pushback on at first and then once it's implemented, it's a game changer – is to get rid of the "drop-in" approach.

Get rid of allowing people to use the service sporadically. Monday this day and Friday next day, and "*Oh, I need all five days after that, but then I'm gone for several weeks after that.*" We really try to teach people to have set and minimum day policies, for example, where all the dogs that are going out are going out every week and they're going out at least X number of days and the same days every week.

It's amazing what happens when they stop allowing drop-ins and sporadic service. First of all, it makes the business so much easier to run because the number of clients you need to have is significantly reduced. So you can take better care of people because there are fewer people to take care of.

So the responsibility reduces. You also don't have all of the scheduling nightmares. For instance, whether you're trying to schedule with Sunday evening texts and emails or however you're taking the reservations... you don't have to do any of that juggling. Your schedule is the same every week. You know exactly the most efficient route to drive. If you're doing group walks, you're able to group the dogs in such ways that you know that those groupings work really well together. That is much less stressful for the dogs because they're not having to renegotiate social relationships every day with a new group.

> BE CERTAIN TO HAVE A SET POLICY REGARDING "DROP-IN" DOG WALKING SERVICE. IT'S BEST TO AVOID OFFERING OCCASIONAL DOG WALKING SERVICES SINCE THE LACK OF CONSISTENCY CREATES A SCHEDULING NIGHTMARE AND IS NOT IN THE BEST INTEREST OF THE DOG IN THE LONG RUN.

It's an amazing way to rethink the service. Yes, there are clients who need drop-in. However, you really need to think about whether you want your business to accommodate drop-ins all the time because it makes things so much more difficult and stressful, and it's also really difficult to predict income.

It's such a benefit to have steady income. We love to see that kind of change. We really see it as a win for the business owner, but also for the dog and the client too. There's so much value in just rethinking things that way.

I really appreciate that. I experienced that in my own business. I had a pet sitting company for 18 years and I sold it last December. I've been coaching for years and loving that, and it grew bigger and bigger, so it was time after 18 years. My business was "ready to go to college and leave the nest." We'd gone through high school together, and it was time for it to fly the coop... cut the apron strings and all that!

However, I did allow drop-in clients in my own business for probably five or six years into my business, and when I stopped making that service available, it made a huge difference. That was also a way of valuing myself and my time and my staff's time, too, because they're counting on that regular schedule.

Like you said, it is more stressful for the dogs. When you have a set group of dogs that know they're going to see each other on a Monday, they do know. I believe they know, don't you?

Absolutely. And they're able to fall into a nice routine with each other.

Exactly. And it brings peace instead of chaos. I really am glad that you brought the drop-in issue up because that is such an important point. I think when they're starting out, a lot of dog walkers agree to anything, which is fine when you're starting out. However, as you get busier and busier, trying to maintain that drop-in experience just isn't possible if you want to keep your sanity. If you don't want to keep your sanity, go for it.

Right. It's true. The thing is we're always thinking about what's good for the dogs, so to recognize how much better a policy like this is for the dogs, and not just for the clients, is very important.

There are various reasons that clients hire dog walkers, but one of the big benefits is coming home to a tired, better-behaved dog. It's hard to get that if the dog is going out intermittently. And it's also harder on the dog walker, too. It's the same if you're running a daycare: The dogs that only come in once a week (or come every now and then, whether it's a walk or daycare) throw the whole tone off for everybody else. As you said, it's harder on the walkers in addition to the scheduling issues.

Yes. I just have this image: It's almost like a substitute teacher instead of a regular teacher. The kids go crazy. The dogs do, too, with intermittent dog walking. It creates craziness with those drop-in dogs.

What are some other policies that you think that are important for dog walkers to implement in their business?

Cancellation policy. It's the kind of business where income can actually be quite, quite good or it can be terribly unpredictable.

One of the things that make it terribly unpredictable is allowing unlimited cancellations. Everything is going along great. Money is rolling in. Then the summer hits and half your clients run off to the Bahamas or the Hamptons or wherever they're going, and all of a sudden, everything plummets. We see that all the time. There is also stress on staff, too, because if you have a larger business with employees, you're either maintaining that overhead for the employees or their income is going down as well, which is a stressor.

It's really important to set boundaries with clients. I recommend enforcing a no-cancellation policy, or, if you want a softer version, we call it a vacation policy. One of my clients calls it "excused absences."

The idea is that you allot clients a certain number of missed days each year. It can be two weeks a year or it can be a certain number per quarter or per month… however you want to do it, but you have to put some boundaries around that. The idea is that once the client has used up those excused absences, if their dog is out of the group or out of the walk rotation, they still pay for the dog space.

A lot of dog walkers are taken aback by that: *"Well, why would the client pay for a service that wasn't rendered, something that they didn't get?"* But stop and think about analogies in other industries. For example, if we enroll our children in a private daycare or a private school and then we take them out for the chicken pox or we take them out to go see grandmother for two weeks, there's no rebate on that, right?

We pay for a term. We pay for a semester. There are 20 spots in this classroom and we're taking one of them up. So we have to pay for it whether we use it or not. Or one of my other favorites is the gym analogy. You pay monthly in order to be able to go every day of the month. If you only manage to get there two or three days, nobody gives you the other 28 days back.

Think about the spaces in your dog walking schedule as really limited and valuable spots and then have clients commit, too. That's one of the differences between pet sitting and dog walking: pet sitting is on an as-needed basis. I'm going on a business trip. I'm going on vacation. However, think about dog walking a little bit differently: it's a lifestyle service. I'm making a choice to enroll my child in preschool. I'm making a choice to enroll my dog in a dog walking company. In order for this company to have the best practices, to have small groups, to have a high degree of reliability so that the clients aren't calling up and saying, "*I really need you Thursday,*" to which we have to say, "*Gosh, sorry. We're full.*" For all of that to be steady and in place, we ask people to use the service on an ongoing basis. Our dog walkers who have switched to that system find their income is so much steadier and the clients understand. The clients value being part of the dog walking schedule and having a spot in this rotation.

I love that. I feel like it comes back to self-worth and respect for one's self and one's business. It's interesting because it's one thing to have these policies, but when I've worked with a lot of pet business owners, they don't have people sign contracts. They forget to have them sign contracts. Or they just get lazy about sending them to clients to sign. They've had the client for a year, and then they ask me, "But how do I enforce this cancellation policy?" I ask, "Well, do you have a contract?" And they'll say, "No."

LIKE THE "DROP-IN" POLICY, YOU SHOULD ALSO HAVE A FIRM, WRITTEN POLICY REGARDING CANCELLATIONS... AND STICK TO IT!

Right. It's so important to have it and to walk through it step by step by step. Dog walkers can do that at the initial intake or meet and greet.

It's not enough to simply have the policy. Clients have to be aware of it. And it's not enough even to have it in writing, but you must walk through it with them and make sure that they've understood it. We're not simply stating what the policy is, but we're explaining why the policy is in place... which is in order to maintain small groups, in order to always be here when you need us. In order to provide the very, very best service, we have these policies in place.

But there's a real fear, isn't there, in enforcing policies?

Even if we know the client knows the policy, there's a lot of fear in enforcing it. So one of the things we teach is what I call the "bedtime strategy." I recently had some friends visiting who brought their 4-year-old. There are strategies you use to announce bedtime. If you walk up to a child who's busy and engaged in a game and say, *"Okay, it's time to go to bed now,"* you can almost guarantee a tantrum. You're setting yourself up for one.

But if you walk up and say, *"In ten minutes, we'll need to put our toys away and go to bed,"* and then we walk up after five minutes and say, *"In five minutes, we'll have to…."*

Then you give them the one-minute warning, and at that point – most of the time – you can avoid the tantrum. So in business, we do the same thing. If you've given a client two weeks (excused absences) and they call up and say, *"Oh, hey, Kristin, I don't need you next week on Tuesday and Thursday,"* you might say to that client, *"Oh, no problem. We've got six days in your vacation policy, so we'll take the two out of that, and you won't need to pay for these and we'll have four remaining."* You do that each time, so then if the client uses up four days another time: *"No problem. We still have four credits on your vacation policy, so I'll just note that and you won't be charged. And then anything hereon after will still be reflected on the invoice, but I really appreciate you letting me know when you won't need us."*

At that point when they call up that third time and their vacation policy time is out, it's really, really smooth because they've been primed to expect it. You set yourself up for success on that.

I love that. When I work with clients, I also like them to explore adhering to the one-strike rule in which they may have a long-time client who wants to cancel tomorrow's dog walk at 10:00 the night before. You might call them and say, "Just to remind you, we do have a 24-hour cancellation policy. I'm going to waive it this one time, but going forward....." You can do the one-strike rule for those clients who you really love who have been there for a while or for everyone the first time they've done it.

Right. I think it's a little bit more gentle and less awkward for both parties, and you set yourself up for success by doing that. *"I've said it out loud, so next time it will be easier to implement."*

Yes. I really recommend, too, role-playing these difficult conversations out loud. You can do it in your car. Get used to hearing yourself enforcing policies out loud and begin to cultivate that confidence of speaking your truth. In a loving, soft way because sometimes when it comes out when it's never been said before, it's might come across like a ROAR!

Yes, right. It's even helpful to put together scripts and memorize them, so that when it's time to say it you can, even if you have to fake it. You have to fake it the first few times. What you'll find is that if you fake it once or twice and it goes well, all of a sudden, the confidence is there and it's so much easier to go from there.

Yes, exactly. In your own dog walking business when you had it, what were some challenges that came up for you and how did you deal with those challenges?

You know, the one that really stands out for me are those moments when you realize that it's time to let go. I remember that I had this dog that just wasn't the right fit. When that happens, I think you know it for a while... and you know it for a while longer and you think it, but the awkwardness of having to go to the client and say, *"I just don't think this is quite working out,"* is difficult.

Like many dog walkers, I let it go on too long. I remember the final straw was when we had been out. It was a beautiful day. It was one of those days that was just gorgeous and perfect. It was so lovely and I didn't have anywhere to be, and I'd stayed out a whole extra hour. So I had these dogs out for two hours on this beautiful, beautiful trail and we'd just been exploring and enjoying ourselves. We get back to the vehicle, and I get all the dogs in and I get myself in, I put my seat belt on, I look up in the rearview mirror just in time to catch Mikey lifting his leg inside the car.

After two hours outside! So I go to throw the door open and I thought, *"No, no, no. No, no, no."* I counted to 20 and got out and cleaned up as best as I could and put him back in. Then I thought, *"Okay, I think finally this is the last straw."* It was so interesting because what I finally had to admit to myself is that although I love all dogs, as we all do, I didn't have a connection to this dog. And it's hard to admit. You feel you should love them all equally and I really didn't. This dog was just not the right match for me.

When I finally made that decision, not only did I enjoy my job so much more every day after that, but also the next walker that Mikey got thought he walked on water, which is what he deserves like any other dog does. They were the perfect match for each other. I think it's really hard when you make that decision whether it's because the dog isn't a right match or there's a safety issue or sometimes we do it because the people aren't a right match for us, either.

But one of the things that I really learned from that is to trust yourself and don't put yourself in a position where you have to say, *"Oh, I wish I had done that six months ago or two years ago,"* when you know it's important to take action.

I had an experience like that too, where there was a dog that I just wasn't feeling a connection with. He acted out all the time. He was just kind of a problem child. And I had a bunch of dogs that were problem kids, but he especially was just so challenging and I knew that I had to let him go to another dog walker. But I had a lot of resistance about letting him go because I was so used to walking him every day. One day, I looked back in the rearview mirror... and he's eating the back seat of my car. And he's got foam in his mouth. It was not pretty. And I just thought, "All right, that's the end."*

> SOMETIMES THE PET (OR THE PERSON) IS SIMPLY A BAD FIT. WHEN THAT OCCURS, DON'T HESITATE TO END THE RELATIONSHIP.

That's a pretty good final straw. So the moral of the story is: do it before the final straw, right?

Right. Before they pee in your car or eat your car seat. Well, anything else you have to say to dog walkers or pet sitters or dog trainers?

First of all, just wonderful, wonderful double thumbs up for the incredible work that you do. I just think it's so incredible... the choice to dedicate our lives to making dogs' lives better and the lives of the people who love the animals, too. I think it's such a wonderful and amazing calling. One of the things that I really notice in our work is that it's really rare for people to come into this industry from an entrepreneurial background. Most of the people who I work with didn't start out or grow up thinking, *"Oh, I'm going to own my own business."* They grew up loving animals, and at some point decided to give themselves the gift of working with animals for a living. When you do that, you look around and realize that the jobs are not all over the place coming out of the woodwork. I think a lot of people make a really, really incredibly bold and courageous choice to start their own businesses.

I think it's such a courageous choice to take your own day-to-day destiny into your hands that way. Let's take a moment to realize what a courageous decision that we've all made to go out there and forfeit an easy paycheck to do something that we really, really love and make a difference in people's lives. I think it's incredible.

That's beautiful. When I work with brand new pet business owners, it's like they are birthing this new baby business, and it really is like an infant in the beginning.

And it's frightening and scary.

I know. It's like, "What do I do with this thing?" It's so rewarding, and if your heart is in it, if you're passionate about it, then there is nothing like it. There is nothing like owning a pet business. It's incredible. Thank you so much, Veronica.

It's been so my pleasure. I'm so glad to be part of the conference.

FOUR

How to Recover from Pet Business Burnout

Interview with Thom Somes

Feeling fried? If you haven't had a break in weeks, months, or (gasp!) years, you'll want to read this. Thom Somes has an ultra-busy business: He leads pet CPR training classes across the country. If he can recover from business burnout with his big business and full travel schedule, anyone can! In this chapter, you'll learn what steps to take to avoid burnout in the first place. And, if burnout does catch up with you, you'll learn what steps you can take now to manage stress (and then leave it behind). Many business owners think that burnout is simply a way of life for a business owner. It doesn't have to be. This chapter will help you get some freedom from burnout today.

In this chapter, you will learn:

- What pet business owners can do NOW to recover from burnout

- How to find the antidote to stress and burnout from one unlikely action

- What rats can teach us about recovering from stress and burnout

- Mistakes that pet business owners make that lead to burnout and how to avoid them

- And more!

Kristin's Musings:

Thom has a heart of gold and a commitment to not only the health and well-being of pets everywhere but also the health and well-being of pet business owners everywhere. This guy is like a big-hearted Energizer Bunny. He's got tons of energy, a sweet spirit, and packs a lot into this conversation. Enjoy!

Thom Somes' Bio:

Thom Somes, also known as The Pet Safety Guy, is the president and founder of Pet Tech Productions, the first International Training Center dedicated to CPR, First Aid & Care for dogs and cats. Thom is a renowned author, speaker, and trainer specifically in the field of health, wellness, and safety for pets.

Thom's career started in the medical field over 40 years ago in Michigan. He trained with the Michigan State Police and worked as an EMT for several ambulance services during college. After moving to California, he worked at Sharp Grossmont Hospital's Cardiac Training Center as an Affiliate Faculty for the American Heart Association. Additionally, he was an instructor teaching human CPR, First Aid & AED training.

Sixteen years ago, Thom went back to school and earned his Veterinary Assistant 1 & 2 and volunteered hundreds of hours at Pet Emergency Hospitals and Specialty Centers to merge the ideal world (Animal ER) with the real world (in the field). With the help of several veterinarians, Thom merged his passion for pets with teaching and medicine and created the premier Pet CPR, First Aid & Care training programs on the planet. To date, Pet Tech has trained almost 1000 Instructors and 15 Master Instructors in seven countries. Together our mission is "Improving the Quality of Pet's Lives, One Pet Parent at a Time."

Thom is the author of *Knowing Your Pet's Health: A Guide to Optimal Wellness from Snout-To-Tail*. You can find out more about Pet Tech at *www.PetTech.net*.

Interview with Thom Somes
Founder, Pet Tech

Kristin Morrison: *I am really happy to welcome Thom Somes. He is the founder of Pet Tech. He is an author. He's a public speaker. And it's just wonderful to have you here, Thom. Thank you so much for being here.*

Thom Somes: Thank you, Kristin. I'm really excited to be included in your awesome project because I think it's really important to help people to follow their passions for pets and get in the pet care industry. So I think you're really providing a great asset for people.

Thank you so much. We're going to talk about burnout because that's so prevalent in a lot of businesses but especially in the pet business industry. So what do you think are some mistakes that pet business owners make that lead to burnout?

Well, we could have a really big list here. First to define it: Burnout, according to Wikipedia, is where you get overwhelmed in your work. They really relate it that way, but in my mind, I redefine it because it's about your whole life. I think one of the biggest ways to burn out is to allow your business to become all encompassing.

Gerber wrote a book titled *The E-Myth*. And "E" stood for entrepreneurial. The myth is thinking, "*Oh, I'm going to have my own company, blah, blah, blah.*" But what you really do is simply own your own job. Although we do what we love, we still have to take time off, eat right, and those types of things.

That's true. That book is incredible, **The E-Myth.** *I read it years ago. They're based – at least they were based – very close to where I live. I think they're in Sonoma County. At least they were when I read the book. I found that book to be so applicable,* *especially since I owned a pet sitting company, which I sold last year. Having owned that for 18 years, I really valued what* **The E-Myth** *talked about, which was really stepping away from your business and creating clones: people who could actually do what you do, so you can get a much-needed break.*

I call it like a "V8 moment." I said to myself, "*Dude, you're right. You can't see the forest through the trees when you're doing everything. Yeah, I'm the president and founder of Pet Tech, right? I also fixed the copier this morning, okay.*" So you end up doing it all.

It's true. Going back to mistakes, what do you think are the biggest mistakes that pet business owners make in the way they run their businesses?

Like what we were just discussing with *The E-Myth*, I think we should take a step back and take a bird's eye view of our company. You have to plan your work and work your plan and put your company out there. Make a time line of where you are now and where you want to be in the future. The only way you're going to get there is by learning. Michael Jordan didn't get there without a coach. I'm a big fan of coaches and mentors and reading books. I'm extremely fortunate because I'm a voracious reader. I read hundreds of pages a day. I read in the middle of the night because I wake up. I read during the day and I read in the morning. I'm really big on reading. Luckily for me, that's a chance for me to step out too. It's allowed me to step away from my businesses and not be in quicksand. So I'm lucky because it polishes me up, but it doesn't drag me down.

I love that. For me, the key has been to step away from my business, so I can get some perspective. If we are always in it, like you said, we can't see the forest through the trees. All you can see is your business... right here. But when you have a better perspective, you're able to really look at, "This needs to shift and this needs to shift." It also has given me an opportunity to be able to relax. If I'm working all the time, there's no way to just chill.

Well, there are a couple of points there. You need to take time out for yourself. That's actually one of the tips I was going to talk about: actually taking time out for yourself. I was a keynote speaker at a conference early last year, and in a room of over 150 people, I asked that question: *"How many of you take an hour out of every day just for you?"* Sadly, I had to follow up: *"Hello, I asked a question. Do you guys still need more coffee?"* Eventually, three people raised their hand out of 150 people.

A long time ago, we went to a financial guru. He said you needed to pay yourself first. You should take ten percent of your income and put it away. My son, who is 17, has already started retirement accounts. I'm stoked. That blows me away. I was more than twice his age before I even got that far. So you need to pay yourself first. I think that same philosophy applies to such a business that demands 24/7/365 plus from you. You should schedule your time out for yourself first. Just because that special client says, *"Well, I need my dog walked from five to six tomorrow"* … and I've got happy hour on my schedule.

You need to schedule that time out for yourself and be stingy. Be selfish with that time because that time is so valuable to be with yourself.

It really is. I love that you said that. When I'm working with pet business owners, I really encourage them to put themselves first. So before they even schedule any clients for the week to really look at where they are. Where's your time for you? Because that's going to be the oasis, you know.

IN TERMS OF BOTH MONEY AND TIME, PAY YOURSELF FIRST. SAVE SOMETHING FROM ALL INCOMING MONEY AND SCHEDULE YOUR TIME OFF BEFORE YOU SCHEDULE ANY CLIENTS.

We're so simpatico, Kristin, in our beliefs and philosophy of business and life. I mean, we've been doing what we're doing for over 16 years. Actually, we're approaching more like 18 years... because I'm not very good at math. We love it; however, we still do the things that we're suggesting. You need to take time off and eat right. I worked with Tony Robbins in the late '80s. That shows you how old I am. One of his favorite sayings is that nothing has any meaning but the meaning you give it. And that is profound on a lot of levels.

That client who's a pain comes at you like, *"Oh, no."* How do you want to have meaning in there? I think another one of your presenters talks about the power of no and firing a client. I know that's really hard. When I first brought that up in 2001 at a conference (about firing that pain-in-the-butt client), people were kind of stuck. When you start a small business, you really come from a scarcity consciousness because you think, *"Oh, I'm a pet sitter. Oh, someone called me who lives 45 miles away. I have to take it."* With gasoline at five dollars a gallon, you lose money going to do that sit.

That goes back to having a network of other pet care professionals who have similar beliefs and values as you. They're a support group. They're a mastermind group. And they're a reference group. You can refer them out. Give someone else business because the universe takes care of us in respect to that person or somebody else will throw business back to you. So there's a ton of business to go around, and you need to manage it mentally, physically, spiritually, on every level.

I agree. Looking at your own life, Thom, how would you say that you recover from burnout? Because I know that you're busy... you do a lot... so how do you personally recover from that?

Well, I don't drink. Been there, done that. Maybe I should start! We have a form of an exit strategy. We have a son who wants to help take over, etc. We're very fortunate. We live close to the beach, and I ride my bike to the beach and I ride along the beach and I can see dolphins. It's all pretty cool. That is a great time out for me. The energy from the ocean is tranquil. It helps you to do that.

I know you don't know all my personal history, but I had a lot of tragedy in my life. Like we said, you can use that to polish you up or to wear you down. I forget the guy's name who said, *"Life is a grindstone."* I don't like that. That's too harsh. Life is a grindstone. It polishes you up or wears you down. But I don't like that grindstone analogy. So, I've had a lot of tragedy and I persevered. I've used it to turn it around and see how I can empower other people, how I can use it to serve me.

It was because of a bad tragedy that I even got back into human CPR and first aid. It was because of human CPR and first-aid teaching that brought me to where I am. This guy in my class asked, *"Thom, this is a really good class, but how would I do this to my dog?"* And I make the joke: I said, *"Cha-ching,"* and people laughed. But I thought, *"Ding-ding-ding, there's a business here."* I was really fortunate that I was able to make that connection. The universe came to my aid and it helped me to merge two big things for me. One is my passion for emergency medicine because I put myself through college working for dozens of ambulance services, cardiac training center, Rosemont Hospital, etc., and my passion for pets. So that one question was delivered to me by the universe, and I was ready to hear it.

I'm really fortunate that I'm on that path and that is the one that works best for me. So, I do get tired and frustrated sometimes because it's still running a business. I wish I had a stronger answer for you, but I do adhere to some of the things. I eat right. Plus, one of the big things is exercising daily. Studies have shown that breaking a sweat and breathing deeply are extremely healthy for you. When you sweat that out and you breathe deep, it helps move the blood through your lymph nodes to get these toxins out of your body. There's no other way to get those toxins out of your body than through the deep breathing and the sweating it out.

So, exercise, deep breathing, sweat. I do that and it helps.

It's so interesting how many speakers I've interviewed during this conference who talk about breathing and how important that is. I'm just blown away. For me it's very powerful too. I do yoga. I work out on the weights at the gym after my yoga class and break a sweat. There's something to taking those deep breaths. We're so constricted, especially if we're really stressed. I've done this before in the interviews and I just want to encourage everybody to just take a deep breath. Use this as an invitation. We're both going to do it. Deep breath.

Deep breathing actually helps to move the lymph nodes so that it helps move those toxins out of your body. So breathing is extremely important. And we actually teach breathing – it sounds weird – in our first-aid classes because breathing is synched up to your brain. If you're not in full control of your breathing, you're not in full control of your mental resources either.

I make the joke that that's why our athletes get paid so much money, because they can function and think when they're on speed, which is naturally occurring speed. I'll give you an example: Maybe you're at a PTA meeting or a meeting at church and the minister points at you and says, *"Kristin, go ahead and stand up. Tell us what project you're working on and tell us your name."* And you stand up and say, *"Mumble, mumble, mumble."* Then you wonder what happened? *"I know my own name."* The reaction occurs because the adrenaline drops into your brain, pushing it away from the thinking part of your brain. So that's why athletes get paid so much money.

We actually discuss that in the training. When you see an emergency, we want you to stop, put your arms out, survey the scene, and take a full breath, gathering all the resources you have available to you – mental, physical, and environmental – so you can respond to this emergency safely. Sorry to jump in on first aid, but it ties right into breathing. We have it in every one of our classes.

That's great. It reminds me of putting the oxygen mask on yourself first before your client.

That's a good point. You have to take care of yourself before you give canine 911.

Exactly. Or human 911. It's so important when you are busy being a caretaker, being a pet sitter, working with the dogs as a dog trainer. It's really about taking care of yourself first before you jump into taking care of others. A lot of pet professionals have a really hard time with that. We're caretakers by nature and we're instinctively drawn to taking care of others first.

You have to take care of yourself, so you can take care of others better and longer.

Yes, it's true. Going back to what you were talking about regarding taking care of yourself by working out: being in nature for me has been a huge way to relieve burnout. I hike in the woods a few times a week and I have this wonderful trail. To me, that's church. It is being with those trees and being in the fresh air and moving my body. I've hiked the same trail for years and it becomes a medi-tation for me.

BREATHING… CONSCIOUSLY STOPPING TO TAKE A HUGE, DEEP BREATH IS A GREAT DE-STRESSOR AND HELPS REMOVE TOXINS FROM YOUR BODY.

Oh, excellent. Cool. It's about creating a habit.

Yes, developing a routine like hiking or yoga or meditation.

One of the things you mentioned earlier is that you do need to take time off because some of the most incredible "ah-ha" moments occur when you consciously stop working on a challenge or problem you're having. When you stop consciously working and allow your unconscious to work on it, that's where the solutions come up. That's where the brainstorm comes in. That's when you wake up at 2:00 in the morning and think, *"Oh, why didn't I see that? It's so simple."* Again, like what you said earlier, we're so into that seeing the tree in front of us that we don't see the forest around it.

It's true. Also in that vein, there's something about being able to really sleep on something. People say, "Oh, I'm going to sleep on it," if they have a big decision, and that can be incredibly powerful. You have a dream that reminds you, "Oh, yeah. This is really important to me," or, "There's the answer." I read a dream book recently about artists, creative people, and business owners who have these big ah-ha's from their dreams. I think just getting out of whatever it is that you're really focused on gives that perspective.

Going back to the short- and long-term plans, which I think are really important, and you touched on retirement. I think a lot of people push that away thinking, "Oh, you know, I don't need to look at that." Yet it can be incredibly powerful and incredibly freeing to begin even setting aside five dollars a week in a savings account for retirement. I'm saying that to all those pet business owners out there who don't have a dime saved. Just start an account and create a container for that.

I remember we had pretzels from Costco. It was a giant thing of pretzels, and we made that our financial freedom jar a long time ago. We made it for our son, Parker, who is 17, and we're very proud of him. He's a lifeguard, a water safety instructor, and as I mentioned, already has started his retirement account.

Another way to avoid burnout is to have something that makes a difference, that's bigger than yourself to which you contribute and that you help, whether it's people and/or pets, whether it's a cause or a charity. Have something that is bigger than you that you can help where you can help get outside yourself with that.

That's what time off is about too. It allows you to let your brain work on it and solve that issue for you. We've got all these little points going.

It's great. And I love what you said about really focusing on others too. Again, it's the ability to – I think when we can take the focus off ourselves and just look at what somebody else is going through and help them – that can be incredibly powerful for us and for them. Oftentimes, we get more than we give when we're helping someone.

Oh, absolutely you get more than you give. We went to Africa in 2012 and stayed with a guy who has become a really good family friend. We were over there for the wedding for a while and spent an entire day that was at an orphanage. I'm not saying Parker's lived a privileged life, but he has. He has his iPhone, his computer and stuff, but he had never seen such poverty in this orphanage. There were 16 of us who came from America to Africa for a wedding. We brought seven suitcases full of stuff. They said that a lot of people had come to the orphanage and this is what they would do: They would drop it (donations) off, snap a picture or two, and they would leave. We stayed there. We were hugging. We were touching the children and that's what surprised them. We were hugging them. I mean, we were doing all these things, and it was so amazing.

But Parker really had a hard time with it. He had never seen such poverty. It was really horrendous conditions. It was in Mombasa, Africa.

It's one thing to see that on TV, but I was in India for quite a number of months during various times in my life and being in contact with people who are really struggling physically and financially can be so intense. But what I've also noticed, and I don't know if you noticed this in Africa, Thom: These people who were struggling physically and financially were some of the happiest people I've ever met. They were incredibly blissed out. It was the simple life. They had their friends, their family, their neighbors, and there was that feeling of community that they were really able to tap into in a way that a lot of Americans aren't able to do.

We Americans are going in the wrong direction, I think. We're always like, *"What can I get? What can I buy? What will make me happy?"* And that's not what it's about. When you do volunteer work, when you give back, when you find a cause bigger than yourself, it allows you to get that sense of gratitude.

Tony Robbins talks about this. I know I talk about him a lot, but he had an impact on me in the late '80s and early '90s. When it comes to empowering questions, if you ask, *"Why didn't I get that raise?,"* that's never an empowering question. That puts you in a negative direction. The question you ought to be asking is, *"How can I contribute more?"* It's like John F. Kennedy's idea: *"Don't ask what the country is going to do for you. Ask what you can give to the country."* It's the same thing with business or clients or relationships. If you want more out of a relationship, give more to the relationship. Don't sit there thinking, *"Why don't I get more?"* That isn't going to help.

So it is about having that gratitude and asking empowering questions.

Also negative energy can really turn people off. Having an open heart and really considering, "Hey, how can I do this better?"... that's really compelling. We'd much rather work with somebody who is fun to work with and isn't a victim.

AN ATTITUDE OF GRATITUDE GOES A LONG WAY IN NOT ONLY PREVENTING BURNOUT BUT IN MAKING YOUR LIFE AND THE WORLD A BETTER PLACE.

When you ask about preventing burnout, you should ask yourself, "Who's your ideal client?" And then don't be afraid to fire the challenging clients because 80 percent of your problems are coming from 20 percent of those clients when you're in the pet care field or any business.

Start weeding those challenging clients out. You know there is a book about building your tribe. You want to have a tribe... and for the pet care industry, I guess we'd call that having a pack. You want to have a pack of clients who have similar beliefs and values as you do, so when you make decisions, they're going to be in alignment with your pack.

I totally agree. Any final words you have as we close the interview?

Make sure you take time out for yourself every day because that's just an incredible investment in yourself and that's so important. One of the things that I truly believe in is to never stop learning. I think that's why people are tuning in to these interviews because they want to get bigger than themselves. They want to take their business in a bigger direction and want to get in the right direction. So don't stop learning.

In our training, we say (within the first 20 minutes), *"This class is not the end all for you to learn how to care for your pet. And what we hope is that we open the door for you to learn how to better care for your pet on so many different levels."* I think these interviews are opening a really big barn door – pun intended – for people to structure and create their business and create their clients in the most powerful and empowering way possible for them.

That's definitely the intention of this conference. It's to open the door and to blow off the roof of what's possible. Thank you so much, Thom. I appreciate you being here.

Okay, great. Thank you very much.

FIVE

Using Improv and Play to Lighten the (BLEEP!) Up in Your Business and Your Life

Interview with Alicia Dattner

Are you taking your business and your life way too seriously? Need a good dose of laughter to lighten the (bleep) up? Being playful is good for both business and for the soul. It also helps you win friends (and clients). This 30-minute interview is chock full of good ideas for leaving your crabby, serious, overworked self behind and becoming the lighter and freer you.

In this chapter, you will learn:

- How improv exercises can help you create more ease and freedom in your business (and your life)

- Improv exercises that you can do right now to lighten the (bleep!) up

- How to connect more deeply with the animals you are caring for through humor and playfulness

- How to be more flexible and not take yourself so seriously

- And much more!

Kristin's Musings:

After interviewing Alicia, I felt like I'd just received a massage… on the inside! She's one of my dear friends, and when I was planning to have mind/body/spirit experts included in this conference in addition to the pet business experts, I knew I wanted Alicia to be one of the speakers. Having known Alicia for many years, I can say that she practices what she preaches. She lives her life with silliness, playfulness, and humor as well as with a deep and profound authenticity and vulnerability. I'm so excited for you to get a taste of Alicia too from this chapter! You are in for a treat… and a bit of a wild ride!

Alicia Dattner's Bio:

After a dozen years of doing standup comedy, Alicia Dattner has been racking up awards for her humorous, insightful one-woman shows. She enjoys helping business owners lighten up and live life more creatively and spontaneously. Her sold-out hit shows and extended runs have garnered her "Best Comedian 2013," *SF Weekly*; "Best Storyteller," *Off-Broadway NY Solo Festival*; "Best of the Fringe" and "Best Female Solo Show," *SF Fringe Festival*; "Best Local Comedian," *East Bay Express*; and more. The *SF Guardian* called her "Goofy, messy, and fun!" The LA Theater Review says she's "Charming, likable, and funny!"

Mentored by several talented comedians over the years, W. Kamau Bell (*HBO, FX*), Eugene Mirman (*Flight of the Conchords*), and Bill Santiago (*Huffington Post, CNN, Comedy Central*), Alicia's played at clubs like The Improv and Gotham Comedy Club, in San Francisco, New York, Hollywood, Bombay, Chennai, and London.

Alicia has appeared on NPR, *The Wall Street Journal*, *San Francisco Examiner*, *San Francisco Chronicle*, *East Bay Express*, The Lady Brain Show, *J Magazine*, BeliefNET, *Elephant Journal*, Elevate, Inspyr, *Integral Yoga Magazine*, The Mindful Word, Awaken.com, Taoish.com, and more. Find out more about Alicia at *www.AliciaDattner.com*.

Interview with Alicia Dattner
Creativity Coach and Comedienne

Kristin Morrison: *It's such a pleasure to welcome Alicia Dattner. She is a creativity coach. She's a comedian. She's also one of my dearest friends. She has been an incredible stand for me in my business and my life. She's been a great support and an inspiration to me for really bringing play and fun into the business realm. And that's why I've invited you, Alicia, because you are so incredibly playful. And you really embody fun. It's such an honor to have you here. So thank you so much. I'm glad you're here.*

Alicia Dattner: Thanks for having me, Kristin.

You are welcome. So a lot of pet business owners have probably never heard of improv before. I know you've taught improv and you've also taken a lot of improv classes. We took an improv class together and had a lot of fun. Can you share with the pet business audience what improv is for those who don't know what it is?

Let me improvise an answer....

Improv is really the process of making things up. I see it as going to that empty blank space and seeing what pops out from nothing as opposed to when we create something and we sit down and we have a notebook and we write it down and then we look at it and we change our minds and we write it down again. The process of using the mind, the conscious mind, to create. So improv is really about trying to open up a space for the unconscious to come through.

What's beautiful about that is it brings something new into the world that was never there before. And you don't know how it happens. It just comes. And it surprises other people. It surprises us. And we create new connections, new moments that were never here before.

How can that help business owners? How can improv help business owners create more abundance and step into their true potential?

As business owners we, I think, carry a lot of responsibility on our shoulders. We have a vision. We have something we want to create. We may have people working for us or we're the only one working in our business. And really, there can be a sense of, *"I have to do this right. I have to make sure I take care of all my responsibilities."* There can be a sense of needing to be in control… because we do. We need to be in control. We need to make sure that we fulfill all of our obligations and responsibilities, that we collect our bills, that we're doing it right.

And that's fabulous, but if you think about the people in your life who you know who are constantly needing to do it right and there's that sort of, *"I've got to do this. I've got to do that. I've got to do that."* There's a tightness and almost a constriction that ends up feeling like it doesn't bring a lot of flow into their life. Look at those people in your life where you have a sense of, *"Wow, everything just sort of works for them."* You know those people where it's sort of like things flow in. They're okay with that. Things flow out. They're okay with that. And challenges come up. They deal with them, but they don't freak out or they do for a little while, and then they start to sort of dance with the challenges.

Improv is a way to learn to be more in the flow of what's happening, to welcome things that come in, usher things that we need to leave out of our lives, and to experience being at ease in the sea… being at ease in the waves of everything.

In the life sea.

In the life sea. And having fun. What are we doing if we're not having fun? We might as well work for somebody else.

I know. One of the greatest experiences that I had in improv class was really understanding that it's okay to make mistakes. I remember the teacher encouraged us to put our hands up and say, "I made a mistake." And it was applauded and really well received and everybody was happy about that. Because, like you said, we can get so tight. We get so constricted. And so to create awareness around being able to just celebrate the mistakes that I, that we, make as humans, that was very powerful for me.

PEOPLE WHO HAVE THE ABILITY TO "GO WITH THE FLOW" ARE INHERENTLY GOOD AT IMPROV. BUT DON'T WORRY, IT IS A SKILL YOU CAN HONE TO REDUCE STRESS AND ENJOY YOUR BUSINESS AND LIFE A LOT MORE.

I'm wondering what other exercises you think business owners can bring into their pet businesses and their lives in order to really step into that improvisational way of being that creates flow?

One game that I love is trying to take a different response. This isn't for high-stakes moments. This is for moments when maybe you're with your family or your friends. That's a good place to practice. Because when you're actually in your business, keep doing the business thing and see how it goes because every area of your life informs your business. So the more that you're doing this in other areas of your life, the more that you can experience the freedom of using improv in your business itself.

So with a friend, with a family member, with a child, try giving the opposite response that you were about to give.

Okay, let's practice that. I'm a little afraid. And that's good, right? That's where you want to be when you are doing improv.

A little fear is good. Okay, how about if I say something to you and you give me a different response and then we switch.

Okay, perfect. Why don't you ask me a bunch of questions?

Well, what did you have for lunch?

I had nothing for lunch.

Why do you like me?

So if you'll notice, I paused there and that's me going into the thinking mind thinking, "*Oh, what do I need to say in order to be polite?*" So I just want to point out for people that there's a way in which we go into the mind and analyze. It can be uncomfortable.

And it's so important to be uncomfortable. Some of the beginning moments of improv – and this happens for people on a long-term basis and also when they're doing an hour of improv – the first stuff that comes out is usually the stuff that we're most afraid of saying. So it can get like, "*Whoa, did you just say that?*" It's like the stuff that we've been holding for so long that just needs to flow out.

That's also a really valuable practice to move things out that have been sort of sitting there.

It's interesting because I work with a lot of coaching clients around creating a morning practice for themselves. One of the practices is called "morning pages" where you journal-write and you spill your guts and you don't think or edit. You just write three pages. This is from the book, **The Artist's Way.** *The author, Julie Cameron, talks about this in her book. And this (improv) is a similar verbal exercise to that. It's just letting it out and taking out that containment and seeing what's underneath. Another exercise I remember doing in the improv class was choosing a response. It was if you asked me, "What did you have for lunch,"*

I might say, "A vegetable sandwich." Then asking again: "What did you have for lunch?" and the response might be random: "I had a meatball party." And to keep coming up with new answers. And that can be really powerful, too.

I love that. Do you want to try it? What's your favorite activity?

Swimming.

Choose a new response.

Hiking.

New response.

Partying.

New.

Playful bantering.

New.

Packing.

New.

Swimming again and again and again through the English Channel.

What's the thing that annoys you most about business?

Being asked the same thing over and over.

New response.

And over and over.

New response.

Having to check emails 25 times a day.

New response.

Writing down my expenses.

What animal would you like to ride like a horse?

An ostrich.

New response.

Giraffe.

New response.

Elephant.

New response.

A gorilla.

New response.

Zebra. That's an image, isn't it? A zebra. That's like a horse, only it's striped. Oh, my gosh. So this is really good for getting out of the head, isn't it? And I'm also thinking if pet business owners are out there thinking, "Well, how can I do this by myself?," is it possible to do this game by yourself?

You can't.

You can't. You really need somebody to bounce it off, so ask your partner. Ask your kids. This is a great game for kids.

I was kind of joking. You can improvise by yourself. It's just a lot harder.

It is. Why don't you do it? Show us how it's done.

Okay. Alicia, what is the – it's hard. All right. Alicia, what famous movie star would you most like to have a love affair with? Barack Obama. He's not a movie star. New response. Arnold Schwarzenegger. New response. Sylvester Stallone.

New response. Keanu Reeves. New response. Miley Cyrus. New response. Blah. Harrison Ford. New response. Jules Verne.

Don't try this at home.

I know, really, it's dangerous. Definitely not where people can see you. So any other exercises that pet business owners can do to get out of their head and into their body and into their truer self?

So I love to make up exercises for me. There is this whole standard set of exercises that you can look up anywhere on the Internet and search "best improv games," and there are great games like Freeze. I'll just give you a couple of titles: "Freeze" or "Three Things." Some great games like group interaction games. But I think for pet business owners to really get embodied, it would be so interesting to try an improv game where – and you might have to do this by yourself – but where you embody your different pets.

Because they all have their unique personalities.

They do. You do. There's Frankie, the Irish setter. And maybe you're by yourself and you just like kind of get into it. You get on all fours and you just do an impression of your dog. Like what does your dog do? Do that. Because they all have that different personality.

Or maybe there's a kitten that you sit for on Saturdays. There's so many beautiful ways. And dogs particularly are so free. They're so loving. They're so expressed.

To really practice, trying embodying a dog. I think it just liberates something in us and it also can expand the heart in such a sweet way in which the more that we are feeling love and openness and expressing love to others, again the more that flows in and out of our lives in such beautiful ways.

That's gorgeous. I love that idea of really connecting to the pets that we care for.

Another question I have for you, Alicia, is... I know with a lot of pet business owners that I coach... they can really get stuck on, "This is what I have to do today." There's a seriousness that business owners often have. Not just pet business owners, but I think business owners in general. They feel really responsible. They have to be really reliable. I'm wondering how business owners can become lighter and freer? I know we talked about some exercises and maybe there are some more exercises to do to kind of very quickly tap into that playful positive kind of flow that comes from being silly and playful.

I think it's so hard when we get into that place of stress to take ourselves out of it because when you're in a hole and you keep digging, it doesn't help you get out of the hole. So I think the first thing is to become willing and open to the possibility that it could be lighter. Not that you're going to eliminate your problems, but that being with the challenges can be a little easier and lighter.

And so really a willingness to say, *"Yeah, I'm open to this feeling different. I'm open to approaching this in a different way."* I think that's really an important decision or choice to make.

Yes. Even bringing that new response "game" into it and maybe exploring different responses to a situation, to a crisis that may arise in the business.

Definitely. One of my favorite ways to bring more lightness is through a practice called laughter yoga, which is basically laughing. And there are, like improv, hundreds of kinds of exercises you can do. The beauty of laughter – and they've done thousands of studies on this by now – is that when we laugh, whether we are encouraging it and not laughing spontaneously or we are laughing just randomly because a stimulus has us just burst out laughing, our body gets the same benefit. So it doesn't matter if we're faking it or not.

The physiological benefits of laughter are huge. It lowers blood pressure. It lowers cortisol. It releases endorphins into the body. It increases actual tolerance to physical pain. It's a great cardio workout. There are so many amaz-

> THERE ARE PLENTY OF PHYSIOLOGICAL BENEFITS TO LAUGHTER WHETHER THE LAUGHTER IS GENUINE OR FORCED, SO GO AHEAD – LAUGH! IT'S GOOD FOR YOU.

ing benefits of laughter. And you can fake it until the point where you start to maybe laugh at yourself laughing, and then you're actually laughing in a genuine way.

I recommend people take something in their lives and think about it and then just to sort of hold it in their hands as if it were a physical thing. So maybe it's a bill that's due or maybe it's a problem with an employee and to sort of look at it and then open your mouth, making a sound. So you may not feel like laughing at it yet. It's really about creating a bridge from where you are to where you want to go.

I like to have people make a sound from however they're feeling. So if you're feeling like *"Ha"* you just start with *"Ha ha ha ha ha ha."* You're looking at this thing thinking, *"I can't possibly laugh at this. Ha ha ha."* And you're angry and so you just say, *"Ha ha ha ha ha ha ha."* And it's really great if you can have a partner do this with you. So maybe you'll practice with me. You're not quite imitating me, but you're laughing along with me in the same way that I'm laughing.

Okay.

So it's sort of like you're mirroring me in a compassionate kind of way. So, Ha ha ha ha ha. <Silly laughing>

Ha ha ha ha ha. <Silly laughing>

That's really helpful for transforming things that are challenging.

It's true. It moves it out of the body, too, doesn't it? I work with a lot of pet business owners who experience a lot of crises in their businesses. So part of that is just getting it out of their bodies. It's like they become paralyzed from that crisis, and they want to avoid the body in that instance too. They want to run away from it, thinking that's going to help. If they get in their head, they can deal with the crisis, but it's still in their body. I have so many of my coaching clients say, "When I'm over this crisis, then I can breathe." I say, "We need to help you breathe now. Not breathing is making the crisis worse." So I see this as a really powerful exercise to be able to move it out.

Definitely. I see amazing transformations with people even when they just come to an hour-long class and we do some improv and some laughter. They really come in with something that's challenging, and we use laughter and playfulness to make a concerted effort to not be making such an effort.

To let go. To lighten up.

To let go. People walk out after an hour and experience, *"Oh, I guess it's okay. It's not so bad. I could maybe have some new possibility or some new solutions for something."* If you bring that into your life as a practice, and especially with other people around you, you can have this. Even you could do it an hour once a week or you could do it five minutes a day and really experience some new level of a kind of freedom and ease.

Well, a lot of businesses are bringing improv professionals into their companies. I know Google has done that and so has Genentech because they understand the power of improv... of how it really helps employees tap into the flow and relieve stress.

I think it's time to take more seriously not taking ourselves seriously! Anyone who has children knows that they have a totally different experience when they go and play with their kids. Kids do that for us automatically. But not everybody has access to that.

Even dogs and cats are like that. They're really in the moment like you were saying. I mean, they're able to be playful very quickly. They may be sleeping, but then a ball rolls up to them and boom. They're into that play mode. It's really inspiring.

You never see a dog be like, "*I don't know. I would fetch, but I just...*"

"I have too many problems."

"*I know. I'm just working on it. I don't know. You take the ball. How much did this bone cost? How many bones are going to be left? Because if I play with this one now, will there be another bone later?*"

Oh, my gosh. That's true. That's how we humans do it, don't we? It's so important to let go, and dogs and kids can really teach us how to do that.

PETS AND KIDS ARE GREAT TEACHERS TO SHOW US HOW TO LET GO AND LIVE IN THE MOMENT.

Anything else you want to share with the pet business audience out there about how to lighten up, let go, create more ease, create more freedom? Anything else?

I think one of the most valuable things to do is to make regular time to get back in touch with the original purpose, the original vision of why your heart called you to do this work, to have this pet business. Remember how it warmed your heart. What's the bigger vision to really get? If I can take care of these dogs and reduce some of their suffering, help them to not be alone during the day, for example, they're going to be happier and they're going to make their owners happier throughout their lives. And it's going to reduce suffering in the world and that suffering is going to create some world peace.

Their owners are happier. People feel less alone in their lives when they have pets. People feel joy and playfulness. I think being able to come back again and again to the original purpose so that we hold that as the bigger context for what we're here for, then the logistical details can fall inside of that, knowing that this bigger context is why we're really here. And that's the context of lightness and playfulness. And just remembering, *"Oh, I'm grateful that I get to do this."* I think that's what I would say to cap it off.

Wonderful, Alicia. Thank you so much for your time. I'm so grateful for the work that you're doing in the world to lighten us all up and the gift of who you are is just wonderful.

Thanks, Kristin. You too.

SIX

How Pet Professionals Can Skillfully Handle Dogs (and the Dogs' Human Parents!)

Interview with Trish King, CPDT-KA

Got challenging dogs you are working with? How about (ahem!) challenging human clients? Handling difficult dogs can be tricky. In this chapter, you will discover the most important aspects to dog handling and behavior... and have we mentioned human handling and behavior? If you want to work more effectively with your four- and two-legged clients, you'll gain a lot of value from reading this interview with seasoned dog trainer, Trish King.

In this chapter, you will learn:

- The most important aspects of dog handling and behavior

- The sad incident that led Trish to the world of dog training

- How to win trust with a fear-aggressive dog

- How to avoid being bitten (and how to emotionally and physically prepare yourself to get back to working with dogs if you have been)

- Best practices for dog walkers to handle very strong or energetic dogs
- How to work most effectively with your human clients
- And more!

Kristin's Musings:

I met Trish years ago when I attended a dog training course she was leading. I found her to be delightful and an engaging public speaker. She is also one of the most outstanding dog trainers that I've ever witnessed. Her work with fear-aggressive dogs, in particular, is something to behold! I almost didn't ask her the question of how she became a dog trainer, but something in me told me to ask. I'm glad I did (although it was hard to listen to). Some of us find our calling through unusual and sometimes painful circumstances, and she certainly did.

Trish King's Bio:

Trish has been a professional in the animal world for over 25 years. As Director of the Behavior & Training Department at the Marin Humane Society (MHS), she built a department known throughout the United States for its quality. Trish established the Canine Behavior Academy at MHS for new or interested trainers. She currently teaches the Academy of Dog Behavior, hosted by Humane Society Silicon Valley, and teaches workshops and seminars on behavior, canine management, temperament assessment, and handling difficult dogs, among other topics. In addition, she and her partner own Animal Behavior Associates, consulting with and helping dogs and their owners.

You can find out more about Trish at *www.canine-behavior-associates.com*.

Interview with Trish King, CPDT-KA
Canine Behavior Expert

Kristin Morrison: *I am so happy to welcome Trish King. She is a dog trainer extraordinaire. I've seen her in action and she is quite something. She's an author of many books, and she's also an incredible speaker. She taught a dog training academy that I was a part of about ten years ago, and I was just blown away, Trish, by who you are, and I'm just so grateful that you're here.*

Trish King: Well, thank you very much. I still teach that academy, although we moved it to Silicon Valley.

Great! Glad to hear it's still happening. So how did your life journey get you to dog training? I realize I don't know how you came to become a dog trainer.

We always had pets when I was a kid, but I don't think I was any more attached to the dogs and cats and birds and flying squirrels or anything than anyone else was. When I was 21, I was living in England, and my roommate and I got a German shepherd, which is called an Alsatian there. He was a wonderful dog. His name was Sebastian. One day I was walking him on the leash in the downtown streets of London, and somebody walked by with a little Yorkie. He picked up the Yorkie, and he shook it and he killed it. It was a horrible, horrible experience as you can well imagine. So at that point, I think I started to wonder what was going on. I had no idea. I didn't know that dogs could be predatory. I didn't know that little dogs could look like bunnies to them. I didn't know anything about them. So that kind of started me. From there on out, I have had a succession of dogs throughout my life, including several more German shepherds. One of them was a stray that had separation anxiety and ended up being one of the best dogs in the world.

So at any rate, I also was a radio reporter and anchor. I did that for many years, for 20 years. At the same time, I was deeply involved in dogs. I was doing dog training. I was teaching classes and all that. I kept trying to make the two roles combine and they didn't very well. So I started teaching classes at the Marin Humane Society. When I took over as the manager, I wanted to change the way we looked at dog training. Positive reinforcement training was just coming into its own. The Association of Pet Dog Trainers had just been formed. I was one of the first 50 members. We were learning a lot from the trainers of wild animals, marine mammal trainers, and the doors were opening to all different kinds of training methods. It was really an exciting time. So that's kind of my journey.

That's great. Wow. What a shocking start, though, thinking about you with the dog dying.

Yes, having a dog that killed another dog, I have to say that's really helped in my world and in my relationships with clients because I have very little judgment of them as people who own aggressive dogs or whatever because the dog you have is the dog you have. And many times people have no idea who they've got.

Yes, it's true, especially if they get a rescue.

Oh, yes, but even a non-rescue. Dogs are like people. They have their own individual personality even if you think you're getting a Labrador retriever that's going to act like every other Labrador retriever. They don't. They all are very different from one another.

It's true. How would you best describe your training method?

Well, I'm what I would call positive and practical. So my methods are positive. I don't use pain to train. That is a moral choice on my part. I probably would not continue to have been a trainer had I continued to use things like choke chains and similar. I have a tendency to be very positive. I am very practical. So that combination sometimes is what people need, particularly for clients because there are a lot of training methods nowadays that are complex, or they're really good but not necessarily as great for individual owners as for people who are like me. You know, dog addicts. You know, a dog addict will do all kinds of things that a normal person probably doesn't have time to do.

It's true. So what are the most important aspects of dog handling that new dog trainers should know or those new to working with dogs?

Well, I actually think that you need to have – and this is why I started my academy – I think the best thing to do is to have an overall knowledge of the dog. I think it's really easy for people to think that they've got a training method and use that training method on all dogs, but all dogs are not the same, as I mentioned. So I think that understanding dogs and understanding learning theory are really important. Learning how to handle a dog. But more than anything else, it's watching a dog and learning a dog's body language.

When I'm training new dog behavior consultants, one of the biggest problems they have is when you're sitting with a client and the client is having some major issues and you can just see the new consultant thinking, *"Okay, I'll do this, then this, then this, and this."* They're just ticking through their brain, and they leap into the advice portion of the consult way before they're ready and they don't get all the information. Then you might actually be giving the wrong advice.

So it's watching the dog and understanding the dog's body language. The other half of it is watching people and understanding their body language. That's also really important.

Yes, it sure is. So let's say you have a fear-aggressive dog. How can you win trust with that dog?

Well, if we're talking about what I do now, which is besides teaching the academy, I go to people's homes. The first thing you would do is to be safe when you walk in the door, which usually means having the people contain the dog in some way. But I think it's giving the dog time. It's the same thing as when you're doing an evaluation at a shelter. If you hurry too much, you're going to overwhelm the dog. Dogs have very different senses than we do. They cannot see as well as we do. They see in their color, but vision is really muted. They can hear much better than we can. They can smell much better than we can. So all the information that they're taking in about us is different than the information that we're taking in about them. And giving them time is really important.

The other thing for most people to understand is that eye contact can be a wonderful thing between a dog and a person that love each other, but not necessarily between a person and a fear-aggressive dog. In fact, yesterday I was at a consult with a person who had adopted a Border Collie mix a couple of years ago at the age of five. The dog has substantial fear issues. They were amazed that the dog got along with me quite so quickly, but it's because of the observation and knowing that a certain amount of ignoring is a good thing as far as the dog is concerned.

If you think of dogs as little children, sometimes it helps, because little kids don't like to be stared at either. They hide behind their mom's skirts or whatever. They don't like it.

And we use our eyes to investigate. Dogs don't use their eyes to investigate nearly as much as they use their noses and their ears.

It's funny that you should say that, Trish, because I haven't thought about this in years. When I was 12 or 13, I was a volunteer at the Marin Humane Society. I just love the Marin Humane Society. I did a dog wash there. They had a fundraiser or something like that, and I was washing dogs. There was this big husky, and I wanted to connect with him. I was washing his head, and I was looking in his eyes and he bit my lip. Not very hard, thank goodness, but it was enough to draw blood. I mean, if he had really wanted to, he could have bitten off my head.

YOU HAVE TO TRULY UNDERSTAND HOW THE DOG PERCEIVES THE WORLD AND USES ITS SENSES OF SMELL AND HEARING FAR MORE THAN SIGHT. DOGS DO NOT PERCEIVE THINGS THE WAY WE DO.

So it was a warning. But when they took the dog away, they said, "Were you looking in his eyes?" And I replied, "I was." And they said, "Uh-uh. You don't do that. You don't want to stare at a dog like that; you don't want to stare at a dog that you don't know."

But it's really hard. I mean, we tend to do eye contact. Even people who know better. The more fearful a dog is, the more he does eye contact, so any scared animal is going to look at what makes them afraid. We would too, if you were staring at the wall and an enormous spider started walking down the wall. You would keep looking at it because you wouldn't know where it's going to go next.

Because of that, the fearful animal will continue to stare at something, but as soon as you stare back, that sparks them into action. And you don't want them to go into action. You certainly don't want them to become aggressive.

What you got when you were 12 is probably, I would say, a disciplinary bite. The dog saw you as threatening him or her, so it was a bite to tell you to back off.

Yep. And I did.

And it worked. By the way, the dog would have done this to a puppy but wouldn't hurt the puppy. But we're rather fragile.

Yes, we are. Our lips especially are very tender. Owie.

Well, if you actually think about it, it's pretty much every place on our face.

That's true. You're right. So going a bit more about the subject of getting bitten, I've had a few pet sitters and dog trainers call me and say they were bitten, and they've been afraid to get back on the horse, so to speak. To be around dogs kind of shakes them to their core after that experience. I just want to say to pet business owners out there that it rarely happens. I mean considering the amount of dogs a pet business owner might care for. I worked in the pet sitting industry for 18 years. I was in contact with thousands of dogs, and I was bitten once in that whole period. So it rarely happens. I don't want this conversation about dog bites to scare those who are new to the pet business world or those who are thinking about pet sitting, dog walking, or dog training. But with you working with the number of fear-aggressive dogs that you've worked with, Trish, I'm imagining you've been bitten maybe a number of times?

Oh, yes. I've been bitten. Usually I say it's my fault when I was bitten. Now for some of them, it was when I was evaluating a dog and I had to invasively handle a dog; however, if you're a trainer, you don't usually have to do any invasive handling. If you're an evaluator, if you work in a shelter and you really need to find out what this dog is made of, you may do something that the dog perceives as being invasive or as being really rude. So there certainly have been times when I've been bitten that way. I've never been really seriously bitten. But other than that, they are usually times when I'm not watching because, as we say, you don't say, "*I'm going to get bitten.*" You say, "*I just got bit.*"

They are so fast. And the worst places, from the point of view of a person who does house visits, is at the doorway because that's where the dog is going to protect its territory, and also you are a stranger walking in. Particularly if you offer your hand, it may get bitten.

So actually, one of my bites was when I was reaching forward to shake somebody's hand after having finished a consult. This was years and years ago. The dog saw my hand approaching as a threat and bit my hand. That was the worst bite I'd ever had. So you learn from those things.

I'd say the whole thing about once bitten, twice shy is true. A little caution when working with dogs is a good thing. The hard part about being a professional after you have been bitten is thinking, "*Well, if I'm afraid then the dog knows I'm afraid.*" They can tell you're afraid. Then I'm not as useful as I might be. So you have to start controlling your breathing. You have to start thinking about what you can do before you touch a dog. And just kind of make those decisions. And it could be hard.

Yes. So you mentioned controlling your breathing. Can you give us an example of how we would control our breathing when we are scared?

Well, I actually give myself time and really think about my breathing. Years and years ago, I took Aikido, and you learn a lot of breath control there. As a matter of fact, I used to teach a difficult dog class, which is kind of a rowdy class for aggressive dogs. One of the side classes that we taught was actually taught by an Aikido instructor on breathing and on controlling your own body because one of the things that happens if you've got a dog whose issue is that he or she is aggressive is that the owner's hold on him tenses up. They can't cope properly. And the dog reads that change in the leash and then thinks there's a bigger threat than there really is… and it's a spiral that gets out of control.

So learning Zen breathing and things like that is very important, again, because the dogs are going to be able to read you.

Those are things that most trainers probably don't think about, but I think that they should. They need to. In fact, we know that because, if you're a trainer, you know that when you take a dog, the dog acts completely differently than it does with its owner. A lot of that has to do with your body language and what you're projecting onto the dog and what your expectations are. It's very frustrating for an owner to have a dog trainer take the dog and say, "*Oh, this is easy.*"

And the owner is thinking, "*No, it's not. It's really hard.*" So it can be very difficult.

I would imagine. So thinking about dog walkers who are having to walk out-of-control dogs, really strong dogs – I know you said you don't believe in choke collars, which I agree with as well – but how can dog walkers control really strong or out-of-control dogs, especially if the dog walkers are petite and they're trying to walk these dogs?

Oh, you mean if the person is tiny.

Yes. I'm thinking tiny person, big dog.

Tiny person, big dog. Well, there's something that I think is really important to remember, and this is going back to a consult just for a second. If I'm in a consultation and the person is coming up with problem after problem after problem after problem and they are just enormous, sometimes I can't think of anything to do. Usually they're out of their depth or I'm out of my depth or we're both out of our depths.

So one of the things to do is to know who you are. Are you a person who can control a big rowdy dog? Does it make you feel uncomfortable to do that? Would you handle two big rowdy dogs? Are you thinking, "*I need the money*"? Because that's not a good reason to take on a dog that's overwhelming or could possibly be aggressive toward another dog.

I think the best dog walkers know the dogs that they're walking. They actually do a little bit of training before they start walking them. And they know their equipment. Usually from the point of view of equipment, what I like are the no-pull harnesses and sometimes a gentle leader, depending on the dog. But developing a relationship with the dog is probably more important than anything else. I think most good dog walkers will do that.

Sometimes I think the new ones starting out think dog walking is a lot easier than it is. It's very hard work. People sometimes think they can control dogs more than they really can. I always think that I might be able to control three or four dogs, but if a deer runs across my path and I cannot hold onto the dogs, then I'm not really controlling them. But that, again, is for where we live in California. There are a lot of deer. There are a lot of prey animals that will go right in front of you, and all of a sudden, you've got a dog that's going, *"Okay, I'm a wolf. I need to go chase him."*

Yes, that instinctual drive kicks in. So you've worked with so many dogs, so many people. Do you feel like you know dogs completely or do you find that you're still surprised by things that come up, or do you have to come up with creative solutions for dogs?

> THE BEST WAY TO CONTROL A DOG IS BY KNOWING THE DOG... AND KNOWING YOURSELF AND YOUR OWN LIMITATIONS.

I like my job because I think of myself as being a detective to figure out what's going on with a dog, what's going on with the owner, and see if I can help them. No, I don't think you ever know everything. In fact, if I ever thought I knew everything, I should just get out of the business because you're constantly learning. When you think about it, we should be really well paid because not only are we teaching an animal – so that's a different species – but we're also teaching a person who is the same species... and we're teaching both of them who don't want to learn.

The people might think they want to learn, but a lot of times, they really don't. The dog has no desire to learn what you're teaching him. So you're teaching interpersonal communication between dog and owner, and you're actually trying to motivate them to learn what you want them to learn as well. I think a good trainer is worth her weight in gold.

Yes, I agree. Thinking back to a recent challenging experience that you had with a dog, how did you deal with that? What happened and how did you deal with it?

I was actually looking back on my calendar to see what kind of challenging cases I've had lately. I think the most challenging ones right now are that I'm working with about three court cases. They're challenging mostly because of what the courts are demanding that the owners do. So the dogs have been deemed aggressive or deemed vicious, so the people now have to take a lot of responsibility where they didn't do that before. The dogs themselves in the cases that I'm working with are actually not that bad. I've had, in the not too distant past, a St. Bernard that actually was downright dangerous. And it was a rescue dog. We didn't know what the dog's history was. He was obviously very, very large. He had integrated into the family really quickly and was protecting all the weaker members of the family, so that was protecting the wife and the children. Unfortunately, the dog had no idea who was dangerous and who wasn't dangerous, so as far as the dog was concerned, everybody was dangerous.

He ended up being returned to the rescue where they got him, which was appropriate because these people were not ready for this dog. He was very dangerous. So when I'm dealing with something like that, I have to make sure that the dog is under control while we're discussing the case and while we're discussing what's going on.

The hardest thing I've had to deal with lately, though, is a client, an elderly couple. They're in their late 80s with a two-year-old Labrador retriever mix that is very, very energetic. And these people are in their late 80s. They've had Labs all their lives, so as far as they're concerned, they are good Lab owners. The problem is that they live on a cul-de-sac, and they let the dog out. They kind of follow him out, so they're watching him. He goes and visits all the neighbors and says hello. And that's all very good, but if anybody he doesn't know comes into the cul-de-sac, he goes after them.

So he bit a pool man, and he scared bunches of other people. To me, this is a really simple case. The dog is very territorial. It's actually a very sweet dog. It's territorial and it needs to be contained. They won't do it.

I said, *"Well, can you put the dog on the leash when you take him out in the morning?"* And they said, *"No, don't want to do that."*

"Can you do a lot of recalls and use treats for the recalls?" *"No, we don't want to do the treats."* So everything I came up with: *"No, can't do that. No, don't want to do that. No."* So that's owner compliance issues. I think out of everything, owner compliance issues are always the worst.

Yes, they can be challenging. It's funny because that was my next question. For a lot of pet business owners, the animals are a piece of cake, but you get these pet parents who can be kind of intense and difficult to deal with sometimes.

> IT IS OFTEN MUCH EASIER TO TRAIN THE DOG THAN TO TRAIN THE OWNER. UNDERSTAND THAT THERE WILL BE DIFFICULTIES, BUT THERE IS ALSO A BALANCE. SOMETIMES YOU SIMPLY HAVE TO LET GO.

Oh, they really can. I had one person a long time ago to whom I was suggesting that the dog be put on a tie-down to control the dog in the house because the dog's energy was explosive. And the male owner was just shaking his head and saying, *"No, can't do that. No, can't do that."* And I asked, *"Well, could you use a crate?"* *"No. No, can't do that. No, we can't do that."* *"How about putting him in the bedroom?"* *"No. No, can't do that."* I finally said,

"Your dog needs to be contained or restrained in some way. Why can't you do this?" And he said, *"Well, when I was a kid my mom put me in the closet, so I just can't stand that kind of stuff."*

I said, *"You know your dog is not you."*

Sounds like he needed a therapist to work through his trauma. Poor guy.

He was a therapist. Sometimes I say I've got my MFCC. That's a marriage, family, and *canine* counselor.

I love it. On some level, a lot of pet business owners need to be like a therapist with their clients because dealing with the humans can be hard.

Well, there are dog trainers — people who, like day trainers, will take the dog out and train the dog… and now we're going to do sit and down and come and stay and all those things that we want the dog to do. Those are dog trainers. They have the easier job, I think. Then there are consultants or trainers who work with the people, which is what I am. But honestly, that's what I like. I find the personalities and the combinations and all that to be fun and interesting. I'm good at letting go, and that is one of the hardest things for consultants to do. If you've got a non-compliant owner – like this person who says, *"No, I'm not going to contain my dog in the cul-de-sac,"* then you need to be able to either deal with this person or let them go as a client. You need to want to deal with those kinds of people. And I can let it go. I can say, *"Well, I'm not going to get through to this person."*

It's true. I know there is a fine balance between keeping clients and letting them go… you know, the clients who are really, really challenging. I think that can be a real issue for pet business owners.

I think so. But I would imagine it's very much the same as teaching children in the school.

Yes. Absolutely. Teachers have to go through it too with parents.

Yes, dealing with the parents. And sometimes they have no option. I think that it's easy to burn out in both of those professions.

I included a chapter on burnout because it's so prevalent in the pet business world, and oftentimes, nurturers are really drawn to the profession. They have caretaker personalities and it can be hard for them to say no.

Yes. It definitely can be hard to say no. It is kind of like when you're trying to set your fees and somebody calls you and says they don't have very much money, so you have to decide whether or not you're going to do something pro bono or not. I tend to do pro bono work with certain kinds of people, particularly people who have adopted from the shelter I'm associated with now.

But you can get yourself drawn in, and you can just care too much. For instance, one of my clients has a dog that has pretty severe hip and knee problems, and they don't really want to do anything about it. Well, I think they should. I mean, it's in both back legs, so this is a pretty big deal. It's impacting the dog's life tremendously. So I have to push for that and talk about what good it will do. At the same time, I realize that I can only do so much. I can't do it. I can't give the dog what it needs. I have to help the people with what it needs. And it could be really hard. It's like a burnout.

Oh, completely. Any final words for pet business owners who are kind of struggling in their business?

You know, I really think just hang in there if you are struggling. It takes at least a year to get known, to actually put yourself out there and have some word-of-mouth referrals and getting yourself involved with other people in the same field but different parts of it. I have a whole list of trainers who do dog training that I refer to and classes and things like that. I also have dog walkers and doggie day cares for the people who need those. So I think getting a whole referral network going is a very important thing. This is a lonely business.

Sometimes you may be working with somebody, and you really want to tell somebody else what happened and there's nobody to talk to. So getting a network, I think, is very important and just hanging in there. And get a sense of humor about it. I think you have to have a sense of humor with everything.

Yes, I agree. It's funny, Trish, because we're including a chapter on improv and how that can help business. I have a friend who is an improv teacher, and she does standup comedy, so we did this whole chapter on how improv can help your business and help you lighten up.

If I can't make my clients laugh… then I'm probably not going to be able to help them. Because you have to have a light heart when you go into this.

You really do. Well, thank you so much, Trish. I really appreciate your time and your wonderful energy and being here.

Well, you're very welcome. And I wish you the best of luck.

SEVEN

The Art of Making More Money in Your Pet Business

Interview with Jerrod Sessler

"Money isn't the most important thing in life, but it's reasonably close to oxygen on the 'gotta have it' scale," said Zig Ziglar, and you know what? He's right! We need money for survival for sure. But how about we take it from simply surviving (blech!) to THRIVING? In this interview, you will learn what works and what doesn't work when it comes to certain types of pet businesses, and how to make more money doing what you love. By the way, Jerrod took time out of his super-busy schedule to do this interview. Thanks, Jerrod, for making yourself available to us.

In this chapter, you will learn:

- Some of the best pet-based business opportunities
- What to do first to make more money in your business (instead of adding more services)
- How to fall in love with your pet business again
- What type of pet businesses might not be lucrative
- What it takes to get your pet business to the next level
- And more!

Kristin's Musings:

Jerrod Sessler is a hero. He's a man who has changed his reality many, many times. His bio reads like the lifetimes of ten different people! From NASCAR driver dream at age four to making that dream happen many years later to running five different companies, this guy is a superstar. Not to mention his recovering from "incurable" cancer through massive diet and lifestyle changes (which, alas, we didn't have much time to talk about in this interview). Want a glimpse into what is possible in your own life? If so, you'll want to soak up some of this man's empowering energy by reading this chapter.

Jerrod Sessler's Bio:

Jerrod Sessler is the founder and CEO of HomeTask, Inc., a multi-brand, service-focused franchisor, as well as the owner of Pet Butler, a successful pooper-scooper franchise, and multiple other highly successful franchises. Born in 1969, Sessler has always had a passion for innovation and leadership. At four years old, Sessler told his mom that he wanted to drive a racecar and in 1998 that dream came true when he started racing as a NASCAR driver. After serving as a Navy Petty Officer and then as an engineer at Intel Corporation, Sessler's life was seemingly destined to come to a screeching halt when he was diagnosed with stage four metastasized melanoma. Sessler was given a five percent chance of life and opted to pursue alternative treatment by moving to a plant-based diet. Now, more than 15 years after his grim diagnosis, Sessler is cancer free and full of life.

In 2004, Sessler founded HomeTask, Inc., a service company, using the franchise business platform, which allowed him to grow great brands such as Yellow Van Handyman, Freggies, Lawn Army, Pet Butler, and Hot Feet Fitness. To find out more visit *www.hometask.com/founder.aspx.*

Interview with Jerrod Sessler
Founder, HomeTask, Inc.

Kristin Morrison: *I am so delighted to welcome Jerrod Sessler. He is the founder and CEO of HomeTask, Incorporated. He's also the CEO and founder of Pet Butler, which is a nationally recognized franchise for pooper scoopers. He also is the owner of four other successful franchises. He's a busy guy, and I'm so grateful you're here, Jerrod. Thank you.*

Jerrod Sessler: Well, thank you, Kristin. Thanks for having me. It's exciting to be on here.

I'm just thrilled. Thrilled, thrilled, thrilled. So, how did you get into the world of pooper scooping?

Let me make a couple of corrections. I didn't found Pet Butler. I am the owner of it, but the vision for it was birthed through another talented entrepreneur. I just happen to be lucky enough to have been able to acquire it in 2010, which kind of ties into how I got into it. I bought my way into the pet business. Before Pet Butler, I didn't have a pet business but am definitely a pet lover and have had pets all my life. I've grown up with pets all my life and really enjoy them. Pet Butler is the largest pet waste cleanup business in the world. We have franchises all over the country, and it's very good, a very successful business and one that was a golden opportunity for me to get involved with. As you mentioned, we license several different service-based franchise brands, and we manage the brands like Yellow Van Handyman, Lawn Army, Pet Butler, Freggies, Hot Feet Fitness, and a couple of others. So all of those locations kind of grew up underneath our umbrella and our responsibility. Pet Butler was started in Dallas. It was built into a pretty decent-sized business and needed to make some transitions in 2010. So we were able to take ownership of Pet Butler and kind of jump in and inject a lot of positive into the business and see it grow.

That's great. So what can people charge for pooper scooping? What's the going rate?

Well, it really depends on the location, obviously, and the neighborhood and things like that. Some locations are a little bit lower; some are a little bit higher. Our average customer requests two visits a week, so they're spending in the neighborhood of around $80 to $90 a month on the service. You can have locations that are operating very small. Startup locations with maybe a few dozen people who they're scooping for... up to some of our larger locations, which have had or have over a thousand customers who they're scooping for with six, seven, eight scooping vehicles and trucks and different things. So it can be a very big operation with a lot of people, or it can be a very small self-run, one-truck, one-person sort of operation.

How long does it take? I'm imagining each yard differs in terms of size and all of that, but on average, how long does it take to scoop poop?

The average is generally somewhere between three and seven minutes depending on the yard. The scoopers get very efficient at it, and we have all the software to manage all of the logistics, so the routing is set up so that they're using as efficient a method as possible from one route to the next. The time in the yard is actually less than... it's about half of what the time is driving to and from. We do the best job we can to try to route them through our custom software called Poop Net, and that allows people to jump from house to house to visit the dogs. A lot of times, they'll spend a minute or two saying hi to the dogs, giving them treats, doing things like that. Then we've got some tools to be able to clean the yard pretty quickly.

Poop Net! That's hilarious. So a huge benefit for Pet Butler franchise owners is that they would get access to that software and that efficiency. That's great. What are some of the other benefits of buying a franchise versus starting their own company?

I would say one of the biggest growth methods or mechanisms that we use and that we encourage our franchise partners to use is acquiring small-owner scooping businesses that start off and might get to 20 or 30 customers but can't grow beyond that for whatever reason. That's a great growth mechanism for us.

A lot of people who start these businesses don't understand how much infrastructure and overhead can be absorbed into the things that a franchise really does for you. So we handle all the billing for our franchise locations. We also do all the routing, scheduling, customer support, and customer sign up. We do all of that from our support center, so the franchise partners essentially go out and talk to people in the community, telling them about Pet Butler. They get people signed up if they want to do that locally or in person, or customers can do it either at PetButler.com or by calling our support center.

So there are a lot of things we do. Our franchise partners pay us 12 percent of their revenue to provide all that support, but think about all of what we're doing for them: Let's say you have a $200,000 business, so 12 percent of that is going to be $24,000 a year. What kind of an employee are you going to hire for $24,000 a year... and are they going to be able to do billing and customer support and web development and scheduling and all these different things that we do, as well as the branding and marketing and all of that kind of stuff?

BEING A FRANCHISEE CAN BE A GREAT WAY TO LAUNCH YOUR BUSINESS AND INCREDIBLY VALUABLE. YOU GET THE BUSINESS SUPPORT YOU NEED AND SKILLS YOU MAY NOT HAVE, WITHOUT HAVING TO REINVENT THE WHEEL.

Look at some of the larger locations. Let's say a location is doing a million dollars, so 12 percent of that is still pretty significant, right? That's over $100,000 a year, but when you look at the amount of volume that's going through that sized business, it still makes sense because you'd have to hire a number of employees and have all kinds of technology and systems and different things to be able to do it. Obviously, I'm a big fan of franchising, but I really feel like that comes from the heart of an entrepreneur and wanting to see others succeed.

I really can feel that from you. I think if someone were to crunch the numbers, it makes so much sense to become a Pet Butler franchisee instead of starting your own business, with all the access to all those tools and resources.

Yes, thank you. I appreciate you saying that.

I'm thinking that hiring a manager can be expensive...

Yes. I would say Pet Butler is on the end of a better overall margin of business because you look at all the overhead pieces. You have a truck, which is really inexpensive, and you have a person scooping, which doesn't require any significant skill other than somebody that loves animals, right? So there isn't a huge dollar value associated with the labor, so labor can be fairly low and those new to the business can even do it themselves.

But I will tell you that selling scooping services is not as easy as some other services. The reason is, we already know that about 41 percent of our population have a dog, but what percentage of that 41 percent is willing to spend $40 to $80 or maybe even $100 or more per month to have their yard cleaned? And that's a small percentage of the 41 percent who owns a dog. Now you're maybe trying to market to a niche of maybe five percent or 10 percent of the population who has a dog and is willing to spend that kind of money on a monthly basis to be able to get their yard cleaned.

The only difficulty that franchisees sometimes have is finding the right clients who are interested and are financially able to pay for the service. It's not a difficult service to sell at all. In fact, we don't really sell. We educate because most people don't realize that there's somebody who will come and scoop the poop out of their yard. They're all like, "*I didn't know there was a service I could pay for that.*" Our biggest challenge is education. Once you find the right people who need the service and we educate them that this service is available, then it's pretty easy to sell it and make it move.

But let me contrast this to a Lawn Army, which is another brand that we have that provides lawn maintenance services. Lawn Army is a great brand, and it's a very powerful brand and very profitable. It's a little bit different because you have a higher-value vehicle that you're driving to the property and using to take care of the property, but the sale is easier because almost everyone who owns a home or property has a yard or something like that which they need cared for. On top of that, almost all those people are programmed or in a place where they feel like or would agree that they are used to hiring someone for that service. So now you're selling to maybe 70 or 80 percent of the population versus five or 10 percent.

So you see, just to be totally transparent, the challenge with Pet Butler is finding people who want the service who are willing to pay for it. But once you do, then I'd say that it's pretty easy.

I would imagine that once they become used to the ease of having somebody from Pet Butler coming in to scoop the poop that they don't discontinue it usually, right?

Yes, we have very good retention rates. We do a lot of things. We have a program set up in our system in which when the scooper is on site, the customer (or we call them members) can have an automatic text sent to them saying, "*Hey, your yard is being scooped right now.*"

That's great. I bet clients love that.

Yes. It's also great because now – in case they want other services added to it… maybe they want something sanitized or maybe there is some stuff on the back patio (maybe they have a kitten that urinated there) and they need it sanitized or maybe they want some special treatment done on their yard or they just want to know that *"Hey, my yard has been cleaned and I want notification of that because I'm paying for it."* We also leave Post-It notes on the back windows or wherever the customer wants, if they want that, saying, *"Hey, you've been scooped,"* just to let them know that we've been there.

So in addition to pooper scooping, which is a good pet-based industry opportunity obviously, although you do have to get clients who are that slim margin, what are some of the other best pet-based opportunities that are out there right now, in your opinion?

Well, obviously, I like Pet Butler and I like the pet waste cleanup business. I wouldn't be in it if I didn't feel it was a really good opportunity. I mean, really, the reason I got the franchise is because I really want to help people own businesses. I think a lot of young owners don't have the skill set and the trust in terms of their overall ability to wear seven different hats to be able to make a business go. I think the franchise really allows you to plug those in. So obviously, the pet waste cleanup I think is good. The reason is because it's got low overhead and it's got decent margins. In other words, you can make a decent amount of money without having a huge overhead expense burden. What that means is that when the economy goes tough, you don't have huge overhead. You don't have commercial space, for example. You don't have to sign a five- or ten-year lease on commercial space. You can operate Pet Butler out of your home.

I would say any pet-based or pet-focused, low-margin business that has a good opportunity to draw people who want to buy that service is great. I think retail is more difficult in the pet industry because retail is being dominated by online shopping. If you're going to sell through Amazon then great, you can do something retail. A gal I know here in Seattle recently started a company called Lean Licks, which is this dog-licking thing. It's like a pushup we had when we were kids that hung around your neck. It's like a dog treat. So when you're training the dog, you just pull the cap on the Lean Lick, and you let them take a lick of it and it's like a treat for them. But that's a retail thing. She has to figure out how to get that out.

Another pet-based business that I like that can have a higher profit margin is pet grooming. I think there are a lot of opportunities. Pet grooming is great because there are so many people who, again, it's a service that pet owners don't really want to do or don't know how to do, but need it. They don't feel like they can do it correctly or that it's done as well as a service that's coming in.

I guess those would be some of the things to think about for some of the different services. I know there are also these pet motels and pet day cares and some of those different types of pet businesses. I think those are good-margin businesses from what I understand. But they also require so much investment. You need a half-a-million-dollar net worth or more just to be able to get into one of those because the build out is pretty expensive to be able to do that in most parts of the country.

So it depends on what a person is looking for. If they have that kind of investment, then they can look at either larger businesses that have really no overhead like Pet

> BE CAUTIOUS ABOUT LAUNCHING A BUSINESS THAT HAS HIGH OVERHEAD, ESPECIALLY ONE THAT INVOLVES PROPERTY. KEEPING YOUR OVERHEAD LOW ALLOWS YOU TO SURVIVE THROUGH TOUGH TIMES AND ECONOMIC DOWNTURNS.

Butler, or they can look at a more expensive business to get into that generates more revenue on the back end.

With the doggy day cares and the boarding facilities, there's also the zoning issues, and it can be very challenging to find a location for those kinds of businesses because of the barking of the dogs.

Location-based businesses make me nervous. I own restaurants also, and we have Data Doctors and it has locations, so I know about that, too. Our headquarters is a location that we lease and pay rent for. However, if you just hone it down to a doggy daycare kind of situation, let's say you it costs you $400,000 or $500,000 to build out or if you're not doing that, maybe you're paying $10,000 in rent a month. If you're on the hook for that lease or that property and all of a sudden your business takes a tough turn, do you have the momentum to be able to make it through a financially rough three-, four-, or five-year period? That's the question. With a low-overhead business, you tend to be able to float through those storms a little bit easier.

There's also the issue if the lease runs out for, let's say, a doggy daycare. Then what do you do?

Right.

It can be very challenging. I sold my business last year. I had it for 18 years. I created a pet sitting company 18 years ago, and it was a really great time because people didn't really know about pet sitters so much then, but there was a need. So I had to educate people a little bit at that point. It wasn't the way it is now. Pet sitting is a really a booming business all over. Everybody knows about pet sitters and dog walkers, but not many knew about them then. When I put my business on the market, the broker had a few other pet businesses for sale. So I would encourage people who don't have a business who might be thinking about having one to perhaps look at one you could buy that's kind of ready-made. It's got all the kinks worked out. I mean, not all the kinks. There's always something. When you have a business, things come up. But looking at something like a Pet Butler franchise where you can simply begin. You don't have to reinvent the wheel. That can be really great for some people. Then there are other people who really have that entrepreneurial spirit who want to start it from the ground up. So it's important to know yourself and what would work best for you.

There are a lot of different options. I agree with that wholeheartedly. With Pet Butler, we've had several successful transitions. We've had owners who got to a place in their lives where they wanted to make a transition, and we help them do that.

The other thing that's really neat is that when you get into the valuation of these businesses, these owners are actually walking away with sizeable chunks of money, which they deserve because they built this business over the last several years. I really like that. I'm a big fan of franchising, obviously, because I like the fact that the success percentage, your success ratio, is going to be better when you partner with somebody who has done it a dozen times or more before and has all these other successful locations. I think that's a really wise way to go.

We have one major market right now that we're basically buying out almost all of the local scooping businesses because we have a new owner who wants a big business right away, and he's got the investment to be able to do it.

There are many different ways to be able to get into a pet business. A more sophisticated owner might have the financial ability to be able to go in and buy a business. When you take ten small businesses that were all scooping say between 50 and 150 and you combine them all into one big business and then you apply our routing software to that, you just shot the margins through the roof.

Speaking of margins, what are some additional streams of income that pet business owners might not be noticing that they could create in their business or add to their list of services or products?

Well, I would say this: The biggest thing that I think service businesses – and this goes for people who are in the industry whether or not you're not with a brand – is that most likely you're probably not charging enough. That would be the first thing I would look at instead of asking, *"Hey, what can I add? What else can I do?"*

Again, I'll give you an example that will answer that question and also give you a caution. Lawn Army is a landscape maintenance business. With all of our brands, we're on the client's property. Yellow Van Handyman is a professional handyman service. We're going to the house and doing something. With Lawn Army, we're going to the property and taking care of the grass. Pet Butler… we're going and we're cleaning up after the animals. It makes sense, you would think, that we would combine Lawn Army and Pet Butler because they're both in the grass. Okay, one guy is going to scoop the poop and another guy is going to mow the grass. We're going to do these. A landscaper would think, *"Hey, I'm going to start offering pooper scooper services and I'm going to do that before I mow the grass."* Or a pooper scooper could think, *"Hey, I'm going to throw a lawn mower in my trunk and I'm going to start mowing the grass after I scoop it."* Right? But if it's not something that the customer needs when you happen to be there, it doesn't make sense for you to add that service onto your business.

I would say one of the most important things is that you are absolutely masterful at whatever it is your core business is. If you're not making six figures or more on an annual basis, then you shouldn't be adding anything else to do it. Adding something is not your problem. Getting traction within the marketplace and getting a blanket of customers, a group of customers who you can throw under a blanket. In other words, you own a community. Because if you're offering a service and it's a mobile-based service and you're driving all over town, you need to shrink your territory and you need to own a certain community. You need to develop at least $100,000 a year out of that community. Once you get to that point, most likely you'll want more. You'll think, *"Okay, how do I get $250,000 out of a little bit larger area?"* You're still offering the same service rather than trying to add additional services onto that.

My response to that is I don't think the answer for most people, especially for very small businesses, is to add different services or products. I think you ought to focus on what you're doing and get better at it. If you don't feel like you can be the best in the world at it, then submit your location and join a franchise and let them help you get better at it or find something different to do. Or they can find a business coach like you who has experience in the pet industry.

> DON'T IMMEDIATELY ASSUME THAT THE BEST WAY TO GROW YOUR BUSINESS IS TO ADD MORE SERVICES. BE CERTAIN YOU ARE THE ABSOLUTE BEST YOU CAN BE IN OFFERING YOUR CORE SERVICE AND DO MORE OF THAT.

When I'm working with new clients, often the first step that I take with them is to look at what they are charging. Often it's very low. They haven't raised their rates in seven years or they've raised them but they haven't raised them enough. I definitely agree with that. Rather than spreading themselves too thin by offering other services, they need to focus on the services they are currently offering and find a way to get those services out to more clients.

It's very important. Here's an easy way of defining it and this will probably offend somebody, but I'd rather offend somebody and tell you the truth than not. If the answer to growing your business is always lowering your rates or providing a coupon, then you need to explore more about business. Lowering your price or giving coupons is not the only way to grow your business, and often it's not the best way to grow your business.

It's true. In fact, it often draws the wrong kind of clients to you too.

Not only that, but it puts you in a position in which you now do not have the financial ability to actually provide the level of service that you want to provide. So it becomes very difficult to stay in business that way.

Any further words for pet business owners who are out there before we end this interview?

Well, let's see. I like Jim Collins, and I like his Good to Great methodology. I think that we should all strive to be the best in the world at whatever we're doing. If you don't have the kind of passion that you feel like you should have or that you see in someone else who you admire as a business owner, then find a business that gives you that ability and that vision and that passion, or try to manipulate yourself to be able to do that. Sometimes you could take your brand or your location and you can inject yourself into a system in which you've got other owners around the country who you can relate with. You've got a group that you can come together with at conventions and that you can wear the same brand and talk the same talk and feel like you're supported.

Sometimes that helps give you the catalyst to be better and to be the best you can be. I don't think that there's anything in our life that we shouldn't do with excellence and the best we can do it. If you are a business owner right now and you have been for a few years, you deserve a pat on the back. Let me give that to you today because you deserve it! It's so cool to see what small business is doing for our society and our culture today.

So it's time to get with it. It's time to get busy and if you don't feel like you have the motivation or excitement to do what you're doing, then find something that you do.

I love that. I had the experience in my business in which it was kind of like having the seven-year itch and I fell out of love with my business. I really had to re-evaluate who I was with my business. What was our relationship and what could I do differently to fall in love with my business again? I was able to do that. I went from working seven days a week to working three days a week and that really gave me the spaciousness to fall in love with it again.

So what I want to add to what you were saying – and I think those were such wise words – is that your business is going to be just like any relationship. We do have relationships with our business. There are going to be days where we feel like we just don't like our business. You might be thinking or saying to your friends and family, "I want out." Perhaps you have a difficult client or things aren't going the way you want. But if you can look at how you can do this differently, that can make a profound shift. Is there a way? For me, after 18 years, I realized I had taken it as far as I truly wanted to go and it truly was time to sell it. But it wasn't out of the feeling of not liking or loving my business anymore.

Don't let yourself get to that point because then it's no fun anymore. The bottom line is that we should be filled with joy daily and we should be having fun with what we're doing.

Live the lifestyle that you want to live and have some freedom with your time. Last winter I took my family to Costa Rica for two months so we could learn Spanish, and I worked a little bit while I was gone, but not much. As business owners, we should all be able to do stuff like that.

I agree. I don't know if you know, Jerrod, but I lived in Bali for six months. I was in India before that. No pet sitter I had ever met had ever traveled for extended periods of time like that and I didn't know if it was possible, but I thought, "You know what, I'm going to try it!" Because that would make me truly happy at that point in my life. And it was the most powerful and incredible experience that I've ever had... I mean, to be living there and not working. Taking a sabbatical. Then I came back with this rejuvenation for my business. It was powerful.

Wow. Sometimes small business owners might need to do a little piece of that to start with. They might need to say, *"Hey, I'm going to take one day a week and I'm going to go and I'm going to immerse myself in something that is completely unrelated to my business."* You know, some passion. Pull something off the shelf from when you were a teenager that you've always wanted to do. I have a friend who was just wrapping up dive instruction or he's becoming a certified diver. It took him several months to do it, but it was just something that he wanted to do and he got it done. I think that there are ways to rejuvenate yourself without breaking the bank as a small business owner. Those are just some of the ways of trying to do it.

I love that. Thank you so much. I'm so happy that you were able to join me, Jerrod.

Thank you. It's great to be here and I hope the information was helpful.

Very helpful. I appreciate it. Thanks so much.

EIGHT

Using Healthy Living and Eating to Create Energy for Optimal Living (and Running Your Business)

Interview with Chess Edwards

If you are suffering from business burnout or even just need a little pick-me-up, this is the chapter to read. In this interview, Chess shares his experience, strength, and hope around how to feel good… no matter what is going on in your business or your life. So grab a glass of water (yes, water). You'll find out why during the interview.

In this chapter, you will learn:

- How to have as much energy as the dogs you care for have
- What one action first thing in the morning will start your day off with vim and vigor
- Foods to eat (and eliminate) to feel vitally alive
- How eating healthfully can transform yourself and your family and friends
- Recipe of The World's Greatest Kale Salad!
- And much more!

Kristin's Musings:

Chess is a friend that I met during my time in Bali. He radiates good health, vitality, and dynamic wisdom, which is why I chose him out of the many others I could have picked for this particular chapter. I recommend you create time to buy the ingredients in order to make this yummy salad tonight. It's incredible. Bon Appetite!

Chess Edwards's Bio:

Chess Edwards is an international Guide for Optimal Living. Whether it be guiding personal development journeys in some of the world's most inspiring locations, coaching business leaders to discover their most potent leadership skills, facilitating corporate team development processes, or coaching individuals to create their most vibrant and fulfilling lives, Chess brings courageous awareness to the life skills that enliven and unlock full potential.

His focus on creating solid foundations of health, mindfulness, and commitment draws upon a lifetime of meditation, photography, healthy and creative cooking, physical vitality, and world-wide adventure travel.

"As a guide, my work is to assist people on their journey through challenging conditions and deliver them to an empowered vantage point of fresh perspectives, clarity and the actualization of human potential." To find out more visit *www.ChessEdwards.com.*

Interview with Chess Edwards
International Guide for Optimal Living

Kristin Morrison: *I am thrilled to welcome Chess Edwards here. He is an optimal living coach. He is a mindfulness teacher. He's a motivational speaker. And he's also a self-proclaimed healthy man. And we need more of those out in the world, and more healthy people in general. So, hi, Chess.*

Chess Edwards: Hey, Kristin.

I'm so excited to have you here.

I am too. I'm so glad you asked me to do this and be a part of this.

I want to let everybody know – because some of the viewers know that I lived in Bali in 2010 and 2011 – that I met Chess the second time I was there in 2011, and he was quite vital then and I can see that he's even more vital now. So Chess, why do you eat healthfully? What's the point of that for you?

Well, you know, you mentioned Bali because those are such watershed experiences. That was an experience for me that really like you said, it opened up my vitality even more and gave me more options. The way I see it, it's a lifelong journey. I've always eaten basically healthy, but when I was a kid, it was frozen burritos in the microwave and frozen pizzas. From there, it progressed all the way along. If you had asked me five years ago, *"Do you eat healthy?"* … I would say, *"Oh, yeah."* But now I look at how I ate five years ago and realize maybe not so much. I eat healthy now because I'm running my coaching business as well. I do corporate client business and I recognize that when I eat healthfully, there are many good things that happen. And one of the first is I feel more vibrant. I have more energy throughout the day.

But there's a great phrase that says, *"It's hard to run your business when you can't even get out of bed in the morning."*

Isn't that true? Unless you want to have your laptop in bed!

Yes. And the middle of the day, if I'm not eating well. I'm in my early 50s, and if I'm not eating well, during the middle of the day I start to crash. I start to go down. So it's about body vitality.

As you say that, I'm thinking there are a lot of pet business owners out there who work with dogs. Dogs have a lot of energy and it's almost like, in a way, we have to match that. We have to come to them with our vital selves to meet their vital selves and to really have that connection.

Right. And our businesses are vital. They're vibrant. They're growing. They've got an energy of themselves as well. If our energy is down, our business energy is going to be down as well.

It's true. Our mojo.

That's exactly it. So that's the body, and the other is for the mind. We feed our brains. We're learning more and more about brain chemistry and brain biology. So coconut oils and different types of short chain fat can be so good for us. That feeds our brain. So we want to make sure we're feeding our brain, not starving our brain. Not overstimulating our brain. It's one of our organs that needs to be really healthy because, as you know, when one is starting a new business or running a business there are lots of decisions to be made. You've got to be really clear. So it's not just our intentions. It's the actual physicality, how clear can we think.

That's right. I know that you said you've made some changes in your life around eating pretty healthy most of your adult life, but then really ramping it up in the last few years. What were some of the changes that you made recently?

One of the most recent ones was because I suffered from candida, which is an internal overgrowth of yeast in the system. It typically happens if you do a long course of antibiotics and then don't rebuild the probiotics in the system. So I did a two-month cleanse with no sugars, no antibiotics, no dairy, all natural food. And one of the things that has shifted since then is that when I eat meat products, they don't contain antibiotics.

I used to think, *"Hey, I'm eating chicken or I'm eating lean. I'm eating turkey. Great, that's good enough."* Now I'm looking at it and recognizing that if they're eating the antibiotics, I'm eating the antibiotics. And that word: antibiotics. I don't want my biotics to be anti! I want my biotic system to be really lively. So that's one of the changes I've made. A lot more leafy vegetables. I'm eating about 60 percent leafy vegetables now in my diet, and I make my own dressings now.

I used to buy Annie's dressings and they're great. But even those I look at when I'm at the store and think, *"I can't quite eat all that stuff."* So I make my own, and I get to put in apple cider vinegar, olive oil, lemon, which is great for the alkaline part of the body, kelp. And I switch it up and I play. So I get to play with my food that way.

Was there a change in your body? Did you feel some lethargy when you went from eating fairly healthy to eating even healthier? Because there is a detox that occurs, I would imagine. I know there was for me.

Right. That's a really good point and people need to be aware of that, especially if you're doing anything kind of radical, like a cleanse.

I recommend folks take small bites in regard to the changes they make. But when you do something radical, you have to be ready for that. When I did the two-month cleanse, the first week I would crash because what was happening was that all the toxins that were in my system were being released. And they were being released into my body, and I was in toxic shock. It took about a week to get rid of those.

The other thing is that I've created a more alkaline environment in my body. One of the things that happens is toxins in our body love a more acidic environment. So if we eat more acidic foods…

CREATING HEALTHY HABITS IS EASIER AND YOU WILL BE MORE SUCCESSFUL IN SUSTAINING THEM IF YOU START WITH SMALL BITES. MAKE A SMALL POSITIVE CHANGE AND LET THAT BECOME INGRAINED IN YOUR ROUTINE. THEN ADD ANOTHER.

Which are what?

Dairy is more acid. Some of the meat products are more acid. Beef is really acid. Lobster is really acid. The alkalines are more kale, lemon, lime, different fruits. When I create a more acidic environment in my body, I have more toxins in my body.

The body's response to toxins is that it needs a place to put them. Where does it put them? Fat cells. So the more toxic or acidic my body is, the more my body says, *"Man, I've got to create more fat cells, so I can store all these toxins."*

Flush the toxins and the body says, *"Oh, I don't need all these fat cells anymore,"* and I become leaner.

Lean and vital. I know. I've done a number of cleanses. In fact, in Bali, I did a juice fast for a week and that was incredibly powerful to me. But I definitely felt this level of sluggishness as I was doing it. But then more recently, I've done three two-week cleanses in the last year at a retreat center. So I actually go away and do it. So for the first few days now, because I've done a number of cleanses, it's easier on my body. I recover more quickly, and I feel more vital more quickly, which is wonderful.

Well, my guess is between the cleanses you're probably always altering and paying more attention to your healthy eating. So that now when you go in for a cleanse, you're going in less polluted.

MORE TOXINS IN YOUR BODY MEAN MORE FAT CELLS – THEY ARE YOUR BODY'S "GO-TO" STORAGE SYSTEM.

One of the other things I find about this, and it's one of the reasons I eat healthy as well, is that it's almost like a role that I can play in my community. When I was doing that two-month cleanse and I'd go to people's houses for dinner and, unfortunately, I can't eat this or I can't eat that, my entire community started to form a new consciousness themselves around what they were eating, how much alcohol they were drinking, how much they were hydrating their body, how much sleep they were getting.

I find that when we do that ourselves, our communities, our clients, they all see that, and we become a leader in that regard. I think my clients trust me more when they see that I'm loving myself and that I care about myself enough to eat well. There's a sense of thinking, *"Okay, there's an integrity here that they can trust."* I think it's really good for people building new businesses to recognize that their clients are going to see that.

I agree. There's a congruency that happens. I love that you said that, Chess, because I noticed each time I've done a cleanse, I've let my coaching clients know that I'm going to be gone for a couple of weeks doing a cleanse. A lot of them know that I am doing a cleanse, but if they don't, they'll say, "Tell me more. I want to know more." Sometimes they'll even do a cleanse while I'm gone. They'll get inspired. I think we all impact each other in how we're living our lives and what we're bringing to the table, and it's so great to be a role model for others just through our example.

Exactly. And then to be a guide because most people don't want to feel lethargic. Most people want to feel vibrant. But they don't know. *"What's the path? Give me some tools that I can start to use to start to increase my healthful lifestyle."*

Exactly. I'm thinking about you having talked about eliminating things from your diet. What were some of the biggest things that you took out of your diet that really led to the most vitality for you?

The biggest one, I don't think will be any surprise, is sugar. I wasn't a huge sugar fanatic, but certainly when I had the candida, which is yeast, it loved sugar. It's like, *"Feed me sugar."*

So that cut my cravings, but even after – and I've cleaned up the candida completely – but even after that, I am much more aware of not feeding myself sugar. I feel more vibrant. I feel more vital. I feel more clear-headed as well. So we've been told as well don't eat fats. But fats are fantastic. That's what the brain feeds on. So cut out the sugars, increase the healthy fats like grass-fed butters, ghee, coconut oil, and that's a really nice balance. But sugar is probably the biggest ones I've cut out… and alcohol. I'm much more selective now in regard to how often I drink alcohol and how much alcohol I drink. It's got a lot of sugar in it as well.

It does. It's true. I know there are a lot of organic wines and beers available, so I've been gravitating toward those if I do imbibe a little bit.

Also with the sugars, I'm thinking one change that I made in my own life is that I have been eating coconut sugar instead of regular sugar. Actually, I barely ate regular sugar, but I was eating agave syrup in my morning tea, and I noticed this dip in energy afterward. But I haven't had that with the coconut sugar because it's a low glycemic food.

That's exactly right.

Yes, it's low on the glycemic index. I love drinking caffeinated tea in the morning. I just love it. And I'm not ready to give it up! But I think having the coconut sugar helps me feel a little bit better about it.

Well, you bring up one good point. We don't want to give up everything. So what I mentioned earlier: small bites as you go through. You choose something that you think you can wrap your head around and wrap your lifestyle around and try it for a week or two until it becomes embedded as a habit and then add something else.

I talk to way too many people who just go whole hog. They've never done a cleanse before. They jump into a major cleanse and five days later, they're thinking, *"The heck with this. I can't do this."* So one of the things that I recommend right off the bat is every morning – when I'm sleeping, and I try to get seven or eight hours of sleep a night – I am dehydrating all night long because I'm respiring and moisture is leaving all night long. And what do a lot of people do? The first thing they do when they get up in the morning is have a cup of coffee. It's a diuretic. It dehydrates them even more. It puts the body into even more shock. So when I get up in the morning before my eyes are even fully open, I stumble into the kitchen, get an eight-ounce glass of water, half a lemon squeezed into it. That alone is fantastic. It creates a really alkaline environment.

I now add just about a teaspoon of apple cider vinegar as well. It brings up my HDL and my hydrochloric acid in the body for digestion. I drink a full glass of water first thing in the morning, and I can feel my body just go, *"Oh, okay. We can start the day now."*

That's great. You're inspiring me. I'm going to have a drink of water. Maybe everyone who is reading this can drink a glass of water now. Cheers!

Yes, water: 32 ounces for every 50 pounds of body weight. Throughout the day. So that's a fair amount of water. One of the big recommendations is have some water bottles around the office, around the home. Carry one in the car. They always get filled up and drank.

> YOUR BODY IS DEHYDRATING WHILE YOU SLEEP. THE WORST THING YOU CAN DO FIRST THING IN THE MORNING IS REACH FOR COFFEE – IT'S A DIURETIC. DRINK A FULL GLASS OF WATER INSTEAD. ADD LEMON TO CREATE A MORE ALKALINE ENVIRONMENT. TOXINS HATE ALKALINES!

I love that you're drinking out of a glass bottle because plastic leaches. And even more of the plastic leaches if it's in the hot sun.

Good point. This is an old tequila bottle. It's this really cool tequila that I got one time. So this goes along with the idea that when I drink out of this, it feels like I'm treating myself well. That's the other part of why we eat healthfully. It's because we love ourselves from the inside out.

What can we do to honor ourselves? If I wake up and I'm just having a stressful day or I don't feel good in the morning, I can ask myself, *"How can I honor myself today?"* I can eat a little bit more healthfully. And if that's the only thing I do, good. That makes a difference.

Oh. Well, thank you so much, Chess. I know you're going to be creating a kale salad now. I'm going to go ahead and let you create that and then we'll come back and talk about the kale salad.

Okay. This is my favorite salad. It is.

Welcome to my kitchen. I'm going to show you how to make one of probably the healthiest salads I know how to make. And what's beautiful about this salad is it's not only healthy, but as you will see, it is easy to make and it's also incredibly delicious. I don't think I've ever made this salad for anybody who didn't absolutely fall in love with it and want the recipe right away. So I'm going to give you the recipe. In fact, I'm going to a potluck tonight, a gathering, and I'm going to be bringing this salad. So I'm going to show you how to make it, and it's going to get eaten by good people tonight.

So this is a raw kale salad. A lot of people hear kale and they think… you know, they may have had kind of either a bad experience with kale or they're not really familiar with it. Kale can have a reputation of being a little bit bitter and kind of tough, especially raw. Cooked kale is fantastic, but raw a little bit tough and chewy. So I'm going to teach you how to make a salad that makes it incredibly appetizing.

Here is the kale we're working with. You want to buy kale that's nice and stiff. You don't want it all kind of limp and soggy. Good stiff kale. The first thing we're going to do is to remove the outside of the kale from this stem. There's a stem right here. That's the bitter part. So if you buy kale at the store, get it in the whole leaf form. If you buy bagged kale, then it's typically chopped kale, and they chop the stem into the mix and that's where a lot of the bitterness and toughness comes from. So what we're going to do is to separate this out. See, I'm peeling the leaves. Peeling them off of the stem. It leaves the stem and that's what we're not going to use.

We're going to peel a variety of leaves. It's very easy to do. Again, I end up with a stem that we're going to throw away. This is all washed. I pre-washed it before making this salad.

Now we've got a bunch of leafy kale. And we're going to take some of this kale and bunch it up into a nice little ball just like that… a nice little ball of kale. We're going to take that and with a nice sharp knife, cut that kale into small bite size pieces and add that into our salad. Here's one of the beautiful things about kale. As you read about earlier in my interview, kale is remarkably alkaline. It's one of the more alkaline vegetables out there. We want to build a really good alkaline system within us because it's hard for toxins to live in an alkaline system and for disease and cancers to live inside of an alkaline system. So we want to go alkaline and kale will do the job.

Another thing I love about this salad is that it just feels so good to eat. As we were talking about earlier, we need our energy. We need to love ourselves from the inside out. Whenever I make this for myself, especially if I choose this over a less healthy meal, there is some aspect of me that feels honored, feels respected, and really feels more robust and alive, and I can do my work better. I can show up in my work better.

So I pre-cut some kale earlier. This is our kale right here in a bowl. Now it's pretty full. When we do this next process, it's going to kind of diminish down a bit. So here is the next process: We're going to take a bit of olive oil, a nice good quality olive oil and we're going to drizzle some of that on the salad. We don't want to drown it. We just want to put enough to kind of coat the leaves. People will ask how much olive oil. And I'm about to add salt and they'll ask, *"How much salt?"* And the truth is: I don't know. I don't really cook that way. The reason that I don't like to cook with amounts is that I want to feel close to my food. I want to build a relationship with it. So I want to just be able to feel into how much olive oil is needed and how much salt is needed. And if I put a little bit too much, then I learn and I do it differently the next time.

All right, next ingredient. First ingredient was olive oil. Now Himalayan pink salt or any good quality coarse salt, a nice sea salt. But you want it to be coarse. You don't want to use table salt or any of the iodized salt, the really fine grain type. A nice coarse grain salt. And you're going to grind that on top of the salad.

Now the next step is to use our hand – and this is kind of the fun part here – we're going to use our hand and we're going to get in there and we're going to massage. We're going to take it and just massage the salad. What that's doing is driving the oil and the salt into the cellular makeup of the leaves, and it's breaking down the bitterness and the toughness of the kale. So this kale is now getting nice and soft. You don't want to over massage it. You just want to get a good coating of all the olive oil and the salt in through the leaves. Use perhaps a little bit less salt than you think you might. You can always add salt later. Now I'm just going to give that a general massage.

Next is avocado. We're going to take an avocado and slice the avocado right down the middle. Open it up, and we've got a beautiful avocado. We're going to take out the seed. It's a wonderful way to take out the seed. We are going to score the avocado. So take the avocado and score it into nice sections. That way you don't have to peel your avocado. We're going to take that avocado and simply remove the outside shell. Take all those nice chunks and drop them into the salad. I'm using my thumb there to push out all the avocado.

Now here is something really important to remember: If you are making this salad – well, anytime you're making it – but especially if you are making the salad for friends and you're over at their house or they're at your house and you're making it for them, wash your hands before you make the salad. It freaks people out if you're in there kind of mashing away and massaging the salad without washing your hands first.

Now we take that avocado that we just added and do one last massage. That's coating all the kale leaves with a nice fine coating of avocado. Again, you don't want to overdo it and over soften the kale, but just enough to get a nice coating on all of the leaves.

Now your hands are going to be a bit of a mess, and that's kind of the fun part. It's like playing in the mud when we were kids. We have permission to play with our food as adults. So I'm going to wash my hands. I don't have to get my hands back into the salad anymore. That's pretty much it. So I've got the kale. I've got the olive oil. I've got the salt, and I've got the avocado. Now we're going to add our ingredients. And you can really play here. But the ingredients that we're going to add are, first of all, scallions. These are spring onions or scallions. We are going to chop off the tips of those guys. Peel off any of the dead skin until you end up with really nice clean scallions. Chop those guys up. Now you can also (or in place of the scallions) use garlic if you'd like. Garlic is a fantastic replacement. If you really want to do a super, super, super healthy blood cleansing salad, garlic might be the way to go. So we're going to put in our scallions.

Next is cucumber… a beautiful cucumber. This is a cucumber out of my garden. Chop off the ends. Probably going to use about a half, three quarters of this cucumber. I'm going to slice it down the middle, turn it over, slice it down the middle again. That gives me nice four wedges. Put all four of those wedges together and chop those into small chunks. That gets added to the salad.

Now tomatoes. This is summertime when I'm making this salad, so I've got all this beautiful stuff growing in the garden. But you want some good organic tomatoes. We're going to chop them in half and then take each of those halves and chop that in half. So we've got four quarters. Take those quarters and chop those into chunks. Now, again, a good sharp knife. A dull knife is one of the most dangerous things you can have in the kitchen.

So why are we doing all of this? We're doing all this so that we feed ourselves well, so that we love ourselves, so we give ourselves a nice treat. And it's got very few ingredients, so it's really easy to make. We've got tomatoes, cucumbers and scallions on top of the kale and that's it. All we have to do now is take that, mix that in. And it's a beautiful colorful salad as well. It gives a lot of the reds, the light color green from the cucumbers.

Here is the final thing, and that is lemon. If you ever make this salad and you find that when you make it you think it just doesn't taste as good as the last time you made it, it's probably because you forgot lemon. You absolutely need lemon. You can use a lemon squeezer if you want to squeeze it. You can use a strainer to squeeze it through. I like to use my fingers. I like to let it squeeze right through my fingers. I use my fingers as the strainer to strain out all the seeds. And this is a fairly big salad because I'm making it for a bunch of people tonight. So we're going to go ahead and use an entire lemon. Again, start off with less. If you need to, you can always add more. If you're not going to serve this salad for a while, if it's going to be hours before you serve it, put the lemon on last. Wait until you're just about to serve. Put the lemon on it and give it a final toss.

And that's it. That is the raw kale salad. You can add other things if you want. You can add feta cheese. That's fantastic. You can add roasted sunflower seeds. I'm going to put on some pumpkin seeds right before I leave tonight. I don't want to put them on now because they'll get soggy. So right before I serve it tonight, I'm going to sprinkle on some raw pumpkin seeds. Pumpkin seeds are also extremely alkaline. Lemon is extremely alkaline as well. So I've got a salad right here that's going to feed me in a really nutritious way. It's incredibly delicious and it's going to get me a lot of love from a lot of good people I love as well because it is so good.

All right, enjoy. Eat healthy and love yourself from the inside out!

Hey, Chess. I love that salad. It's so good!

Isn't that phenomenal?

It is. And I think what's most surprising to me about that salad is the lemon juice that you squeeze in there. And also the massaging with the avocado.

It makes it fun. I get my hands all messy.

I know. I'm glad that you tell us to really make sure to wash your hands, especially if you're going to be preparing it in front of others, so they don't freak out.

I learned the hard way. I was at a friend's house and I said, "*Let me make you a salad.*" And I'm making it and she's looking at me like, "*Oh, man.*" And she asked me, "*Did you wash your hands?*" And I thought I could lie, you know. "*Sure I did.*" But I didn't want to lie so I said, "*No, I didn't. I'm sorry.*"

Yes. So really good to do that as a visible experience for people, so they can really see. "I'm washing my hands now and then I'm going to be playing with the food."

Well, thank you so much, Chess. This has been incredibly informative and fun.

Kale Salad Recipe

(Use amount to best suit your taste and appetite.)

Fresh organic kale

Olive oil

Avocado

Scallions (or garlic)

Cucumber

Tomato

Lemon

Roasted sunflower seeds (optional)

Feta cheese (optional)

NINE

How to Develop a Powerful Online Presence with Social Media

Interview with Therese Kopiwoda & Danielle Lambert

Feeling a bit confused about what social media sites to be on in a sea of so many? You aren't alone! Therese and Danielle shine the flashlight of clarity on what works and what you shouldn't waste your time on when it comes to social media.

In this chapter, you will learn:

- Specific social media sites that pet business owners should be on

- How to manage time effectively, so social media doesn't take over your time

- Topics that pet business owners should (and shouldn't) post

- Mistakes that pet business owners make when it comes to social media, and how to easily remedy them

- Tips for ease in managing social media

- And much more!

Kristin's Musings:

These ladies know their social media. I found myself wanting to take notes as I was interviewing them! (But I held myself back.) They are both delightful and are able to talk about social media in plain English. This is a very rare skill with social media experts. Social media is often explained in ways that sound like it's a foreign language. Hearing about it can often cause pet business owners' eyes to pop out and steam to come out of their ears. Not with these gals. They keep social media simple. As it should be!

Therese Kopiwoda's Bio:

Therese Kopiwoda has worked in online communities/social media for over 20 years and uses her success to help other business owners grow their online presence. She is the founder of Social Media Hound and currently works primarily with owners of pet businesses as a WordPress web designer and social media consultant.

Therese operated her own pet sitting business for ten years and is the founder and former owner of PetsitUSA, which she grew into one of the top online pet sitter directories. She has been interviewed for several news articles and podcasts and has spoken at conferences including SXSW and the former Cyber Sitters United. To find out more visit *www.SocialMediaHound.com*.

Danielle Lambert's Bio:

Danielle K. Lambert is a veterinary practice manager and the founder of Snout School, a website dedicated to teaching social media to the veterinary industry. Danielle focuses on coaching veterinary businesses on social media in a practical way. When she isn't working or spending too much time on Pinterest, she enjoys hiking with her Brussels Griffon, Archer. To find out more visit *www.SnoutSchool.com*.

Interview with Therese Kopiwoda
Social Media Consultant **&**

Danielle Lambert
Social Media Consultant

Kristin Morrison: *I am so excited to welcome Therese Kopiwoda. She is a social medial consultant. And I am also so happy to introduce Danielle Lambert. She's also a social media consultant. We're going to be talking about social media and how to develop a really powerful online presence using social media. So, Danielle, what social media sites do you think really need to be utilized by pet sitters, dog walkers, dog trainers, and any pet business owners really?*

Danielle Lambert: First and foremost, hello everybody. I am so excited to talk about social media for pet business. But in terms of which platform you should be on, I think it's really important to know your audience, know where they spend time online. If you haven't established a client list, just do a quick survey. I like to use Survey Monkey or something like that and send out an email asking where people are online. Other than that, you can also pick the social media that best suits your business. If you're a dog trainer, something like YouTube is going to suit you because you can show your services off via some training videos. If you're a pet business that creates pet clothing or something like that, you might want to use something more visual, like Pinterest. So all said and done, everybody needs a Facebook page, and you need to start there. But it depends on your business, so you have to find what's the right fit for you and what you feel you can really commit to.

I love the idea of asking your clients where they are online and really tapping the pulse of that to be able to see and do some marketing in that way. And what about you, Therese? What do you think?

Therese Kopiwoda: Well, I agree with everything Danielle said, but I also want to encourage people, too, to get on Google Plus. Just about everybody uses Google for their search engine, and Google Plus is a Google product. Of course, they're going to like their product. I think Google Plus is getting more and more important these days. In addition to finding out where your audience is, you want to make sure that whatever social media platform you choose – if you're a small business and a lot of pet sitters are sole proprietors – you want to choose a platform that you are going to feel comfortable with. If you absolutely hate Facebook, you're not going to do a very good job with it. So you want to pick something you're comfortable with, too.

I agree. I do a lot of coaching for pet business owners and I work with a lot of people who are introverts, so even the thought of being extroverted on Facebook makes them cringe. I think it's really important to find social media that really works for whoever is doing it. I love that.

Because there are so many things to choose from, which social media platforms do you think don't really matter that much for pet business owners?

Therese: There are a lot of them out there. You really want to stick with some of the bigger ones, the ones that people go to. You might find a really small one that looks really cool, but if nobody is using it, it's not going to be very effective. So stick with the basic bigger ones: Facebook, Pinterest, Google Plus because not only are your clients and prospects going to be there, but if you need help with it, you're going to have more luck finding somebody who can help you with those. Also like Danielle said, find out what's going to work for your business. If you're a dog trainer, Pinterest may not be the best place for you. So go where it makes sense for you and for your clients.

And what do you think, Danielle?

I agree with Therese and with what we were all saying before where you definitely have to pick platforms that you're actually going to invest the time in using. As a small business, I don't think it's a good idea to have more than two to three platforms at a time. You want to avoid the platforms that not as many people are using because you want to use your time efficiently.

> TO PICK THE BEST SOCIAL MEDIA PLATFORM, LEARN WHERE YOUR PROSPECTS AND CLIENTS ARE, AND ALSO SELECT THE ONE OR ONES WITH WHICH YOU ARE MOST COMFORTABLE.

That makes sense. I know a lot of pet business owners wonder what they should be posting about. They get a little like a deer in the headlights not knowing what to post. Danielle, what do you recommend that pet business owners post about?

I know for the veterinary hospital that I manage, we really focus on posting content that shows the behind the scenes of our business. It shows the new patient pets that came in that day, or if we're having a staff training, it shows what we're up to. That definitely applies to any sort of pet business. Anytime you can show that behind the scenes of what's going on can make it super personal. People like that.

I think it's also important to be a resource in your area of expertise. So we have a blog for the veterinary hospital, and we share parts of the blog out on social media. By doing something like that you can really establish your knowledge and your authority. If somebody is going to be watching your pet, you might want to see that they know about pet first aid or similar topics. Anytime you can be resourceful or show behind the scenes, I think that's the best kind of content to share.

Great. And what about you, Therese? What do you think pet business owners should be posting about?

First off, I think they need to make sure their content is upbeat. People are looking for something pleasant most of the time when they're walking around. You want to remember what your main focus is in your business. If you're a dog trainer, then you want to give information about dog training. Think about giving people some free great advice. You're really good at this, Kristin. So when people think of you, when people think of a coach, they naturally think of you because they've been on your Facebook page so much. So you want to give them snippets of information that centers on what you offer.

Also, if you're a local company, if you're a groomer or a pet sitter, you have a good local base. What you want to do is set yourself up as an authority in your local area. For example, every Thursday you might want to post about the pet-related events that are going on in your city. Post about your expertise and then expand a little bit so that you become an expert in that area, so people actually come to your page or your social media site to see what exactly might be going on for that week.

That's great. I know, Therese, we've had discussions about what people shouldn't be posting about. But those who are reading haven't heard our discussions, so I'd love to hear what you think pet business owners definitely shouldn't be posting about just to clarify what's right content and what's not right content.

Well, you want to stay away from the obvious: politics and religion. That kind of stuff you don't want post about. And you also want to not post about things that are just totally off the wall. If this is your business page about pet sitting, you probably don't want to go on and on about your husband's car breaking down and you don't want to complain. As I said before, you want to keep it upbeat and relevant to what your site visitors' needs are.

Yes. Any additional comments, Danielle, on what people shouldn't be posting about?

I think definitely keeping everything positive and remembering that, especially in veterinary medicine, different topics are a little controversial. It's kind of like how people don't want to be told exactly how to raise their child. They feel the same with their pets. So you want to definitely not be too strongly opinionated on things. While you think it's good to share a lot about your personal side, especially if you're a sole proprietor, you obviously don't want to go on a rant about your husband or something like that.

Exactly. I would also add not ranting about clients. I've seen some pet business owners who start posting about bad experiences they've had with clients, and I just cringe when I see that because their other clients are reading that. How we treat one person is usually how we treat everyone. So I would also add: Don't post about your clients with whom you've had bad experiences.

Danielle: Also, don't post pictures of the inside of your clients' homes or pictures that might identify where your clients are or give their names. I've seen pet sitters do all of the above, and like you, it makes me cringe because they're really compromising their client's security by doing that.

I agree. Any mistakes that you've seen pet business owners do online that you would recommend against, Therese?

The one that I see quite often is that some pet businesses, not just pet sitters, will post repeated posts about a dog that's going to be euthanized. It breaks my heart every time I see it, and I want so desperately to go out and save that dog, but it's just not possible. Rather than it making me feel better that I can do something, it makes me feel worse that I can't do anything. So once in a while I understand that, but there are some pet sitters or – I keep saying pet sitters because those are most of the people who I deal with – pet business owners who will every day post five or six messages of these dogs or cats that are going to be euthanized. It's kind of a double-edged sword because we want to help them because we're big hearts, but we can't. So go easy on those types of posts.

Yes. I would say those posts might be really valuable on a blog that's going out to particular clients perhaps where these clients might want an additional dog and they're able to rescue a dog or something like that. I've also seen – I don't know if you've seen this, too, Therese and probably you, too, Danielle – but I've seen really violent pictures and I find it disturbing when pet business owners are posting these really graphic shots. I would imagine it's disturbing to their clients too. I completely get the motivation behind it... the big heart behind it. But I noticed for me there's this contraction that happens inside and it can be really intense. What do you think about that, Therese? Is that something you think you would avoid pet business owners posting?

Definitely. You can actually lose followers by doing that too often. So, yes definitely avoid that.

Going to a happier topic, what social media sites do you really enjoy using and which ones would you recommend? I know we've talked about Facebook and Pinterest, but what are some that are really fun and that you think pet business owners who maybe aren't tech savvy would have a real sense of ease in using? Why don't you answer that, Danielle?

KEEP YOUR POSTS UPBEAT AND POSITIVE... AND BE VERY AWARE OF POSTING SOMETHING THAT MAY COMPROMISE A CLIENT'S PRIVACY.

I personally really enjoy anything really visual. I like Pinterest. I like Instagram. I think people are getting more and more into Instagram, and I think that's a really fun place to share your pictures. That way you're not hurting your Facebook followers by inundating them with pictures all the time there. And since it's a mobile app, I think it's fairly easy to use Instagram. Pinterest is a little trickier to get the hang of, especially if you're creating your own original content. I do definitely enjoy using that, but I think Instagram is one people should look at a little bit more.

Right. And what about you, Therese?

I'm on Pinterest. I love Pinterest. I'll admit this. I don't do Instagram yet, which is probably something I shouldn't confess, but I will. I'm actually going to be doing a long road trip soon and I'm intending to get on Instagram just to chronicle my road trip with that platform. But definitely Pinterest. And I like LinkedIn. So I really enjoy LinkedIn and Facebook. As you know, I'm on Facebook quite a bit.

I am, too. It's a lot of fun to be in a conversation and connect with people all over the world that way. Any solid tips that you would give to people who really want to boost their social media presence? Maybe three tips from each of you that you would really recommend. Why don't I start with you, Danielle?

I think my number one tip would be to make sure you are collecting email addresses. It might seem like a little out of right field when we're talking about social media, but email is how most people log into their social media. I think it's really powerful to be able to leverage those emails for advertising, for example. So that's number one. Don't forget about an email list. It's powerful and you own it instead of being at the mercy of the platforms.

As I mentioned before, I think knowing where your clients are is the second most important tip and knowing what platforms suit you, so you know you're going to really utilize them to their full potential.

The third one is, even though I know some people are more introverted than I might be, to actually jump in and be conversational and be social. I think that is really important. If you're in a local area and you have a Twitter account, you can search your local area for certain terms and jump into conversations with people. I think that's a great place to start actually being social or like Therese mentioned, on LinkedIn, sites like that. So actually be social would be my third tip.

That's great. And really, it's an opportunity for us to be able to reveal a little bit of ourselves on social media without revealing too much, going to the other extreme. Really letting some of us out to be able to connect with people online can be so valuable on so many levels. It's so important. I also love what you said about the email list. I think those emails are gold. It's important for pet business owners to really collect and gather and harvest those email addresses and to not go crazy with the newsletters. No more than once a week, I would say. But really use that as a tool to be able to connect with clients. It's incredibly powerful and I'm really glad you brought that up. How can pet business owners best get those email addresses, Danielle?

Well, I think it depends on whether or not you have a brick and mortar location or if you're mostly online. If you're online, I think you could very easily do some sort of giveaway in exchange for the email address. For example, if you're a dog trainer and you have a video series of tips that people could sign up for, they'll easily hand over their email address for that. If you are a brick and mortar store, it's just important to actually remember to ask them for their email and gather it. If you have a staff, that involves a lot of training sometimes. I know that personally, at my veterinary hospital, that it's much easier if you have the person in front of you and you can ask. Again, making sure you're not going to abuse that email once you have it is very, very important to keeping that list.

True. What about you, Therese? What simple tips would you give that pet business owners can powerfully leverage on their social media?

I'm going to back up just a little bit here. In addition to your social media platform presence, I think you have to have a website. Your Facebook, your Pinterest, those are all great. You have to be there if you want to be found. But the thing is you're not in control there, so you want a website so that you have... I call the website your world headquarters. So you want to have your world headquarters. It's always going to be there. Then you want to have your branch offices, which are your Facebook page, Pinterest, all the social media platforms. Because when you have a Facebook page or a Pinterest or Twitter, you're at the mercy of those people who are running the show. And if they decide, like Facebook does, to change the way they play their game, you may lose out a little bit or, God forbid, if they just pull the plug, which I know has happened to people on different social media sites. Then you're kind of lost. So you really want to have your website well established so that people can still find you.

In addition to that, if you're just starting out, you want to pick one social media platform that you think you can really commit to and then get used to that. Like Danielle said, try not to do too much. Just pick a few that you know you can do and add to them as time goes on. You don't have to start out with all of them right at the very beginning. So do one, master it, and move on.

Then when you work on your social media, because we're all so darn busy these days, you really need to set a time limit. Write out a list of the things that you want to accomplish with your 10 or 15 minutes of Facebook time and

SOCIAL MEDIA IS GREAT, BUT HAVING A WEBSITE IS CRITICAL. YOU HAVE COMPLETE CONTROL OF YOUR SITE, AND IT SHOULD BE YOUR "WORLD HEADQUARTERS."

stick to it. If you have to, set an alarm clock. I think we even talked about this before, Kristin. Time yourself and once that time is up, you're done. If you have that time limit, you're going to know that you have to get these things done and you're not going to wander off. You're going to get your work done.

I was going to ask you about setting time limits. One app, I don't know if you've heard about it, is the Freedom app. It's very cool. I actually haven't used it yet, but I keep hearing about it and I will use it at some point. Basically, it's kind of the opposite of logging in and doing your social media. It really doesn't allow you to go online. You set a time limit for when you don't want to be able to log on and go online, so it won't let you access the Internet. Let's say you have a Word doc or task that you need to do. You set the Freedom app and you can focus on it. Or let's say you definitely don't want to be online between 9:00 a.m. and 5:00 p.m. You would log into the Freedom app and set that time constraint. It won't let you log in at all, so you can focus on the other non-online items that need doing.

I really love what you said about setting a timer. I do that a lot with different projects that I have. I also think it's really important to do that when it comes to social media because it just sucks us in, doesn't it? It's one of those things where we can go down the rabbit hole, so to speak, and I think holding a mindful, conscious attitude around it, so we're able to focus on all the other actions that we have as business owners is really important. I think that's why some people aren't on social media because they're afraid of going down that rabbit hole.

What about you, Danielle? What do you think are some strategies that pet business owners can use to not be on social media very much and set time limits?

I think it is so important. Going back to what Therese said about having a website: If you have a blog on your website, I think it's good to sit down and get that blog done and then you can schedule posts that all go back to that blog. That's what I do at my veterinary hospital. I schedule out my tweets and then I schedule out my Facebook posts. I spend maybe like an hour a week setting everything up, and then I have all the apps on my phone that can allow me to be responsive because I think it is important to have a good response time. But it doesn't have to be a huge time suck if you just schedule something. I love the idea about setting a timer. I could probably use a little bit more of that! But it definitely helps if you base everything off of a blog post and schedule things out that way. You can get pretty effective in a short amount of time.

Okay, great. Anything else? We're going to end this interview soon, but any other tips or insights that you have for pet business owners? What about you, Danielle?

I think we've covered a lot of the really important stuff. But I think the most important thing is not to be so afraid of social media. Again, if you find a platform that you're comfortable with and you can actually dive into, you don't have to have nine different platforms going at once and be totally overwhelmed. I think the most important thing to realize is that you can gain a lot of traction if you use, for example, something like Twitter and get really involved in a community. You can really build up your business that way. It doesn't have to be scary. It doesn't have to be overwhelming. Just actually start is probably my biggest word of advice.

I love that. What about you, Therese?

I think Danielle's comment to just start has a lot of merit to it. Just get in there. Jump in and just get out there. If you're at a total loss of what to do, look at some of your competitors or some people who you admire. Don't copy them, but emulate them. You can learn from watching other people.

I agree. There's power in that. Really looking at who is doing what you want to do. How they are expressing themselves on social media and really looking at that. Thank you so much for being here. I really appreciate it. I appreciate your wisdom and your expertise. Thanks so much.

TEN

How to Create More Freedom in Your Pet Business and Your Life

Alicia Dattner Interviews Kristin Morrison

Guess what? We get to create our reality through our words and actions. What kind of life do YOU want to create? Kristin made a decision one day, and it powerfully altered her business and her life. It's time for Kristin Morrison, the creator of the Prosperous Pet Business Online Conference, to be in the interviewee seat! Join Alicia Dattner, Kristin's long-time friend (and also one of the conference speakers on improv and humor in business) as she interviews Kristin. You get to be a fly on the wall: They are such good friends that they almost forgot you were watching.

In this chapter, you will learn:

- The surprising moment that propelled Kristin into the world of pet business years ago

- Powerful morning practices that can help you live your life with intention and set the tone for ease and joy

- How changing unconscious beliefs can help you make (a lot) more money (and have more fun making it!)

- Some first steps that pet business owners can take to create more freedom in their business

- The many gifts of creating a life filled with enough time and ease
- And more!

Kristin's Musings:

It's funny, I was a bit nervous as I sat down to do this interview. And I was surprised to feel a little nervous because I've very much enjoyed speaking at various pet business conferences in the last few years. Here's the thing: Alicia is one of my very closest friends, so I knew if anyone could have me feeling relaxed and forgetting I was on camera, it's Alicia. I came away from my interview feeling like we'd just hung out at a coffee shop for a while. I wish for everyone out there a good friend like Alicia, one who makes you laugh and really "gets" you. We all need that!

Kristin Morrison's Bio:

Kristin Morrison is the founder and host of the Prosperous Pet Business Online Conference. She has coached thousands of pet business owners from around the world through her webinars, pet business programs, and private coaching. She's also a nationally recognized pet business conference speaker. Kristin is the author of the books *Six-Figure Pet Sitting* and *Six-Figure Pet Business* and creator of 40+ empowering pet business products and recordings for pet sitters, dog walkers, pet groomers, and dog trainers. She is the founder of Six-Figure Pet Business Academy, Six-Figure Pet Sitting Academy, and Prosperous Pet Business. You'll find her free podcast for pet business owners on iTunes. Kristin enjoys making business easy, fun, and lucrative for pet business owners. Visit her websites to find out more: *www.SixFigurePetBusinessAcademy.com, www. SixFigurePetSittingAcademy.com,* and *www.ProsperousPetBusiness. com.*

Interview with Kristin Morrison
Founder, Six-Figure Pet Business Academy
and Prosperous Pet Business.com

Alicia Dattner: *My name is Alicia Dattner, and we are here with the creator of the Prosperous Pet Business Online Conference, Kristin Morrison. She is a good friend of mine and she is the founder of the Six-Figure Pet Business Academy and Six-Figure Pet Sitting Academy. She is creator of over 40 pet business products and recordings. She is a business and life coach for pet business owners, and she is the author of the books* **Six-Figure Pet Business** *and* **Six-Figure Pet Sitting**. *I'm really excited to get to have this conversation with her and excited to help you guys and talk about how to create more freedom in your business and your life. Welcome, Kristin.*

Kristin Morrison: Thank you. It's kind of funny to be on the other end of this. I really appreciate you being available to interview me, Alicia.

I want to hear everything about how you got to this place where you've created this online conference. I mean there is so much work that goes into it. There is so much passion. There is so much that you have to give, and you've done so many things along the way to get to this place. I want to hear how you are in this magical position today. How did you get started just in the very beginning in pet care?

It's funny that you bring up the word "magical" Alicia, because I feel like my start in the world of pet business was very divinely inspired and magical. I don't use that word lightly. I mean I really feel like I was called to do this work because I had always loved animals. I had always wanted to work with animals. I was studying or pursuing becoming a vet, really exploring that option and

I ended up becoming a vet tech. It was so wonderful to be around animals and to help them, and I went into surgery one day and I fainted when I saw blood and realized, *"Oh no I can't be a vet, what do I do?"* So I got a regular job and was pretty upset about it, not really sure what else I could do with animals. I just wasn't sure.

I had my heart set on being a vet. One day, in my early twenties, I was walking down this bike path near where I lived, and there was this woman who walked by me with a couple dogs on leashes, wearing a shirt that had a dog walking company name. I didn't know that; I wasn't sure. It had a phone number on it, and I asked, *"Are you getting paid to walk dogs?"* She said, *"Yeah, I own a dog walking company. Do you want to work for me?"* I said, *"Yes."* She told me to meet her the next day. We met at a café for an interview. She hired me on the spot, and I began working for her. A few months later, I started my company, and I had my pet sitting company for 18 years. It was just when I started that business I felt like, *"Oh my God. I found what I am meant to be doing,"* and it really was that profound inner sense of *"yes"* and it was so wonderful.

I'd had a lot of anxiety about what I was going to do with my life in the years leading up to that. So there were about five years between when I was going to be a vet (then I realized that I couldn't because of my blood reaction) and the time that I began working for this woman in her dog walking company. During those five years, I would often wake up in a panic thinking, *"What am I going to do with my life?"* I felt like I didn't want to keep doing what I was doing, but I felt like I wanted to work with animals. It was very confusing for me and I felt pretty anxious about it. It would wake me up at night, and then about a year before I met this woman on the bike path, I realized, *"You know what, my brain isn't figuring this out. I can think about it until the cows come home but I'm not figuring it out. I've got to let it go and just trust that either whatever I'm supposed to do will come to me, or I'll find fulfillment in other ways besides my work."*

So I really did let it go, and I think I found that being able to manifest things in our lives – at least in my life – requires letting go. It's kind of this fine balance between letting go and taking action, and I had taken action. I had read books. I had really been looking and that wasn't working, so I let go. Finally, that balance of really taking action and then letting go helped me really find my right livelihood.

The thing that I got so curious about was where did the origin of your love of animals start?

Oh, that's a great question. You know I had a cat named Suki who was part Siamese and part something else; we weren't sure what Suki actually was.

We had a cat named Suki.

What?!

We had a cat named Suki.

Now that you mention it, I remember you saying that when I talked about Suki with you years ago. So Suki was just such a great cat, very dog-like. I've had an affinity for dog-like cats all my life, and then we also had a dog that was part wolf named Wolfie. I named him; very clever name, huh?

They really were incredible creatures who were great listeners. I could really tell them my problems at age five, six, seven, eight. You know, they got it; they understood. Having them in my life really gave me a love for animals, and my mom was very passionate about animals. So we had turtles, ducks, chickens. I had a horse. I got a horse for Christmas one year and that was incredibly thrilling for me. So I was really surrounded by animals growing up. In fact, we raised guide dog puppies because the Guide Dogs for the Blind center was a few minutes away from where I lived growing up.

We raised guide dog puppies for a year of their lives, and then we would give them to Guide Dogs for the Blind, and they would train them to work with blind people. That was always really bittersweet because we would get to know these incredible puppies that were super smart and loving, and then we'd have to give them up, which was very hard. But it was so fulfilling. One of the puppies that we raised was "rejected" by Guide Dogs for the Blind. I don't think they call it "rejected" anymore. I think it's now called "career change" to help the dog's self-esteem. So we got to keep one of the German shepherd puppies because he got a career change. He became a family dog instead of a guide dog. So that's really how my love of animals came about.

Wow, thanks for telling that story. I didn't know all about that. So how did you start coaching?

I had my pet sitting company and about a few years into it, I received a call from somebody in New York who saw my website, really liked it. She said, *"Oh, it's so professional. I love it; I see you've been pet sitting for a while, would you be willing to help me in my business?"*

So I began coaching her, and she began experiencing a lot of shifts in her business as a result of the changes she was making, and she told some of her pet sitting network friends about me, and they started calling me for coaching.

I had all these New York clients within a very short time. I live in California and word spread, and I began coaching people from all over the United States. Then people in Canada and the UK started contacting me for coaching; then pet business owners in Australia asked if I'd coach them. It kind of grew and grew through word of mouth for a while. Then I was asked to speak at a pet business conference. Somebody found out about me who was hiring speakers. I created Six-Figure Pet Sitting Academy followed by Six-Figure Pet Business Academy because I began to work with all kinds of pet business owners: dog trainers, groomers, doggy day care owners, dog walkers, so that's how I started. At this point, I've coached thousands of people, and it's been incredibly fulfilling for me to help them, to nurture them toward success... whatever that looks like for them because it's so different for each of us.

For me, success is about having the freedom to travel and be with the ones I love and having time. That's really what it is for me; that's what success means for me, but

> SUCCESS ISN'T WHAT WORKS FOR SOMEONE ELSE. YOU DEFINE YOUR OWN SUCCESS, SO DETERMINE WHAT THAT IS!

for other people it's very different. It's usually not about money though, for any of us, but money is often a vehicle to get what we want that helps fulfill whatever need we have that's behind our business. Money can be the fuel that funds our dreams.

So it sounds like the way you grew your coaching business was crazy organic and I just kind of... I need a little of that in my own business!

Well, it's funny because I've had a lot of people ask me about this because my life, especially my work life, is very divinely guided. I feel that on so many levels, and I take a lot of actions to really stir that and open the channels for that, and some of those actions are the morning rituals that I have. One of the morning rituals is doing journal writing every morning. I've done it for about 20 years. I write about this process in my books, *Six-Figure Pet Sitting* and *Six-Figure Pet Business*. They are called "morning pages," and they're based on Julie Cameron's book, *The Artist's Way*. I don't know if you've heard about that book though I'm imagining that you have. It's such a powerful book on many levels. It's not geared for business owners, but it's really powerful for business owners because I found a lot of the tools in that book were really impactful for me and my business. Especially the morning pages. Basically you write for three pages straight, and it's stream-of-consciousness writing. You don't think. You don't edit. You're not spell checking. Some people prefer to do this on their computer and that works great for them. For me there's something about holding the pen to paper. It's like... it's almost like the brain goes through my pen into the paper. I just feel more connected to what's coming out than I do when I'm typing morning pages on a computer.

Natalie Goldberg, who is a writing teacher, talks about how the energy goes from your heart, through your arm, into the pen.

I love that. I really feel it too after having written and done this practice for 20 years. I have a huge amount of journals as you can imagine, and I just love them. Sometimes I review them but just writing them helps in so many ways. In a way, it's like therapy with yourself where you work things out. For me, I work out a lot of business decisions and challenges that I may have going on. I get a lot of action steps that arise through the morning pages practice. I find it connects me to my true self, and that has been a really powerful force in my life. I think that's led to me really listening deeply to the signs that come and my intuition.

Also, I meditate in the morning. I don't do that every day, but I do it often enough that it really feels like it makes a difference for me. I also love to be in nature, so I hike. I try to hike at least a few times a week on my favorite trail that's near my house, and it's an hour-long loop and there's something about walking in a place that I've walked so many times that it becomes a meditation for me. I don't think about it. I don't even observe what's around me. Nature is there, and I feel like it's an old friend and my thoughts are flushing out; you know, the ones that I don't need leave me and the ones that I need to really focus on are there. I feel really recharged and rejuvenated when I finish my hikes. That's another thing that I've written about in my books: the power of having exercise practice, and for me it's even more than an exercise practice. It's really a meditation.

You know, it's funny Alicia, because you were saying how my coaching happened organically. The birth of my business products for pet business owners was very organic as well. Those arose one day when I was in the midst of hiring pet sitters. I found that it was so challenging. I would put an ad out on Craigslist, and I would get maybe a hundred people responding in the course of a week, and it was overwhelming. I wished that I could get somebody, a hiring assistant, to basically field these emails, so I could move on to knowing who to interview. Then I would only interview the ones who seemed right.

That was such a vision for me because hiring was such a pain in the butt, but when I thought about hiring a hiring assistant, I realized that I didn't know anybody like that who has that good gut instinct. At least at that time I didn't, so I created an application packet for my own business, and it is eight pages. It has a cover sheet that explains what I want the applicants to do: fill it out and mail it back to me by a certain date. It has job descriptions for each job. It has applications, and one is specific to working as a pet care provider and the other is a basic application. It has questions that the applicants would fill out and answer. I emailed the application packet to them and then I would have them snail mail it to me. I found the snail mail process really weeded out the bad from the good because if they could just email it, it would be very simple. The packet is eight pages, so it's kind of intense, but it weeds out the people who aren't good.

It weeds out the people who aren't serious, I imagine.

That's true. It weeds out the people who aren't really committed to the job in the first place. They think that it'll be a fun job. So I was working with one of my coaching clients many years ago and he was really going through a hiring crisis where he wasn't hiring the right people and I said, *"Oh, I've got this application packet and you might want to create one."* I was telling him how to create it and he said, *"I don't want to create it. I'm so stressed out.*

175

Can you just sell it to me?" He bought it, he loved it, he told his pet sitting friends about it, they contacted me to get their own Pet Sitting Application Packets, so that was my very first product I created, and it's helped a lot of people and it certainly helped me in my business. It's almost like a lot of the next right steps have come from my clients who need something and it gets created for them.

I can just imagine. I've had some wonderful coaching with you and loved it. I get how you having that connection with your intuition has a really special effect on the people who you coach because you have this way of customizing your coaching for each person. Different people need different things, and you get to share your "toolbox" of all of these different pieces and intuitively help them create what they are looking for and what they want.

I love that you said that because it's reminding me how I've had a few people ask, *"Hey, can I do Skype coaching sessions with you?,"* and I've said, *"Absolutely if you want to do that you can, but here's the thing: I find that my intuition works better if I'm not actually seeing you."* There's something about the phone in which I'm not seeing the people, but I can really feel what's happening behind and even underneath the words, so if people want to work with me by Skype, I definitely am available for that, but I really encourage people to talk on the phone because you'll get more from me.

Same thing with my coaching. One of the things that I love about you and what I love about how you've created your life is that you just say, "I'm going to do this," and you go do it. A huge piece of that is travel, and I'm curious because something amazing you did a few years ago is that you went to India and Bali for eight months. You said, "I'm just going," and you found a way to make that happen. I'm curious for people who perhaps see that as something of an impossibility. What were the first steps that you started taking to do that and then how did that progress?

I love that question and I'd like to first back up a little bit and explain what spurred me to think about traveling. I did a workshop, and it was kind of a life-changing workshop. I do those every now and then because I find that it really helps me in my own life and also helps in my work with my coaching clients, so it's continuing education for me. I was doing one of these workshops and in one of the exercises, the facilitator led us on a meditation in which she had us imagine what it would be like for us if we only had six months to live. What would we do with our lives? I closed my eyes and saw myself wearing a travel backpack that I had traveled with around the world many years before I had my pet sitting company. I'd gone to Europe, Thailand, and Bali, but it was years ago. It was shocking for me to see that traveling was what I would be doing if I had six months to live.

I had this idea when I started the meditation that I would be with my friends and family and connecting with them. That was not the image that was popping up! It was me with my travel backpack, and you know what, Alicia? I had this huge smile on my face, and I realized that was a soul desire that I had not been paying attention to. It's funny because I would go in my shed and see my travel backpack, and I would feel this feeling of, *"Aww… that's not possible for me. I have this huge pet sitting company; I've got all these coaching clients."* I thought that traveling for an extended trip was an impossibility, and when that vision of me wearing my travel backpack popped up, I realized that if we don't take care of our soul desires, they'll sabotage us in some way. I really have seen that over and over in my coaching clients' worlds and in my own life too. I know the power of the soul desires and if they're not listened to, they can really wreak havoc on our lives. They're there to really lead us to our next step in life.

I knew I had to listen to it, but it felt totally impossible. I had a couple managers working for me, so I thought maybe I'd just ask them if they'd be willing to work for me while I was traveling, but I was afraid to ask. It's funny… it was almost like if I ask them and they say no, then what? I felt like I'd feel even more hopeless about it.

I got up the courage one day, and I called one of them up and I asked, *"What do you think about this?,"* and I told her my idea about traveling for a few months. She was my main manager. She said, *"I think you should do it."* I said, *"Really?"* She said, *"I'd be happy to help."* It made it so much easier for me to call the other one and say, *"Hey, so and so is available to help, would you be willing to be that other person?,"* and she agreed, and nine months later I was on the plane, and it was, again, very divinely inspired. A very organic process. There was a lot to prepare for both with my life and my business obviously, but I gave my managers incentives to reach a certain mark in the business, like if the sales grossed more than X amount, they would get a bonus that month and that really inspired them to make it happen, to really increase the sales.

> LISTEN TO AND UNDERSTAND YOUR SOUL DESIRES. THEN TAKE THE NECESSARY STEPS TO MAKE THOSE A REALITY. YOUR SOUL WANTS WHAT IT WANTS. PROVIDE IT AND YOU WILL LIVE A FULLER LIFE.

Actually, we did the best that we had ever done. Each year we'd increase our profit, but that year, the profit was profound and I was gone and not working for eight months! I had been leading up to this in a way without even knowing it because at that point, I was only working three days in my business. At the very beginning of my business, I worked seven days a week and often 12 to 14 hours a day when I started. It was really stressful, so I ended up hiring pet sitters and dog walkers to help. Gradually throughout the years, I began to stop pet sitting and dog walking; then I hired these managers and I went from working seven days a week managing my business to working three days a week managing. When I came home from that trip, I realized I really want to work two days a week, so I was only working two days a week in the business and coaching and doing webinars during the other time. After being back from my trip for a while, I realized that I've had this business for 18 years; it's really time to sell it. Years before, I had dreams of franchising and even acquired domain names for franchising and was thinking that that would be a vision for me, but it wasn't a soul desire. Again, it's important to listen to the soul desires, and I knew that my next step was really to make myself even more available, so I could help pet business owners because the two days that I was working in the pet sitting business were days that I couldn't help others. So that's kind of the progression that has happened for me around traveling and making it happen.

Did you feel like when you finally got to Bali, it was everything that you dreamed?

Oh gosh, in some ways it was. I mean it's such a dreamy place and I really encourage those of you who are feeling drawn to go to Bali to go. It's incredibly beautiful and the people are so filled with heart, and they're lovely and the food is magnificent and the yoga is great. I did have some things come up there that were really challenging for me and part of it was that I was traveling alone, so I did feel some loneliness when I was there. That was really hard for me to experience. I had a lot of people who I met there, so it wasn't even like loneliness for people, but it was more like loneliness for the people back home that I really missed: my friends and family. It's funny that we have this idea about traveling that it's going to be being on the beach, hanging out. It's kind of hard work, especially if you're going from one place to another with a backpack on, which I was doing. If you're traveling alone, it really requires a lot of energy, in a way, to make your own way. So there was a slice of it that was kind of challenging for me, but I would say if I have to break it down 80 or 85 percent was just incredible and wonderful, and it was very transformative for me.

It almost sounds like the part that was this soul desire with the backpack that called you there gave you this experience of freedom and ease, and the challenging part could have been the piece that called you back home and had you appreciate what you're continuing to build in your business and the friends and the family and the people who you have at home.

Exactly. I didn't work for eight months. While I was on that trip, I told my coaching clients that I was taking a sabbatical, and I came back hungry to work. I was ravenous. I missed it so much. I missed working with people. I missed creating things. I missed my work and being away was a great break for me. I really needed that time because I had been working a lot prior to that, not just in my pet sitting company but with my coaching clients and the webinars and writing my books, things like that. So it was a great break for me, and I also came back hungry to work. It was really wonderful.

Wow. I'm curious to sort of sum up what are some of the really biggest gifts that you've had out of creating a business that allows you to have that kind of freedom and time. What is your life like now that it wasn't like before?

I really feel like what gives me the most meaning is being with the people who I love. That trumps everything else on the planet, so having that ability to be with people who I love gives my life meaning. I would say that the richest piece for me of having freedom and time is to be with those that I really love. It's funny because I haven't had that so much while I've been creating the conference, and I really miss hanging out with you, my dear. I'm going to schedule time with you when we are done with this interview. I want to hang out with you!

When I'm working on a big project, there is that kind of tunnel vision that needs to happen with a big project like this. So it really makes it clear to me how much I do appreciate the freedom and time when I have it because it's really about people for me. It's not about possessions, although those are great. I don't say no to nice things! I love nice things, yet what really motivates me is having time to spend with the people who I love. So that's the biggest gift. Also having autonomy: the ability to do what I want when I want to do it. I like that, and I think that's often one of the reasons that pet business owners contact me: *"Hey, I created this business because I wanted to be self-employed and be able to create my own life, but now I'm chained to it. It feels like a ball and chain."* So they'll work with me to get some freedom in their pet business.

One thing that I really want to bring up, Alicia, is that I had to really work through some beliefs that I had around money and business.

I had this belief early in my business that if I had a business, I'd have to work all the time because to be a business owner means that you have to work all the time. I believed this and a lot of people believe it. If you survey people asking that if being a business owner means you have to work all the time, most people would say, *"Yes."* I had that belief and even though I wasn't aware of it on a conscious level, it really ruled my time and my life, and I began to look at that in my journal writing and really looking at, *"Is that true for me; do I want that belief to be true for me?"* I started asking myself and exploring how I could make my life a different experience because I didn't know any business owners who had a business and a life.

I wanted to create a really rich life. I only knew business owners who were working all the time and totally stressed. I didn't have a role model for having a successful business and a great life, so I had to find it within myself. I decided that I didn't like that belief, so I was going to change it!

CHANGE YOUR MIND AND YOUR ATTITUDE ABOUT MONEY IF YOU BELIEVE THAT MAKING MONEY IS HARD. THE SAME IS TRUE IF YOU BELIEVE THAT YOU HAVE TO WORK ENDLESSLY TO MAKE YOUR BUSINESS SUCCESSFUL.

One of the beliefs that I actively worked on changing was the belief that money is hard to earn to a new belief that money is easy to earn. That new belief began to be my motto, and it began to be reflected in my business. Beliefs are so powerful… what's happening inside always gets reflected on the outside. So that belief became my new belief. I also began playing with the belief that running a business is easy and allows me a lot of time and freedom. That began to be a new belief and a new motto for me after I felt like I'd mastered the "making money was easy" belief. My new beliefs began to be reflected in the choices that I was making in my business; having managers help me manage, so I could go from working seven days a week to working three days a week and then two days a week and then traveling. It feels good to talk about all of this and articulate it. Thank you for your great questions!

Is there anything else that you want to share?

Just that I would really encourage the people who are reading this to just go for whatever you are wanting because you are the only one who holds you back from your most luscious dreams. Really. I mean, we may think it's somebody outside of ourselves or our friends, our family or society, but really, we're the ones who can make it happen, whatever it is that we want.

I really want to encourage people that if their desire is to work less in their business to really begin to make that happen. If their desire is to travel to really see what you can do today to begin that journey. It may be a tiny step but go for it. You are really the only one who is holding you back from whatever it is that you want to create. If it's that you are going to work less, put an ad on Craigslist today for a manager or look in your own business and see who among your staff might be a good manager to work with and help you and delegate more, too. That's a big thing. I think the more we can delegate, especially the things that we don't like to do with our business, the more we'll be excited about our business and really jump out of bed in the morning thrilled to start our day.

I love all of those ideas. Everything that you share is energizing, it's grounding, and so is my connection with you. Any time that I experience you, I love the way that you bring so much of yourself and how much positive intention and how much care you bring and how much you are here for people. Like this is what you're creating and this is your art, your creation, your joy. I love when you call me and tell me you have a new idea for a business, and I ask what it is and it's a life-filled, delicious thing. I want other people to get to have some of that through you. I feel so honored to know you.

Thank you so much for that, Alicia. You are such a delight. You are just one of my dearest people, one of my tribe.

Thank you so much for this conversation and thanks to everybody who came and showed up and enjoyed it.

Thanks, Alicia. Have a wonderful day my friend.

ELEVEN

All About Franchising: How to Turn Your Pet Business into a Franchise and What's Involved in Buying a Franchise

Interview with Paul Mann

Are you thinking of turning your pet business into a franchise? Or are you exploring buying into a franchise? Paul Mann is CEO and founder of FETCH! Pet Care, and in this chapter he shares all the ins and outs of franchising. Regardless of whether you have your sights set on being a franchisor, a franchisee, or are just curious about franchising in general, you'll want to read this.

In this chapter, you will learn:

- What's required to turn your own pet business into a franchise
- Challenges and gifts that come from creating a franchise
- If you are the type of person who is best suited to start a pet business vs. buying a franchise
- Benefits of buying a franchise instead of starting your own business
- And much more!

Kristin's Musings:

Paul Mann is wonderful. I contacted him a few months ago about speaking at the conference, and he suggested we discuss it in person since we live in same county. I agreed, so we met at a nearby coffee shop a few days later. I was really impressed with him! Paul is a rare blend of super smart, silly, and playful. I encouraged many of the speakers to make funny faces at me prior to recording their interviews, so we could loosen up, laugh, and relax a bit before going "on air." I have to say that Paul's faces were the most outrageous! The reason I chose him for this particular chapter is because I've worked with a lot of his franchisees who had great things to say about the FETCH! Pet Care franchise.

Paul Mann's Bio:

Paul Mann is the Founder and CEO of FETCH! Pet Care, the largest pet sitting franchise in the United States, serving thousands of clients in hundreds of cities and towns from coast to coast. Paul founded FETCH! Pet Care in 2002 as a San Francisco Bay Area local pet sitting and dog walking service, and, after experiencing rapid growth and profitability, launched this first-of-its-kind franchise-based business in 2004. Through Paul's leadership, FETCH! Pet Care has established itself as the nation's largest and most sophisticated professional pet care network. In his current capacity, Paul oversees all FETCH! Pet Care franchise sales, corporate marketing, and communications.

Prior to founding FETCH! Pet Care in 1996, Paul co-founded and subsequently served as CEO and a board member for Informative, Inc., an Internet software technology company and a pioneer in online survey technology. There he was responsible for the development of strategic business alliances with potential business partners and was integral in securing the company's investor capital from Nokia Ventures. He also developed an automated training program to reduce costs of training the company's large customer base. During Paul's tenure as CEO at Informative, Inc., he grew the business to over 70 employees with over 300 Fortune 500 customers generating $5 million annually, before selling the company in February 2001 to an international software development firm.

Throughout his distinguished career, Paul has amassed a diverse set of business skills, having between 1994 and 1996 served as Director of Technical Training and Sales Manager for TeamAlliance Technology Partners, a technical job placement firm, and, between 1990 and 1994, served as both a National Sales Manager and Quality Assurance Manager for health and beauty aids manufacturer Inverness Corporation. From 1989 to 1990, he worked at Two C Pack Corporation designing, developing, and selling high-end packaging to Fortune 500 companies. Between 1997 and 1998, Paul also completed packaging engineering and quality assurance internships with cosmetics behemoth Estee Lauder and with IBM, a leading computer hardware and software manufacturer.

Paul earned his B.S. in Packaging Engineering in 1989 from the Rochester Institute of Technology and has completed multiple areas of business coursework with the American Management Association. He has a nine-year-old son and two cats, and currently resides in the San Francisco Bay Area. To find out more visit *www.FetchPetCare.com*.

Interview with Paul Mann
Founder, FETCH! Pet Care

Kristin Morrison: *I am so happy to welcome Paul Mann. He is the CEO and founder of FETCH! Pet Care. I am just so thrilled to have you here, Paul. Thank you.*

Paul Mann: Hey Kristin. Thank you. It's great to be here.

You live very close to me, and it was such a surprise to know that you live so close.

Practically neighbors.

I know. It's great. So how did you get into the world of pet care?

Well, that's a funny story. I bought a house in early 2001 and I took some time to renovate it. As I was taking some measurements, the dog walker came in for the tenant who lived there at the time and I had never heard of anything like this, and she told me that she makes about $20 for 20 minutes. I was just amazed by that. I'd never heard of somebody that did dog walking. I didn't think about it until later in the year when I was looking for a pet sitter for my dog and two cats, and I called everybody. A lot of people were booked or they didn't cover my area, or I just didn't feel comfortable giving them the keys to my home or my pets. I didn't do anything about it, but then later when I had the same problem, I had this "aha" moment and realized that I'm not the only person having this problem.

I did some research and basically found that almost 2/3 of households have one or more pets and only about a quarter of the households have kids. I remember how hard it was for my parents to find a babysitter when they were looking for one for me. I thought, *"Wow, it's probably a big, big problem for pet care."*

So I did some more research and realized just how big the market was and yet how much it was underserved by professional reliable sitters. I used to work for companies like IBM and Estee Lauder doing systems process reengineering, which is streamlining an organization. I realized pet sitters are awesome. I mean they're out there. They're loving, they're caring, but the problem where they usually fall down is all the other business stuff that they have to do, whether it's marketing, or billing, or collections, or customer service; even answering the phone when they're out with pets, and that's where we got the idea of FETCH! Pet Care. We wanted to put great people who love pets on the front line and have a streamlined back office operation with a franchise owner running that part of the business. So pet sitters could do what they love, and the franchise owner could be the business manager.

Got it. Did you start out starting your own pet sitting service and then turned it into a franchise or how did that work?

Yes. Well, I started pet care in 2002 and did the dog walking and the pet sitting in my local area, and we got a lot of business quickly. Word of mouth spread, and we realized that we needed more help, so we hired more sitters and within a year's time, we had probably about 75 sitters on staff. And we were serving over a thousand clients.

The reason we could do that was that we had built all those back office systems to really support that growth and deliver reliable and professional service each and every time.

Having worked with so many pet business owners, the infrastructure is really often times very weak, if it even exists at all within a company. Often times, it's mom-and-pop businesses, and they don't have the support that they need, like the software system and the ability to grow their client base easily and effortlessly and also handle scheduling and invoicing.

I'm a techie and I'm also very detail-oriented, so right from the start, I figured out Internet software systems to run all of my business. I sought those out. I worked with some of the early founders of those pet software companies and really tried to develop it to a level where I felt that it would work for customers and pet sitters. The other thing that I was really picky about was having an operations manual; something that wasn't just in my head, but that I had something that was replicable and with which I could share the values, mission, values of my business with everybody… whether it was my staff who worked at the back office, the franchise owners, or the pet sitters themselves, and we all operate under the same guidelines as a recipe.

That's great. So everything is congruent.

Yes. It's all about consistency. Think about a brand. A brand is a promise and you want that promise to be of high quality every time; otherwise, you know what happens, people will go out and say bad things about your brand and before you know it, it's dete-

UNDERSTANDING YOUR BRAND IS A CRITICAL COMPONENT OF YOUR SUCCESS. BRAND COMES FIRST, AND YOU HAVE TO HAVE CLARITY ABOUT IT AND YOUR CORE VALUES, AND ALWAYS DELIVER ON THOSE.

riorated. So it's really important for the brand to come first. To do that, you have to ask what is the brand, what are the values or core beliefs of that brand that you will always deliver on and that are nonnegotiable, and make sure that everyone understands those and acts on those.

I talked to a lot of pet business owners who don't even have a mission statement or even know what their core beliefs are for their business, and I'd love to hear what FETCH's mission statement is and the core beliefs, if you care to share.

Sure. Our vision is a safe and happy world where our pets live life to their fullest every day. We really want to embody them with the love that they deserve and the care that they deserve. The other thing that we look at is the mission, and our mission is to provide the highest quality pet sitting and dog walking services to pets and their owners through a trusted national brand, and that was pretty key. We started off in the beginning saying we want to be a franchise system. Would you like me to talk more about that?

Sure.

Going back to pet sitters being great people. They're going to get out there and do a great job with the pets, but to manage the pet sitting business on a local level, you need somebody like a manager who is truly dedicated and committed. So I look for entrepreneurs, people who really want to own their own business yet want to follow a proven system. That combination allowed us to create a household name across the country. That was the idea.

That's great. I hear from a lot of pet professionals who say that they have a pet business and they want to create a franchise with their business. What's really involved in franchising?

Well, there's a lot. First of all, you have to have a concept and something that the marketplace really needs. There are probably about 3,000-plus franchisors out there today. There are over 300 lines of business… just to give you an idea. So a restaurant would be one line of business. Pet sitting would be another. So that's 300 of those, and then there are 3,000-plus concepts, and they're constantly coming and going in the franchise system community. That's a key thing that you want to look at, but the thing that you really have to understand is the concept of development. You have to develop and understand what it's going to look like, how you're going to take that to market, how you're going to go out and market it, and how it's going to be received. You have to create operations manuals, as I mentioned, and these are really detailed because you're basically creating a recipe book. For those who are interested in creating a franchise, we are talking about the specific, exact recipe that you want people to follow.

You also have to create a franchise disclosure document (FDD), which is required, and it's kind of like being a public company. It's a thick document! I think ours is a 180-page document, which has all the disclosures. It has all the financials. You have to disclose any history, maybe bankruptcy, things in your life, and everybody on your staff has to be disclosed. You have to update this every year. You have to submit it, and be registered in about 16 states across the country, and they go through it with a fine-tooth comb. It's actually the Federal Trade Commission that looks at this to make sure that you're on the up and up because they want to make sure that no one is going to get cheated.

You need a support plan as you bring on franchise owners. You have to know how to support them from day one and as they grow. You need an operations team. These are people depending on the franchise concept. It might

> FRANCHISING YOUR BUSINESS IS NOT FOR THE FAINT OF HEART. IT IS A COMPLEX UNDERTAKING WITH A LOT OF LEGAL IMPLICATIONS THAT MUST BE LETTER PERFECT.

be a storefront, so you have to help them in terms of finding and zoning a location for their business. You need to have a sales and marketing team, whether it's marketing to get franchise owners, having a sales team to talk to them at trade shows or around the country, to a national sales marketing team that's going to focus on national and regional consumer marketing to drive customers for the franchise owners. You need lawyers and accountants. They have to keep you in legal compliance. There's a lot that you need to know. The franchising world is very complex, and different states have different laws. Here in California, it is horrendous and you cannot make a mistake.

I know this personally from experience, and it costs a lot of money and a lot of aggravation if you do.

You then have to deal with the franchise owners. Once you have the system and you've built this whole business, you have to understand that you're never going to satisfy every entrepreneur in your business. They're all individual people with different ideas of how the business should be run.

I talk to many, many franchisors in different industries, and they all have the same complaint. You know you will never be able to satisfy everyone, and in fact, we try to do what's best for the entire system. At some point, you have people who are doing really well, some people are doing fairly well, and some people are doing horribly in your system. Then how do you meet all of their needs? It's very difficult. Having this system in which you bring them all on together is a great idea, but markets are different.

There are different demographics and different marketing conditions that make it almost impossible to have the same business everywhere around the country. So you have to be ready to deal with that and of course the investment. It costs a lot of time and money and effort to start a franchise, to be a franchisor.

How much realistically would it cost to create a franchise? What's a ballpark figure would you say?

To start a franchise concept that you're going to have franchisees buy?

Yes.

You know, that's going to vary. It's really going to vary because the key thing is, you want to do your research up front and you know a business like mine, FETCH! Pet Care, was a home-based business.

It always has been, and we have a corporate office now, but we were able to test the concept for a year with no overhead. We were making money, but that's pretty rare. You can have a one-store creation if you have a retail outlet and test it that way, but at some point, you have to invest in infrastructure, and then you have to invest in all those people. Depending on the kind of franchise concept, it could cost hundreds of thousands to sometimes millions.

It really depends, and it also really depends on your goal. There are many franchisors who come into this business. You know they want to run a decent business. They would be happy with five or ten units, but if you want a hundred or five hundred units, you have to plan for that, so I brought on investors for that growth because I simply cannot afford that growth out of my pocket.

I have to say I've worked with a few FETCH! Pet Care professionals, franchisees, and they've been extremely happy with the system, which is the reason why I contacted you for this interview. I've heard so many wonderful things about you and about FETCH! Pet Care, that it was really clear to me when I was going to interview someone that had a pet care franchise, you were the one that I wanted to talk to.

People may be thinking, "I wonder if I would I be right for a franchise as far as getting into the pet sitting industry?" Let's say they want to be a pet sitter. What kind of person would be better suited to become, let's say, a FETCH! Pet Care franchisee versus being their own business owner? What would be the distinction for that?

That's a great question, and you know it's a really good idea for people to do soul searching ahead of time before choosing franchising or going independent to determine what kind of person they are.

In my opinion, there are two types of people. There are independent business owners. That's someone who needs the freedom to innovate and experiment on their own. Perhaps they want to grow

KNOWING YOURSELF IS THE FIRST STEP IN DECIDING IF YOU SHOULD RUN YOUR BUSINESS INDEPENDENTLY OR BUY A FRANCHISE.

at a slower pace. They want to be left alone to do it the way that they want to do it, and they're also willing to take some of the risks involved. You know they are going to make some rookie mistakes. Everyone does and they're okay with that. Somebody who goes into franchising is really someone who knows they're able to follow a prescribed system, and they really want that. They understand that what they get is a lot of training and support and they bypass a lot of the headaches and possible pitfalls of a business startup. So what we look for at FETCH! Pet Care is someone, first of all, who believes in the brand. You know they have to be as excited and passionate as we are, and I always tell my people that we don't want to sell anybody a franchise. We're not trying to sell them on anything. We believe that we're going to present the characteristics of our franchise and if something connects, resonates, they're going to feel that, and we're going to feel that. That's somebody who we really want because they really get it.

They believe in the brand; they know what it stands for. We obviously are looking for people who are customer focused. With this kind of business or any retail business, you have to have a high customer focus to be successful, especially in the days of Yelp and all the other online reviews. Reputation is so important these days.

Obviously they need to have the time and money needed to grow their business, so if somebody doesn't have a lot of money, they might want to do an independent business and grow it slowly; whereas, in a franchise, you have to put in money upfront and you're paying royalties, but the whole idea is that it's a faster path and you've got brand recognition. You get the support. You get the training. You get the peers who are working with you, whether it's the other franchise owners or people at the franchise support center. You get a lot there.

We want people who are going to sweat the details. So although we want people to manage the business, not be in it, we want people who are detailed oriented. It's also the little things that count and that they're willing to drive that to their staff as well. Obviously, if someone is going into a franchise system, we want someone who is willing to follow a proven system. We want someone who is a good communicator. They need to communicate with us, the franchisor, with other franchisees, with their clients, with their sitters. You have to be a people person that way. Lastly, I think, at least in our business, being active in their community is really important because this is a business where they're going to become known in their community. They're going to do a lot of things and the more that they can get engaged and enjoy being engaged in the community… it makes such a difference.

It really does. A lot of the pet sitters that I've seen who have become very well-known in their community are often very active in their local pet communities, rescue organizations, humane societies, and just diving in and making themselves known to the pet community.

So let's say someone has heard all that you said Paul, the good and the bad about creating a franchise, and they realize they do want to start a franchise with their company whether these business owners be dog trainers, pet groomers, pet sitters, dog walkers. What advice would you have for them if they were really serious about starting a franchise?

I think they should think about really choosing a business. When you think about choosing a business model, it should be a business decision. You know, there are lots of things that we can get passionate about. You know, I have a 9-year-old son who comes up with all kinds of business ideas every day. They're great. He's so passionate about it, but they probably wouldn't fly because there's not the business need for it. It's an emotional need that he's excited by, and you know it should be a business decision. You want to basically weigh the benefits and the cost of franchising a non-franchise business versus becoming a franchisee.

It also should begin with a really solid assessment of yourself. Are you up to taking on all the legal stuff, all the managing of people, bringing on your staff, writing the operations manual, dealing with franchise disclosure documents, dealing with all the states, dealing with lots of people who are going to have issues at various times and probably will very rarely thank you?

It's just the nature of the business, and if something goes wrong, they will probably point to you as the problem maker. I don't mean to say that franchising isn't great, but it's just the reality. It's a lot of people reporting to you, and if you're not guiding them properly all the time, it does come back to you. You want to look at the pros and cons and weigh those against the benefits in terms of both investment and personal values and goals and really do those all meet?

If someone is looking at buying a franchise, you want to do your homework. You want to read the franchise disclosure document. There's a thing called "Item 19" which actually has a disclosure of how much the franchise owners are making, so you can see if that meets your financial needs. You want to speak to existing franchise owners. You want to check your finances to see if you can really make all this work. Bottom line, it's about looking at all aspects of the business and understanding them and not turning an eye and saying, *"We don't have to do that,"* but really treating it as a professional business that needs to have every aspect of it done professionally... and then asking yourself if you're up for it.

You also want to test the concept. I did it for a year and I figured, *"Well I got a thousand clients who love the service."* We were doing customer surveys and getting a 93 percent customer satisfaction score. We were doing all the right things. We didn't know if we could franchise it, but we knew we could do this business well. Once we got really clear that we could replicate it through our systems, then we knew we could franchise. So there's a lot of effort, whether it's securing suppliers or negotiating deals or getting your software systems. You need a lot of patience to really do it right because if something is missing or not put together properly, it's going to affect your franchise owner, and they're going to tell you about it and not feel so good about it and they're your reference. When you try to sell new franchises, you need them to say great things about your business.

That's true. I was thinking about it when you were talking about how, if the franchisees aren't happy, they'll talk to you and make it very clear. It reminds me of simply owning a pet sitting business and how your clients make it very clear if they're not happy or they just leave, but with franchisees, they can't leave very easily.

It just sounds like clients on steroids in a way. You're dealing with people who really have made an investment, they want to know that you're doing what you need to do as the franchisor to help them.

That's right. They've paid into a system to get certain benefits and you are partially controlling their fate at that point. So it's a big responsibility.

It really is. I would encourage pet business owners who are considering creating a franchise to not take it lightly and to really think about it. I like what you said about soul searching and really looking at, "Is this part of what I want to create for my life, because it sounds like a lot of work?" It also sounds really rewarding in a lot of ways. What have been the rewards of owning FETCH! Pet Care?

Obviously, the personal satisfaction that we're helping pets everywhere to have a better life. That was the vision and it's coming true. We're also helping franchise owners have the business of their dreams. They're having a lifestyle business that they enjoy and they're building jobs. They're employing people around the country. We have over 3,000 pet sitters on staff nationwide.

That's real and that's exciting to know from my standpoint that all that is happening, but the franchise owners personally gain satisfaction in knowing that they are providing jobs and doing something that they love and that they are helping pets and the pet owners to enjoy their lives as well. That's personal satisfaction. I'm a perfectionist, so for me a franchise system is the ultimate. I come from an East Coast Jewish family who will tell you everything that you're doing wrong, so I have the skin for that and you get that in the franchise system where they will tell you everything that you're doing wrong. In this case, it's like I have over a hundred family members telling me, from time to time, how we can improve.

It's a constant reinvention, and for me, that's exciting because I simply want to provide the best service possible out there and the marketplace is demanding it. The franchise owners demand it, and then we have to deliver on that. So it's a personal challenge and not everyone is up for it, but my team and I… we love that stuff and we're geeked out by that. We just think what can we do, and ask ourselves, *"How can we push the envelope, how can we innovate to provide the better service every day?"*

I know that there are a few other pet sitting franchises out there. What would you say makes FETCH! Pet Care different than those franchises?

So many things. First of all, there are other pet franchises and it's a variety of things, whether it's a pet food store or it's training or it's boarding, utilities or daycare facilities, grooming; there are a lot of other choices besides pet sitting and dog walking.

What I like about the specific industry that we're in, dog walking and pet sitting, is that it's a low-cost, low-risk business first of all. But let me take a step back a minute. I think all of the businesses that I just mentioned are pretty much in a recession-resistant industry. That's the good news and we've seen it. When I came into this market, into the business, in 2002, it was a 28 billion-dollar-a-year pet industry. I think this past year we're upwards like $56 billion or something like that.

Significantly higher.

So, the good news is it continues to grow and a lot of the reason is that you have baby boomers whose kids have moved out and they have pets and they have money. You have the young working professionals who have relocated, and they miss their family and they have pets, and then you have the dual-income family households who have kids and they want pets in their family, and that is continuing to grow exponentially. We don't see any slowdown in our industry. In fact, we have seen growth every year since the day we've started, and our system-wide sales, our franchise owner sales, just keep growing so that's good validation.

Getting back to why FETCH is great... First of all, it's a low-cost, low-risk business. It's a home-based business. So it can be run from the comfort of your home. It offers a lot of flexibility. With us, it is a very fast start-up period. We can get people up and running within about 30 days, maybe 60 depending on the timeframe of what they need to do, but we can get people up and running very quickly. We have brand name identity. I'm not saying that's all over the country, but certainly in many markets, people know about FETCH!, and we do a lot with PR, with social media, and when I say PR, I also mean we're on TV, radio, print, online. We do a lot of things with search engine optimization, with search engine marketing. We really guide our franchise owners locally with events and other things. So we're creating brand name identity. We assist in a lot of the national and the local marketing. So this is phenomenal.

In the last two years, we've created more marketing than we've ever done for our franchise owners, and we have some pretty innovative systems that are helping them to be there in social media, in reputation management, in the directories, in blogging, in email marketing, the website, and so much more, and of course SEO, search engine marketing, search engine optimization PR. We provide ongoing training and support, and I think this is really the key thing. We spend a lot of time with our franchise owners doing live, in-person training, and then we bring them here, but then we have weekly one-on-ones ongoing.

We do this until they hit a certain revenue number and we know that they've really gone beyond the point of being a newbie, and then we take them to the next level and they can really go beyond. To that point, we even match them up with buddies, other franchise owners who can assist them. I think that's a big part. Not only do they get training and ongoing support – you know we do webinars here in the franchise support center regularly – we're constantly putting out new information. We have the knowledge base. We have franchise forums. We have a Facebook-like application where they all talk to each other.

But I think the biggest thing is their connection with the other franchisors because these are people who have experienced the challenges that a new business owner will come up against, so when you can ask a question and a hundred other people who are doing exactly what you do, but they have invested interest, they're not your competitors, but they actually know that, *"Hey actually this franchise in Los Angeles does well… that may actually benefit a franchise in New York because that LA client might travel to New York and bring their pets for destination care."*

So the franchise system is really key and lastly the really key thing about us is we've invested a ton of time and money into developing outstanding systems, processes, and procedures, so it's a turnkey system and the franchise owners simply need to follow that.

It's a recipe that I go back to. All this is just a recipe for success, and we understand that no franchise owner can understand everything about business, whether it's legal, accounting, human resources, customer service, marketing operations. Who could? But we put that all together, and we understand that one person will come in with one skill and another will have another but no one will have it all. So we work with them where we are to help them understand holistically how to run their whole business.

I love that. That was the word that was coming up as you were talking about it. It is holistic. It's very thorough. It sounds very empowering for the franchisees to work with you.

Thank you so much, Paul. I really appreciate you taking the time out. I know you're a busy guy, so it means a lot to me to have you here.

Well, thank you, Kristin. This has been really fun.

TWELVE

Branding and PR: How to Brand Your Pet Business to Gain Clients and Get on TV

Interview with Caroline Golon

Are you feeling a bit lost when it comes to branding your business and getting your business seen? In this interview, Caroline shares what it takes to get your brand seen and recognized, even if you have a lot of competitors in your area. And branding and PR don't have to be expensive; there are some actions you can take to make your pet business visible for free (or very inexpensively). Let's get your business seen and talked about!

In this chapter, you will learn:

- What a brand is and how to make your brand stand out in a sea of other pet businesses

- Important steps to take to create your brand

- How to avoid the biggest mistakes when it comes to branding and PR

- Branding and PR on a shoestring budget

- How to get your pet business on TV

- And more!

Kristin's Musings:

Caroline is a radiant ball of light filled with lots of good tips on branding and PR. What a great lady who really knows her stuff. If you want to get your business "out there" and visible in front of your right clients, she's the one to listen to!

Caroline Golon's Bio:

Caroline Golon is the president of High Paw Media, a content development firm that helps businesses and organizations in the pet industry share dynamic, inspiring content with their audiences.

Golon spends her days researching and writing about pets for clients and for her own blogs, where she's raised more than $85,000 for homeless pets. Golon is also a regular contributor to Vetstreet.com and Petfinder.

Golon also co-founded BlogPaws, the premier online community and annual conference focused on pet blogging.

Golon's work has been featured in *USA Today*, *The New York Times*, The Associated Press, and more. Find out more at *www.HighPaw.com*.

Interview with Caroline Golon
President, High Paw Media

Kristin Morrison: *I am so excited to welcome Caroline Golon here. She is the founder of High Paw Media. She specializes in branding, blogging, and PR.*

Caroline Golon: Thank you so much. I'm thrilled to be here.

I'm so happy to have you here. So, a lot of pet business owners think about their business, but they don't really think about their brand. How would you define "brand" to pet business owners who don't know what that is?

I think the term brand kind of describes several different aspects of what we're talking about. To me, brand is the core essence of your business. It's the intersection where what you believe in, what you're all about, what your customers experience when they're interacting with you, and what your reputation says about you kind of all come together into one.

I mean everything is a brand. You are a brand; I'm a brand. Businesses are brands. Movie stars are brands. You know, it's really how the world sees you, and like I said, it's that combination of your reputation and then people's actual experiences with you. That kind of encompasses what your brand should be all about.

So, how can pet business owners really make their brand stand out and be visible in a sea of other pet business owners?

I think that the first thing that a pet business owner needs to do, whether it's a pet sitting business, a dog training business, or a dog grooming business, is think about why they're in business. Again, most small businesses, if not all small businesses, start with a person, an idea, a passion, a reason for starting that business and for staying in business.

In the service-based pet industry, it's about animals. So there is always that passion to it which is different from many other industries. We're so fortunate to be in the pet industry, but I think that starting with the reason why they

> BRANDING OCCURS AT THE INTERSECTION OF WHAT YOU BELIEVE IN, WHAT YOU'RE ABOUT, HOW YOUR CUSTOMERS PERCEIVE YOU, AND YOUR REPUTATION.

started the business in the first place and knowing that reason is the first place to start. That's number one. Why are you in business and what's the whole reason and what's your passion?

The second is asking what your customers want from you. I think a lot of people, a lot of businesses, miss that. They think they know, but they don't really find out. So I think the second piece of it is finding out what your customers think about you and what they want from you, and that's usually done through a customer survey, for example. It seems like it's very basic, and you can give somebody a survey card, "yes, no, yes, no," but it actually is a great opportunity to glance at some insights about what you may not realize about the kind of brand you are presenting to the world. So that customer survey, that discussion with your customers is very, very important.

What specific questions would they ask in that survey? Are there any additional questions that you would recommend?

Yes, absolutely. I would start with the basic questions. You know, *"Why do you do business with me? What's your favorite part about doing business with me?"*

If I'm a dog groomer, I will use that example again, *"Why do you get your dog groomed?"* Find out why they go to a professional as opposed to trying things at home. Do they have any other pets? What's important to them in a dog groomer? How far away do they live? Are they traveling 25 miles to see you? That's pretty telling. Or are they just around the corner? So there are a lot of things like that that business owners should not be afraid to ask their customers when they're doing that type of survey. That will tell them a lot.

I just did an article last year for *Pet Age* magazine, and it was about families with pets, busy families with pets, which is a passion of mine because I've got a busy family with pets. So I did a survey with about a hundred different families that had children and pets to find out the types of things that I was just describing to you: what was important to them, why they shop where they shopped, what they were looking for.

One of the things that I thought was very interesting is 70 percent of them told me that they had more than one pet or more than one species of pet. I thought that is really interesting. If I have a dog and a goldfish, wouldn't a retailer want to market to somebody that has multiple species in a bit of a different way so that they can get in business for both of those types of animals? That type of information that comes out of a customer survey is powerful information.

That's great. I love that. What form of survey should they do? I know there are a lot of online surveys available. Is there one in particular that you really enjoy using?

I use SurveyMonkey. It's very easy to set up. It's free. The first level is free, so I think up to about a hundred responses is free and then you pay a nominal fee for more responses beyond that.

It will tabulate the responses. You'll see percentages. You'll see trends. You can create open-ended questions that may not have an A, B, C, D option. I have people fill in an essay. Those types of surveys can be emailed to your newsletter list if you have one. You can post it on your Facebook page and have your customers fill it out that way. You can do some sort of drawing or giveaway and have people log on with a certain URL. Put their name at the end of the survey, and then you'll do a drawing or something like that. That's a very easy way of doing it. That's how I would suggest. There are other survey programs, but that's the one that I prefer.

Okay, great. I've used Constant Contact before for surveys and for regular members; it's a very low cost per month to send out surveys to your list. I agree, I think it's so important to really tap into the pulse of your clients and really get a sense of what they're looking for, what they want. It's so illuminating.

It really is and also how they view you. You may think that you are providing exceptional service. They may not. Or they may. So if you think you're providing exceptional service and your customers think that you're providing exceptional service, that's one piece of your brand that you really need to promote.

The most important piece.

Yes. So it's back to the whole "what is a brand" thing. It's the things that are important to you, what your reputation is out in the world, and how people's interaction is with you.

Going back to what you were saying about how your clients see you, I've encouraged pet business owners I've worked with to send out surveys to their clients. What I found most beneficial in my business with my own pet sitting clients was to snail mail them a short survey and then include a self-addressed stamped envelope because there was something about having that stamp on the envelope....

Yes. It's wasting if they don't use it.

Yes, and people feel guilty. You know it's kind of like tapping into clients' guilt a little bit and it works. Keeping the survey short and sweet is a good idea. What I found is people are more apt to write something than they would be to call if they're unhappy.

Because of that, I was able to change some things in my business and really address certain staff members who weren't living up to expectations that the clients had and that I had for them.

It also was such a positive experience too, because it gave clients the opportunity to really say how much they loved us, and those comments became testimonials for the website. So it was such a positive experience on all levels, even if it was a negative comment. It enables change.

> THE BEST WAY TO SERVE YOUR CUSTOMERS IS TO GIVE THEM WHAT THEY WANT. THE BEST WAY TO UNDERSTAND WHAT THEY WANT IS TO ASK THEM!

Absolutely. Those are actually more valuable. You know, positive is wonderful because it reinforces that you're doing some things right. And it makes you feel good, but man, when you get some feedback that's not so positive, it makes you take a really hard look at what you're doing.

It forces you to look at why you're getting the negative feedback that you're getting. If a customer is letting you know that, that really needs to be on your priority list and something to take care of immediately.

It's true, and you know the truth often hurts a lot; we all want to avoid pain wherever it is. It's kind of a human inclination to avoid it, but my advice, and I think yours too, is to really look at what's not working in order to create the most successful, empowered business that's possible. An empowered business that's congruent with who you really are and your values, and when we provide an impeccable service, we sleep better at night, we feel great about ourselves, and it impacts every area of our life.

It's powerful. So what mistakes have you seen that some pet business owners make when it comes to their brand?

I think that there are a couple of things. One is a pet business that really tries to be all things. We didn't really cover this exactly, but who is your customer? Who are you really trying to do business with? Yes, of course, we're all going to say everybody, anybody that has money who wants to send their dog to me to be groomed is my customer. But really, that's a big universe and so part of that is the branding process. You really want to define who your customers are, who you want to work with, and who your ideal customer is. So if you're a dog grooming business and you just want to work with women, women dog owners, then you know that's one aspect of your brand that is really going to be something that sets you apart. Right?

If you are a dog grooming business that only wants to work with crazy busy families with pets who are bringing in their golden doodle to be groomed so often and they're manic, and you know you have to get them on a schedule and on a regular basis, so they make sure to come in, that's one customer that you might want to be focused on.

Maybe you want high-end customers; people who will spend a lot of money regularly with you. I mean, we all want that. That's a different type of approach, right? So a dog groomer who is focused on… we'll use the high-end customer for example, probably doesn't want to worry as much about marketing to that busy family or marketing to the women. They want to focus on the people who are affluent, who live in a certain area, that type of customer. You'll be branding yourself and marketing yourself a little bit differently to that person because that's who you want to reach. I think that the biggest mistake a lot of pet businesses and businesses in general make is not finding that focus, not finding that customer who they know they want to reach out to. So when you spread yourself too thin and you spread yourself in your branding and your marketing or you're trying to reach everybody, you're not going to do a great job reaching one person.

It's really true. You know, I'm thinking of two photographers who I have worked with that take pictures of me for my branding, and they only work with women. They have women call and ask, "Can my husband come to the photo shoot?," and she says, "No." It comes down to setting boundaries to really keep your brand intact. I love what the photographer says: she doesn't want to dilute the brand. People see her as a women's photographer.

That's strong… a strong brand.

It is. You know, they are some of the most incredible businesswomen. It's a couple. They are booked solid. There's something about having that niche where people know what you're providing. It makes it very simple. I think about pet business owners who I work with who are cat sitters. They only take care of cats. They are so busy because there are a lot of people out there who just want that sitter who doesn't have the smell of dog on them.

It's very true. So really having that focus is very important especially when you are first starting out. It can be tough to narrow down your focus because you want all the business that you can get, wherever you can get it. But the focus you mentioned, really having that focus actually will bring you more business in the long run.

The other thing that you also mentioned was the photographer who you used. Another mistake that a lot of pet businesses and small businesses in general make is not investing in professional design and photography. I can't stress that enough. I do PR for businesses, and I also write for several pet outlets, so I can live on both sides of it. There have been times when I have been working on a story about a business and my editors have killed the story because the owners I was interviewing didn't have good photography for their business and it was a missed opportunity for the business. I even recall sending an email to the business owners about whether they had any great shots of that dog food bowl that they wanted me to write about, and they didn't. That's the opportunity that's missed.

Having the photo available when somebody needs it, sending it to them right away. Having their logo ready to send to somebody who needs it, having photos ready to send to somebody who needs them. I think that's a miss that many businesses don't do because they're too busy. It falls to the bottom of that priority list, but I think having a suite of tools, both marketing tools and branding tools, available to them to send to somebody at a moment's notice is really key.

I love that you said that because I'm thinking about different pet business owners who I worked with and I've asked to see their website, and first of all, sometimes the design is really just horrible. It looks like it was a very cheaply designed site and that's usually a starting point when I'm working with people. I'll say, "We've got to get you a better website here," and sometimes they don't even have a logo. Those things need to be congruent with each other too. So the logo and the website have matching looks. Like you said, having a nice picture for the About Us page. I work with people who are wearing sunglasses on their About Us page.

On their head.

Or over their eyes and you can't see their eyes. People really want to see who this person is that they going to be calling. The home page and the About Us pages are the most widely viewed pages on a site. They're the ones that people immediately go to: the home page and then the About Us page. Who is this person? Having those pages be a reflection of you because, whether we like it or not, we are perceived by how we look, and how we're presenting ourselves in the world matters. The photographs are really important for those pages.

Someone may have the most amazing business and have the best customer service and have the best dog grooming abilities in town, but your junkie website is going to turn people away. On the flip side, you may be mediocre but having a nice, clean, well-designed website and really great photos of the dogs, your dog customers being groomed makes a positive impact. Visuals can make all the difference in the world if I'm coming to your website to decide whether or not I'm going to call you for the first time.

That first impression is also another important part of your brand. Going back to the great reputation—if they come to your website and their experience there is *"Ewww!"* then you just diluted your brand, but if they say, *"Wow these guys really look like they got it together,"* you've created that whole essence of how you want people to perceive you and you've done a good job there. Look and feel is very important.

It is. When I'm working with people and helping them with search engine optimization, I say, "You know you may be number one on the search engines after we do this work, but if your site isn't nice, they're going to click on it and go away within seven seconds." So it's really about having that be congruent. And the flip side of this is you can have a beautiful website, but if you're not providing quality service, that's not going to help you grow. What is it...? It's something like if somebody likes your business they'll talk to maybe two people about it, but if they don't like your business then they'll talk to about 20.

And there's a big danger there. That kind of thing can spread quickly, especially online.

It's a shame in some ways and good in other ways. You may have heard wonderful things about a business, and then you're cruising around the web and you see a Yelp review that's like one star, and the person is saying, *"Oh, these guys are terrible, they didn't return my calls, they did a horrible job when I finally went in to see them."* That's got to impact somebody's opinion regardless if they heard five great things about you.

That's true. Going to the subject of actually creating your brand: A lot of pet business owners are starting out and they're on shoestring budgets. What can they do? How can they create their brand with few resources... like money?

I think that's a great question because I think that's always a challenge with anybody and their branding and PR and marketing efforts. The good news about branding is that branding is for the most part one of the cheapest things that you could do for your business. Understanding what your brand is, understanding how you want people to perceive you. Understanding the type of experience they want to have with you is key and then executing is key.

There are several different parts of that. The first is understanding what your customers want. We talked about that customer survey. We talked about knowing who your customer is, understanding what they want, and then delivering it in ways that are not expensive. Good customer service is not expensive at all. It's free. Answering the phone with a smile makes a humungous difference. I know these seem elementary, but people forget, they get busy, they get focused on the bottom line, and they forget that the most important aspect of their business is how the customers are perceiving them. How they're interacting with customers. Being on time is another huge branding opportunity for a pet sitter, groomer, photographer, any type of service provider. Show up on time. Show up five minutes early. People notice. If you show up ten minutes late every time, they're going to really notice.

So those things are all free. If you have a retail store, or you're a groomer or any place where people come in to see you and your staff, it's important to have your team all wear the same uniform, or their own clothes. Like khakis and a black shirt. It doesn't have to have a logo on it. Those are things that cost money, but most everybody has khakis. Most everybody has a black shirt. That will show a very put-together, well-branded business. We talked a little bit about how important it is to have the logo and professionally done website. So those are things that cost money, but they don't have to cost a ton. You can certainly go to an agency that's going to say that they can do that for five grand, or ten grand, or twenty.

There are ways to find less expensive services by people who can do things that look professional. Art students for example. We have a great college here, a design school, and the students are always looking for projects on the side, and they're a lot less expensive than an agency. Maybe you can find somebody who will trade with you. Perhaps they have a dog and maybe you'll do some grooming sessions for them in exchange for them developing your website or your logo or doing something like that. There are ways to get around that hefty cost of creating your branding and creating your website or your photography. But it's so important. It's something every business owner really needs to find a way to make happen, but it doesn't have to have a huge price tag on it.

That's true, and they can start and get a very simple website, and then as they get more business they can get a little bit more elaborate.

No homemade websites. You have to have a website. Not a homemade one.

So, talking about PR, what are some simple tips that pet business owners can do to get more PR and exposure for their pet business?

Well, I touched on this, but having some photography images is so critical in PR these days. Everything is image based. If you want the local news to come out and do a story on you, you have to think in terms of what kind of great images you will be able to provide to them. If you're a dog groomer, are you going to have ten dogs in a row lined up getting groomed or do you have the new pet paint? Are you going have some cool colors on the dogs that you've been grooming?

It depends on what it is or what your event is or the reason why you want the news to come out and cover you. You need to have some great visuals to share with them. Tell them what those great visuals are going to be upfront so that they can imagine that would be great on camera. That's television. Print or online, again the same thing: photographs. Really good quality photographs, not junky photographs with the smartphone, although many of them can be good, but it's better to have high-resolution photographs as they will always help you in any kind of PR outreach.

Those are some tips for the logistics of it, but as we talked about in the beginning, we are in a wonderful industry where we're talking about pets and pets do well in the news. They do well with PR. You know news stations and reporters and editors love covering pet stories. So you have to find something that's going to be unusual or interesting or sweet or heartwarming that will help pique somebody's interest, but just having the pet aspect to it puts you miles ahead of any other business that might be doing some PR that day. I mean would you rather cover an insurance company or would you rather cover a dog training business?

Always capitalize on that pet aspect of your business and try to find sweet, unique, interesting, cool, unusual, heartwarming stories about your clients, about your background, about the pets that come in, about the things that you're doing in the community, and definitely leverage that pet aspect.

That's great. So let's say a dog trainer really wants to get on the news, how do they go about doing that?

Well it depends on what the story is. And it depends on who they're reaching out to. So if they want television, for example, they need to have a good idea of what they want the news to cover. Say they're doing a training session or a class that they're doing for little kids to learn how to work with their pets. That's cute. You've got kids and you've got dogs. Right?

GETTING PUBLICITY IS EASY WHEN YOU THINK ABOUT THE NEEDS OF THE NEWS OUTLET: WHAT DO THEY WANT TO COVER? PETS ARE AN EASY IN. DO YOUR HOMEWORK AND ENSURE YOU HAVE GREAT VISUALS TO SUPPORT THE STORY.

So, then you contact the news station, and the best way to do that is to call the front desk and ask who the producer is. Typically, something like that would be a morning show story or a noon story. Probably not a 5:00 or 10:00 p.m. news story because that's much more hard news, but morning news is always looking for stuff like that. Noon shows often have that ability too. So I would focus on those two shows, and I would call the front desk and ask who the producer is for these shows. Tell them, *"I have a story I want to send them,"* and they'll give you either a name or they'll give you an email address, and even if they offer a generic email address, those emails do get checked. They do because they're always looking for great news stories. I would reach out to them via email and say, *"I'm holding this training event and I'm going to have kids there and I'm going to have dogs there and it's going to be great and the visuals are going to be wonderful, we will get releases from all the kids, and come out and film it and it'll be a lot of fun. And I can give you five tips for parents who are watching the segment or give them five tips on how to train their dogs at home."* That's an easy little package for them to get their heads around and might be something that they pick up.

That's great. I love how you spell it out for them and make it really easy for them to go after that story.

Absolutely. Just to further that point: the easier that you can make it, the better. Don't make people create a story themselves. Again, it's this world we are in, everybody is so busy. We're moving so fast. If you can create that package and give it to them on a silver platter….

Then do it.

A lot of times, they're going to do it. They're going to say, *"This is easy. Let's do it."*

Why wouldn't I do this?

Absolutely.

That's great. Thank you so much for sharing all these great tips. I'm really grateful to have you on and this has been great.

Thanks very much. Take care. Thanks for having me.

THIRTEEN

How to Train and Motivate Dogs and Humans (Including Your Clients and Staff!)

Interview with Dr. Ian Dunbar

Got some challenging client and staff issues? The way we train dogs can be very useful in training the people we surround ourselves with: our clients, staff, and even our partners! You'll also learn about the biggest mistakes dog trainers and owners make when they are working with their dogs. Oh, and if you want to motivate your clients or prospective clients to buy your service or product, you'll want to read this!

In this chapter, you will learn:

- Qualities of successful dog trainers (and dog owners)
- Biggest mistakes that dog owners make when they are training their dogs
- How to become skillful in the behavior and training of humans
- What makes clients motivated to buy your service
- And much more!

Kristin's Musings:

Ever heard of the expression "cheeky monkey"? That's Ian. He's a rascal! I never knew what was going to fly out of his mouth, which makes him very fun to interview… and, I will admit, a little nerve-racking! Ian's a generous soul who made himself available to all of us pet business owners in the midst of his extremely busy worldwide travel schedule. (Thank you, Ian.) Many people think, *"OH MY GOD, IAN DUNBAR!,"* and he is all that (and even more). He's also a really kind, down-to-earth guy who knows how to treat people and dogs with love and respect. What a guy!

Ian Dunbar's Bio:

Veterinarian, animal behaviorist, and dog trainer, Dr. Ian Dunbar received his veterinary degree and a Special Honors degree in Physiology & Biochemistry from the Royal Veterinary College (London University), plus a doctorate in animal behavior from the Psychology Department at UC Berkeley, where he researched olfactory preferences and the development of aggression in domestic dogs. Dr. Dunbar has authored numerous books and DVDs about puppy/dog behavior and training, including *How to Teach a New Dog Old Tricks* and the SIRIUS® Puppy Training video.

In 1982, Dr. Dunbar designed and taught the world's very first off-leash puppy socialization and training classes — SIRIUS® Puppy Training. Subsequently, he created and developed the San Francisco SPCA's Animal Behavior Department, the American Kennel Club's *Gazette* "Behavior" column, which he wrote for seven years, and the K9 GAMES®, which were first held in San Francisco in 1993 and continue as annual events in Japan and Europe. He hosted the popular UK television series, *Dogs with Dunbar,* for five seasons and has appeared on numerous radio and television programs, including the *Today Show* (US) and *Dash Village* (Japan).

Additionally, Dr. Dunbar has consulted on a variety of movies — full-length features, documentaries, and animation (including Pixar's UP), and he has twice spoken at the prestigious TED Conference. Over the past 40 years, Dr. Dunbar has given well over 1000 one-day seminars and workshops for dog trainers and veterinarians in an effort to popularize off-leash puppy socialization classes, temperament modification, and owner-friendly and dog-friendly dog training.

After he founded the Association of Pet Dog Trainers in 1993, Dr. Dunbar was inducted into the *Dog Fancy* Hall of Fame along with four of his heroes: James Herriot, Konrad Lorenz, Lassie, and Balto. Currently, Dr. Dunbar is President of the APDT Foundation, Top Dog (CEO) of the Center for Applied Animal Behavior, and Scientific Director for *www.dogstardaily.com*, a free online, multi-media educational website for puppy and dog owners. For more information visit *www.DogStarDaily.com*, and to download Ian's free puppy training workbook visit *www.jamesandkenneth.com*.

Interview with Dr. Ian Dunbar
Veterinarian, Animal Behaviorist, and Dog Trainer

Kristin Morrison: *I am so happy to welcome Ian Dunbar here with me. He is an animal behaviorist. He created SIRIUS® dog training school where he was the first instructor to do off-leash puppy training in the world, and that's pretty brave to take them off the leash. He is also the author of many books. Anything else that I'm forgetting? That's right! You're a veterinarian, too.*

Ian Dunbar: That's true. Such a life!

And so, Ian, what are some mistakes that dog owners make when they're training their dogs?

I think the biggest one is that they don't look ahead. They get a dog and before they know it, they're out of control because the dog is growing up and developing so quickly. You know, especially if we get a puppy or even if we adopt an adult dog, because it's the first week that makes the dog: new house, new rules. They learn very quickly.

I think they should look on it like driving a car. You don't just buy a car, get in it and turn it on, and then off you go without knowing how it works. People should think ahead a little when it comes to getting a dog too.

The classic is when people come up to me and they say, *"Oh Ian, I've got a problem with my dog,"* and I ask, *"Oh no, what is it?"* And they say, *"Well, it barks."* I say, *"No! Oh, no! Of all the dogs you got it's really unlucky that you pick one that barks!"*

We laugh at this, but the thing is, all dogs are going to pee and poop, chew, bark. They're going to be hyperactive. They're going to be happy over-the-top to see you. They're going to run away off leash. They're going to pull on leash unless you teach them otherwise. So I think a little prior preparation and learning what your puppy is going to do. If you follow mentally, when you get it, week eight, week nine, week ten, and know exactly what you've got to do, and then the puppy raising becomes so much easier.

And what kind of training style do you prefer when it comes to training dogs?

Basically, it's a three-step process. The first step is to show the puppy what you want him to do. You have to let the puppy know what the rules are, and in other words, find a way to communicate to teach the puppy ESL, if you like, to teach the puppy human words; the doggy behaves in action, so we can, *"Here's your toy, get the chew toy."* So we can communicate what we want them to do, but honestly, 90 percent of training is motivating the dog to want to do it as opposed to the approach where people tend to look on the dog as their adversary in the training arena and say, *"I told you to sit down, now sit."* So motivating them is the second step. First, let's make sure the dog understands what it means and then figure out how to motivate them.

The third step would be that we must communicate to the dog when it's a "must do" command. I mean there are times when we need absolute compliance: on-demand compliance, and that's the biggie. I think that's where dog training is sort of split down the middle. A lot of people are saying, *"We get them to comply."* Other people are saying, *"Well, we are reward trainers."* So what do you do when the dog misbehaves? *"Oh, we turn our back on him when he jumps up. We're going to extinguish the behavior."* It's insanity! That's why I think a lot of pet owners are frustrated that they go to a class and they do it with the trainer and they're having a great time.

The training is very, very positive with the dog, but the trainer is not teaching them what to do when the dog misbehaves or when the dog is not compliant, and I think this is the biggest change in dog training in the last hundred years. We now have ways to insist that the dog does what we'd like them to do without causing fear or pain to the dog. Of course, the analogy here would be a parent to the child and an employer and employee or teacher and a student. I mean we don't want to beat that child to get them to do what we want. We want to teach them and to motivate them but occasionally we have to acknowledge daddy or mommy knows best: You must do this now for your own safety.

Punishment just inhibits the behavior that we don't want, but even if it works, which it seldom does because it's pretty inconsistent, it's so woefully insufficient. What we want is to stop the behaviors. We don't want to get the dog back on track as soon as possible and occasionally communicate to the dog how serious noncompliance would be or how dangerous it would be. Say the dog is running through the front door and by using that voice, you can do this in one word. You can communicate, "*Stop running away, I want you sitting and this is urgent so you must do it.*"

> THERE ARE THREE STEPS TO THE TRAINING PROCESS, WHETHER IT'S PUPPIES OR PEOPLE: SHOW THEM WHAT YOU WANT THEM TO DO, MOTIVATE THEM TO DO IT, AND REQUIRE COMPLIANCE WHEN NEEDED.

It sounds like you are saying being in partnership with your dog instead of you being the boss?

I think sometimes you need to be in charge. I mean being in control because we're humans with human brains, and we can foresee the dangers of the future, so we occasionally have to tell dogs not to do something. "*You will not jump up on the child.*" You know Labradors would frighten the child. If you're a Rottie or a Pit and you do that to a child, you're in big, big trouble.

So I think the process more is about communication. It's living with the animal. What has happened in dog training is the most peculiar thing in the past few decades. Many years ago, most books on dog training would say to basically ignore your dog for six months to a year and then put a leash on him and jerk it when he doesn't do what you want without telling him what you want him to do.

A silly way to train. I think if a dog or a child gets it wrong, we have to explain to them why it was wrong or at least we have to explain to them what exactly we want to do rather than just saying no, and jerking or zapping them. We have to say, *"Get your chew toy."*

See, by using words, correction becomes an easier process, but then the very ironic thing is when clicker training came along (which is a fantastic technique to doing specific things with dogs, complicated things, teaching dogs behaviors which aren't in their normal repertoires) that we kind of lure them. What clicker training did was took words out of praise and rewards and instead we go click then give a treat.

Clicker training does require consistency and impeccable timing, which sometimes are not always present. It takes words out of the loveliest side of training. I like to say to dogs, *"That was a really good pee."* I've seen some pees in my life that had volume, that had style, that had the leg lift. I mean serious! Like hot damn buddy that was faster than my brain could process.

I think it's such a shame that we're trying to teach so many owners to be technicians and then just go click and treat. So please, I don't want people to say, *"He doesn't like clicker training."* No. I was responsible for getting the very first workshop together where clickers were used to train dogs. It was run by Puppy Works just around the corner here and I promoted it. We got 200 people. That's a great training technique for specific uses. I don't think it's a starter technique for someone who's trying to develop a relationship with a growing puppy.

I agree, and I think dogs do like words and they like hearing our inflections.

The inflections. You see, if we use feedback… I mean we've almost reduced dog training to a click or a shock or a jerk. These are quantum feedback. It's always the same. Where is the behavior? Oh, the dog's response is always different, so our feedback needs to not just communicate whether you get it right or wrong, but how well you did or how potentially dangerous the mistake is. We can say thank you, which means minimal requirements have been met. You know the response wasn't brilliant but at least you did it. Then we say good dog. Good dog. Good dog. Or hot damn, diggity, man that's so cool. You get it. It's such a natural feedback because it's a binary feedback and it's analog, so we can communicate the various qualitative aspects of behavior and how well you did.

We do that with people, too.

Oh, yeah. Well… some people do.

That's true. Some people don't.

Other people have communication problems there and they will never tell someone when they're doing something wrong. So they fret over it, and they never praise people when they get it right.

Either way the people who they're around don't know how they're doing.

Yes, and I think with a dog, I mean… to me the whole reason for having a dog is he's your buddy. I mean he's like your little cute, furry psychologist, home companion, exercise coach, and everything! You know, I think it's so nice when we talk to them. I remember we had a big old dog called Clure, and I had some things that I was worrying about and I would talk to him on my walks and my neighbor actually came up here and said to Kelly, *"You know, your husband is talking to that big red dog,"* and Kelly says, *"Oh, he always does,"* and she said, *"No, no he is talking to the dog as if the dog is replying to him."* It's true; I did and it really helped me through the problems.

I get it.

Why worry my son, Jamie, and Kelly when you have a dog that you can talk to? He pretty much solved everything. His solution was, *"Walk me more often."*

There you go.

Yes, let's do this five times a week.

And cheaper than therapy too.

It is.

That's great. I remember in some email exchanges that we had, you were talking about the behavior and motivation of humans and that you're very interested in that. Tell me more about that.

Well, I think that I'm interested in it simply because I'm interested in it from the viewpoint of the focus of this, which is running a successful dog business. To me, two things just pop out in what would make a successful dog business. I'm talking about growing the business, and the first, obviously, is that what you do has to be reproducible. You need people to do it for you now, with you, for you. Eventually having employees is the only way to grow because you are only one person and you can only do so much. Well, as soon as you get people working for you, we now get into, I think, the most important aspect of dog training which is people training. We are not just training the dog. I mean that's one aspect of it. There are many layers of the onion. I mean, train the dog a little, get him up and running, and then we are teaching a person how to train the dog or to work with the dog's people.

More importantly, the person that we're usually working with is mom in the family, so we're actually teaching her our job – which is how she can go home and train other people in the family, extended family, friends, and guests how to train a dog that we just helped train.

So a lot of it is people training. I think that's important in any profession, and especially in dog training, because it's so emotional. People care about their dogs so much that people training skills are everything. If you want a successful business, you need to know how to make people feel good and to motivate your employees to work for you, to motivate your dog owners to do their homework. It's that three-stage process again. It's not just telling them what to do. It's motivating them to want to do it and then very occasionally you have to say, *"Look I am the boss here."*

I am the dog trainer, and I see what happens if you don't do this, so I really want you to do this. I'm going to check on you next week. I'll ask your dog and I do. When I see the dog the next week, I actually put my forehead down on the dog's head and I say to the owner, *"The dog's telling me that you haven't been home feeding him around children,"* and they reply, *"Well Tuesday we had houseguests…"* and then they totally blab, and I say, *"You've got to do this because your dog doesn't like children. Do you understand what your dog is going through? Every time he sees children, he is stressed and anxious and it's just not fair. You've got to solve this problem."* Occasionally, for the third level, I will say, *"You're going to do this,"* and I'll do everything to convince the person, but by and large, if you motivate your staff properly, they are going to work for you because it's as if it's their company and the clients and pets are their family.

> PET PROFESSIONS – WHETHER YOU'RE A DOG TRAINER, PET SITTER, GROOMER, OR DOG WALKER – INVOLVE EXTENSIVE PEOPLE SKILLS. YOU HAVE TO MAKE CLIENTS FEEL GOOD AND MOTIVATE YOUR EMPLOYEES TO DO A GOOD JOB.

And your dog owners are going to want to do the homework because it's a fun thing to do with the dog.

It is, and you know I'm thinking about my own pet care business. I had a pet sitting company for 18 years and 35 staff members when I sold it.

It was a pretty big company, and what I found through having staff members for so many years is they really did work better with praise rather than, "Hey, you did this wrong." I mean, I had to learn that the hard way early on and I had to also learn that it wasn't money that motivated them. It was gratitude and really letting them know how grateful I was that they were there, and once I started doing that and really paying attention to appreciating them more, I found that they stayed with me longer. The staff members that I had stayed with me on average five to seven years.

A lot of people make this big thing about money. Even for the business owner, it's really fulfillment that you want. You want the feeling that you're doing a good thing and you're making people's lives a little happier, but in terms of motivating employees, money is not a good motivator because it's on a fixed schedule. Either fixed interval or fixed ratio, and we know that doesn't work to train puppies, so it's probably not going to work for humans either. The crazy thing is that 100 percent of the entire work force of the world is maintained on these two schedules and it doesn't work. I did a massive survey once of vet techs. This was at a veterinarian retreat in Lake Geneva and I asked them, *"What do you want from your job?,"* and the number one thing by far was recognition. The second choice and most popular thing was fulfillment or a chance to grow and expand my knowledge base. So I have done quite a lot of reading into motivating people and from… like the industrial psychology viewpoint. Boy, this is a heavy-duty subject now.

It sure is! I love it.

One of the books that I really liked was *Swim with the Sharks,* and this was an envelope salesman who then became a multi, multi-millionaire. Why? Because of the way that he sold envelopes. He did the typical male fashion, he developed a questionnaire, 66 questions I think it was. Questions I want to ask my client like: "Are you married, did you go to college, what college was it, do you have children, what are their names, what are their interests, do you have a dog, do you have a cat?" Then he would come back and meet them to try to sell his envelopes. He would ask, *"How is Johnny's soccer going? Did he get onto the team?"* Bam, bam. You're meeting with the person on a personal level. You just made the sale. So in the doggie world that is so easy for us because it's a dog and all you have to do is get down on the ground and say, *"Oh, how's Sparky? Hey, how's my favorite cocker, who's a good dog? Has mommy been training you?"* Yeah. So that's the greeting and then when you leave, there's a little nice thing that you say to the dog. Say, *"I'll see you next week. I can't wait. You're my favorite consultation or I've got a little present for you and it's addressed to Sparky Johnson."* See that? You used the dog's first name and the owners last name and it's a little chew toy and some treats and it's just a little present. But not every time. Not a birthday card. Not a Christmas card. These things are not motivating.

> MONEY IS RARELY, IF EVER, A MOTIVATOR. PEOPLE FIRST WANT RECOGNITION, FOLLOWED BY FULFILLMENT.

It's when you do it out of the blue. In fact, when everyone is depressed because the holidays are over and where is the sunshine and you send the dog a little card saying, *"How is the training going? I'm missing you. You know I'd like you to come to another class,"* and it makes the owners feel so good to receive something like that.

I'm thinking also about a lot of pet business owners that I work with. And we'll talk about how to motivate referrals to come from pet groomers, pet storeowners, etc., and what I recommend is giving them gifts during the non-holiday time because everybody is giving them cookies and candy over the holidays. Bring something in on a February day or an April day that has nothing to do with the holidays.

I think when you think about where the referrals come from, you've only got to find out what breed the referral sources have and that's the little thank you card that you send. You don't send a Labrador card to someone that has a German wirehaired. So you send a German wirehaired card and you just say, *"How's Trix? How's he doing and thanks by the way for sending a referral. It's really, really appreciated."*

And that's it. It's that small connection again which shows that you care and it's amazing. It's the little things that really matter and that go so far because money is not the motivator. It's not the motivator if you're paying someone to work for you and it's not the motivator when you earn it. You can earn a lot of money and you think that's cool, but then next month you get depressed if you earn less. You see it's a very dangerous thing that you're in there if your motivation is money. So it's about the little things and that is really what life is about because now I'm finding in the dog world so many people get so wrapped up in their dog and the dog world and there's nothing else there. It's very dangerous. You're setting yourself up for real hurt if anything goes wrong. And you've got to have other hobbies as well.

You've got to have a life to be a really good dog trainer because you've got to be able to relate to people on that level.

A lot of pet business owners may love animals and they're working in the pet business world, but some of them don't really like people. They love animals, that's why they got into it, but they don't really like the people, the human clients so much.

That's a very delicate way of putting it. So many people come to me and say, *"Well I don't really get along that well with people. It's why I became a dog trainer,"* and I thought, *"Wow you're in the wrong field."* I mean if ever you need people skills, it's when you work with animals.

If you're a vet, groomer, dog walker, daycare, or dog trainer, you've got to have people skills because this is a very delicate thing that you're dealing with. It's very emotional. You better have people skills. I look at all my friends I went to college with and we were a pretty fun bunch, and they were all amazingly successful as veterinarians. Why? They were just fun people and their clients loved going to the vet to see them even though they were upset when they would go to the vet because their pet is sick. You've got to relate to the people. It's an irony that so many people who are so positive – a million percent positive with dogs – are actually so nasty with people and saying things like, *"Then you shouldn't have gotten a dog in the first place."* What are you doing?

My view is this person has come to me with their dog. If I insult them in any way, if I belittle them, then I'm distancing them from me so now I can't help that dog. So actually what I visualize is – and this is a very weird thing: If someone is doing something to a dog that I don't like or if they're training in a way that I find reprehensible, I imagine a little syringe floating over their head. A little syringe of euthanol, and I think the dog has got a lucky break and all because he's here with me, and I can help him if only I can get the owner to listen to me and that's what gives me great patience and I come up with some nice styles. Like if I want to say, *"That's wrong,"* I'll say instead, *"You know, that used to be a very popular way of training dogs 50 years ago, but we just do it much quicker now, let me show you."*

I won't make an issue out of it because if I distance the person from me I know they're going to another dog trainer, and if you think about it in any profession whether you go to a dog trainer, doggy daycare or, say we go to a lawyer or a doctor, half the people you're going to see are below average in that profession. I like to think if someone has come to me because of their dog that they really got lucky, so if I frighten them away because I'm a bit of an asshole, then they're going to have to play the lotto with a trainer again and they can quite as easily get someone who is using methods which aren't quite so great. So that's what I tell people. Don't take the bait. I know you're upset. Bite your tongue and imagine this syringe of euthanol.

What's euthanol?

That's what you use to euthanize animals. Basically, it's a heavy-duty barbiturate. When I see dog trainers I disagree with, I imagine an enormous syringe of euthanol because our dialogue will influence the lives of so many dogs now.

It's true.

So it's about seducing people to see it your way and not get into an argument. But so many people… they just love to have arguments. They love to point out when you're doing something wrong, and when I lecture around the world, it's kind of interesting in some places they are really accusatory and saying, *"Well this isn't right. You know you're stressing the dog,"* or something like that. They can't really see a problem with logic and I say, *"Well yeah, the dog is a bit stressed here because he's dog reactive,"* but what we have to compare that with is if we do nothing and the dog remains dog reactive for the rest of his life, and this dog is seven years old… he's been dog reactive seven years and you haven't done a damn thing about it.

That's what's stressful every day of your life. So I'm going to do something and yeah it's a little bit stressful, but I'm going to make your dog better. So you know we don't want to just tell people this is wrong. Those were ways to train dogs many years ago, but now we do it differently.

I don't use the word "better" and I don't use "inhumane." That's the volatile one. When you say, *"No, that's inhumane or that's cruel"* … oh my word. That person is not going to listen to anything that you say now, and I don't care if you've been to a hundred clicker workshops, they're not going to listen to you because you insulted them.

You belittled them. You shamed them in public and their dog now can't benefit from your experience and expertise.

Words are so powerful. They're important. So any other final tips you have for pet business owners?

I think there are some important things to think about when you're dealing in a profession where if you get it right you're doing a lot of good, but if you make a boo-boo then you fail and you can actually cause harm. It's very important to be a representative about what you do because I see a lot of people who crucify themselves with a single failure, especially in the rescue world and the shelter world, and you've got to fail. You're going to fail a few times. Let's face it. You didn't mean to do it, but there's a lot going on. Dogs have baggage and they have owners we have to convince. So you've got to look at your successes and then at the end of the day you've got to say, *"Well, I had trouble with one class."* And don't focus on that one class. You gave it your best shot, now focus on the 11 puppies that you really helped to have a better life and actually that's my principle. In fact, college taught me this, and I was told that being a veterinarian is a great profession, it's going to be very fulfilling and you're going to love it, you're driving around the countryside seeing animals. It really is the James Harriett thing when you are a veterinarian in the country. And three things are important.

Number one: your colleagues, your employees. You work with them for so much of your life. Well, you are with the people you work with over a third of your life. Treat them as individuals. Value them. More important than your colleagues, though, is your family. That's what's life is about is family and friends. So don't let go of your family and friends because of your work. Then what I heard next absolutely stunned me. *"More important than the veterinary profession, your veterinary colleagues, than your family, is you."* I thought, *"Wow."* I heard, *"If you don't look after yourself, if you don't see what you do reprehensively, the good that you do; if you keep focusing on your mistakes and the screw ups that you've made, you're going to be useless as a veterinarian, horrible as a colleague, and pretty pathetic as a family member."*

I think that's it. Let's take the principles that we use for training and motivating puppies, apply them to people, but especially apply them to ourselves and to look at the good time that we're having in life and have a good time in doing it.

Thank you so much, Ian.

Well, thank you.

FOURTEEN

How to Keep Track of Your Numbers in Your Pet Business (Yes, It Can Be Fun, Easy, and Illuminating!)

Interview with Susan Briggs

Feeling overwhelmed with keeping track of your income and expenses? You are not alone. Many business owners find themselves scrambling to get their records together at tax time because they haven't kept track of their income and expenses on a regular basis. Let's face it: Numbers are often on the bottom of most of our to-do lists. And even if you have pet business software that keeps track of your income and expenses for your business, you'll want to read this chapter because you are sure to learn new tricks. (Yes, even if you are an old dog in the world of pet business.)

In this chapter, you will learn:

- Easy steps to make recordkeeping a habit, to make tax time – and the rest of your life – easier

- How to use your numbers as a flashlight on your business

- Healthy financial habits to cultivate on a regular basis for optimum ease and joy

- How looking at your financial picture each month can generate more money

- How to use simple financial spreadsheets as barometers for where you've been and where you want to go in your business

- And much more!

Kristin's Musings:

We all know that numbers can be kind of boring to talk about, but somehow Susan manages to make it fun and even exciting! She explains how to keep track of numbers in a clear and simple way (which I really love), making this information user-friendly for all. Many business owners have math issues (I know I used to), and the intention for this interview was to make numbers less intimidating for the average pet business owner, and I think she did a splendid job! Susan also has an effervescent, radiant spirit. Thanks, Susan, for sharing yourself with us!

Susan Briggs's Bio:

Susan Briggs is founder of Crystal Canine and, with over 14 years' experience operating a large pet center and as an author and speaker, is a recognized leader in the industry.

In 2009, her second book, *Counting Noses*, was published and inspired the Financial Health Check-up course. Through the online course or personal consulting, her presentation style makes it easy for all owners to increase profits and feel more comfortable with their financial responsibilities.

The pet care industry is Susan's passion, but her professional career began as an auditor. She has a Masters of Accountancy and passed the CPA exam in 1984. Visit her website at *www.CrystalCanine.com.*

Interview with Susan Briggs
Founder, Crystal Canine

Kristin Morrison: *I am so excited to welcome Susan Briggs. She was formerly a CPA, an accountant, and then she started a doggy daycare, which she owned for over 12 years. That's fascinating: CPA to doggy daycare owner! She also is an author and a speaker, and I'm really excited to welcome you here, Susan. Thank you so much.*

Susan Briggs: Well, it's great to be with you, Kristin. I do have an interesting past, so you just never know what is in store for you.

It's true. It's very true. So tell me, CPA to doggy day care owner. How did that happen?

Well, I wanted to take my dogs to work with me. To me, it felt very natural. I actually moved out of my CPA career into kind of operations of management at a mortgage company and then a travel company and then from there I was acquired twice by a bigger corporation, and my job was eliminated.

The second time it happened, I really wanted to follow my passion and enjoy my next career move, and I had the opportunity to start a doggy daycare back in 2000. So we were one of the really early pioneers of doing doggy daycare, cage-free sleepovers, grooming, and training. It was a big multiservice center that I loved.

That's great. What were some of the challenges that you experienced in your doggy daycare when you owned it?

I had partners so that always brings a layer of challenges, and there were three of us who we were trying to support with the business. It was a very large business, and we were doing cage-free sleepovers back in 2000. This is when we were very early, so our niche was narrow and I learned that in hindsight. We were still explaining to people what doggy daycare was and why they might even want to take their dog there.

It's just unbelievable today!

You were educating people on what doggy daycare is.

Right. So starting out, our niche was narrow, so people are kind of surprised with my background to find out that I had a lot of financial stress and struggles operating my business even with my background as a CPA.

I felt very much like a failure because of that for a long time. But it's something that I'm very passionate about: that people can learn and it is such an important part of being a business owner. We've got to make it more accessible and achievable for folks. That's one thing that I hope to help to do as we talk through some issues.

Great. I know a lot of business owners in general, but especially pet business owners, have a lot of challenges when it comes to dealing with their finances, keeping their records clean, orderly, and accurate, and it's one of those things that gets shoved to the bottom of the to-do list.

Right, because it's not the fun stuff. It's much more fun to go play with the pets. To me, one of the best parts of having my center was I could get out of the office and go play with the pets, and in hindsight, I probably did that a little too much instead of looking at my finances. Hindsight is so 20/20.

I think what we'll talk about are some tips to make it easy and kind of fun and rewarding for yourself and your business in the long run.

I love that. Why don't we just start right there and see where we end up.

Okay. Well, I think one thing that I learned, and hindsight is the best teacher, was because I did understand accounting and finance that the time that I could allocate to it in my business I needed to use to do the actual bookkeeping work. I was in the trees and I never took time to step back and look at the forest... which was looking at my business and doing the planning and what I needed to do to have the financial prosperity that my business deserved.

I think that's the first lesson that I really want to encourage to all business owners and especially pet business owners. I know you have a limited amount of your time that you can really allocate to finances, so make it the role of strategic planning because nobody is going to care more about your profits and how much you make in your business than you do. You really can't outsource that or delegate it to anybody else.

YOUR TIME WILL BE BETTER SPENT UNDERSTANDING THE IMPACT OF YOUR FINANCIAL REPORTS (I.E., SEEING THE FOREST) THAN DATA ENTRY (I.E., ONLY SEEING THE TREES). OUTSOURCE THE BOOKKEEPING IF YOU NEED TO, AND FOCUS ON STRATEGIC PLANNING BASED ON YOUR FINANCIALS.

So you are saying the way that pet business owners will be able to look at the forest instead of being in the trees is to really do the finances themselves versus outsourcing.

Yes.

I recommend that a lot too, Susan, because I found that really helpful in my own business. When I'm the one tracking my numbers on a weekly and monthly basis, I'm really getting the ability to tap into the pulse of my business. You can really see the life force of the business when you're looking at the numbers.

The numbers are your guidepost of where you are and where you've been and where you are headed. A lot of people think about accounting as only looking at histories, so part of what's important is building a strong foundation for your business and that's easy to do. Let your CPA and bookkeeper help you do that part.

Let them do that: be in the trees doing the entry of all of your expenses and income, and then once a month you get the big picture financial reports. I think what's really important is when you look at these reports it's just like data on a page.

If you don't have a budget, then I would compare what you are earning now to the same period of the prior year. Then you can at least see how you're doing compared to last year. Then you have data that is information.

From that, you can make decisions. One thing that I started doing in my own business is every month I set a meeting with myself and I go over my business financials.

I do that too. It's a powerful process and really helps create a clear picture of where you are and where you want to go.

Yes, and I make that part of my marketing too, because the financial analysis and marketing really go hand in hand. If you look at your business numbers and you want one segment of your revenue to be higher, that's where your marketing comes in. What are you going to do to increase revenue in that segment? Look three months ahead and put down two or three action steps that you can take to improve that revenue number.

That's such a great tip, and in looking at the data comparison, I think it's also so powerful to look at expenses and income and really track it. And not just track it, but investigate it. When you've been in business for a while, that can be so revealing. It's like, "How did I do in January for the past five years?," and really be able to look at whether, historically, January is one of the slow months for me.

It gives you so much power when you know that information.

It really does. It is empowering.

Yes, because the pet industry is cyclical. We have our slow months. We have our peak months. Then what you need to make sure you do – if you're offering multiple services – is make sure you're tracking your revenue by your key services. If you're doing dog walking versus overnights versus boarding or doggy daycare, track all the revenue separately, so you can see how much each revenue stream is contributing to your overall income.

Some of them will vary. What I found in my business is when we had peak boarding, that the daycare portion of my business tended to naturally drop and then when boarding was really low, daycare would go up, so they were great complement services.

Yes. They kept the financial flow going for you.

Yes. The more you combine complementary services like that the more it smooths out your overall revenue. So it's not quite as cyclical as it might otherwise be.

Because I keep track of all my revenue streams for the last ten to twelve years and spend time really looking at those every month, I am able to really see and track where my income is coming from each month.

For me, it was so helpful and actually, perhaps even saved my business from failing, because at one point I thought about letting go of dog walking in my own pet sitting company. I was finding that dog walking was one of those services that was so stressful for me. As the owner of the business, I was finding that having to deal with cancellations and additions was really taxing to me, my staff, and my business. I was thinking about letting the dog walking portion of my business go, but I didn't do that before looking at how that income stream performs every month. How much is it bringing in for the business? When I really looked at those numbers for dog walking for the last few years, I realized dog walking was 40 percent of the income in my business!

So I decided not to let that service go but instead look at how we could work the dog walking differently so that it works for me, it works for the clients, it works for the staff members. The numbers can be really revealing and helpful on so many levels, and I think doing it in that experience really saved me from making a fatal business mistake.

What I challenge people to do is to look at labor numbers and then you can see the net and whether each revenue stream is actually contributing to the profits of the business given the amount of money you are paying staff members.

That's a really good point, Susan, because it can be one thing if the gross numbers are really high for a service you are providing. But the gross isn't the true number. Let's use dog walking for example. If the amount of expenses that are sustaining that service is too high, expenses like marketing or payroll, and if you are finding that those expenses are costing you more than you're making, you will want to look at how you can adjust those numbers or perhaps this is a service you might need to let go. Because if the expenses for the service are more than the revenue, it's obviously not worth it.

> IT'S CRITICAL TO UNDERSTAND THE IMPACT YOUR VARIOUS SERVICES HAVE ON YOUR OVERALL BOTTOM LINE. KEEP TRACK OF INCOME AND EXPENSES (AND PROFITABILITY!) OF EACH SERVICE YOU OFFER.

Right. Or you could reprice according to where it is profitable to you because I think a lot of the pricing that's done in this industry is strictly based on market rates and everybody's cost structure is different.

I really think when you're pricing services, you need to look at what the market competitors are doing, and you really need to understand your cost to provide that service and make sure your pricing is correct, so that the service is profitable.

I agree. So what are some other tips that you would recommend for pet business owners when it comes to their business finances?

Well, one thing that I find in this industry is that we're very compassionate and we have big hearts and we like to serve and we like the pets, so I do find that sometimes we give big discounts. So maybe our rack rate is a profitable rack rate, but then you look at how many discounts we give for multiple pets, seniors, military; and I'm not saying don't give any discounts....

But I think if you think about other professional services, and I'm very much about this being a profitable service, that we're knowledgeable and we're providing a real professional service to pets and their families. We need to be paid accordingly. You don't see dentists and doctors and other service providers that discount near as much as we do in the pet industry.

That's true.

Families with five kids don't get 50 percent off the third, fourth, and fifth child when they go to the dentist. When it comes to pet care, time is our money. So I challenge people to really think about discounts differently and look at those low periods and perhaps only offering discounts in your slower periods.

I'm a big person on also tracking occupancy, especially in boarding and daycare, but I can see it also in dog walking. You have only so many slots to walk dogs, what's your percentage that you're full? On the months when that goes lower, that's when it might make sense to offer discounts to fill it up when you have capacity.

Right. What I've noticed with a lot of pet business owners is they sometimes automatically give discounts without the client even asking for it, and when I'm coaching pet business owners that's a big no-no. It's so important that pet providers honor their time by not giving discounts.

Get really strategic about what the discount is doing for making your business more successful. Does it make sense to give discounts to everyone? I think perhaps discounts to new clients or clients who refer your business might be good; also discounts for the military, police, and fire employees. All of those can be good "give backs" to your community.

Let's make sure our discounts are truly a win for all involved and not simply us being unable to say no. I think that's the other thing. We don't always stand up and value the service we provide. It can be very hard work and clients really do appreciate when you bring professionalism and knowledge and that whole focus on safety when it comes to pet care. People will pay for it and part of that is you, the business owner, valuing what you're bringing to the client.

Yes. I think most of us get into this profession because we have big hearts; we're very nurturing, which is wonderful. You really want those qualities when you're starting a service-based business like this, and one of the drawbacks that I've noticed is that the big hearts can lead to failure in setting boundaries.

It can lead to an inability to say no, inability to take care of ourselves, and also like you said to just discount where we might not need to or want to. Also where it doesn't make sense, especially if your client didn't ask for a discount.

And that discounting is often not beneficial for us. It can really impact our bottom-line profit margin if we are discounting.

Often, pet providers determine that whatever is left over after expenses and discounts is going to be their pay and often it's not enough. If you look at it on a per-hour basis, most of us are probably making less than we were in other careers, and that shouldn't be.

You are right.

I want people to feel empowered to take control and increase their pay, and if you don't want it for yourself and your family, give it to a charity, but really get the value that you deserve for the services that you're providing.

DON'T GIVE DISCOUNTS JUST BECAUSE YOU THINK IT MIGHT DRIVE BUSINESS. MAKE SURE YOU UNDERSTAND THE IMPACT DISCOUNTS HAVE ON YOUR BUSINESS AND ENSURE THAT DISCOUNTS ULTIMATELY HAVE A POSITIVE IMPACT ON YOUR BOTTOM LINE.

I think that everyone will feel better about the experience when we are valuing ourselves and our service.

I love that. What are some tips and tools for managing your own finances?

What really helped me was having this monthly meeting with myself and when I became intentional and began empowering myself to take control. For me, the financial side comes a little easier because of my background. It was the marketing half of it that I had to really say to myself, *"Okay there's no reason that you can't do this and do it better. I can just jump in there and embrace the social media. You can figure this out."*

So I have this monthly meeting that I schedule on my calendar and I spend a couple hours going through the reports and then setting up three action items, and I make this meeting fun. I really recommend people go out to the coffee shop, turn off your phone, and don't let anybody interrupt you, and get your favorite beverage and really make it a time for you.

Then the first thing I did was reward myself for actually having that meeting. So on Friday afternoon, my dogs and I quit work early and we have a little happy hour and all of us are rewarded for having this meeting. That's the first step.

Next, especially if your business is cyclical, I would set up a base pay that you pay yourself so that you have your base salary and then maybe every quarter give yourself a bonus. If you exceed your financial goals for the quarter, then you get a bonus and then take part of that money and either do self-care or something fun for yourself so that you're rewarded for all this hard work, because I don't think people realize how much you can come to resent your business.

So that's important. I think pet care should be the best job in the world, so reward yourself and make sure you're taking care of yourself as part of your business... and that means treating yourself to some perks that you wouldn't normally get.

Absolutely. Give yourselves rewards the way that you would with the dogs that you care for. You give them little treats. You need treats too.

Exactly. My thing is frozen yogurt. I love to go to the yogurt store, so that's going to be one of my rewards for myself because I try not to do that too much, but make it something that's very rewarding. I also really recommend that people create a budget. I think it's the best thing to compare to because if the numbers don't look right when you're going to pay yourself, you can make the changes when you do your monthly and annual budgets. That's the time when you can look at which service will be focused on to increase revenue or where can you cut costs in order to meet your budget.

Then every month if you're comparing the actual numbers coming in to your budget, you know where you're out of line and maybe you need to make adjustments. So you're not just looking at historical numbers on a page. It becomes something that you have control over and can do something about.

That's great. What budget software do you recommend?

Well, I'm a big believer in QuickBooks because I think that you can get a lot of nice reports. I've been using the online version and it's actually very user-friendly and the reports are easy. There is a level where you can actually get a budget based on your history of your business numbers. QuickBooks will basically do the budget for you.

And then the reports easily come out. So I think if you can't do QuickBooks then look at Quicken or something else where you're actually getting a monthly profit and loss statement for your business and that you can put in a budget for comparison. That would be the most important thing that you need to do.

I agree. You know, one of the things that I've been doing for a few years now, which has been really helpful and is kind of nerdy, is I write down everything that I spend money on, whether it be for personal or business. I have a little book and whenever I spend money, I highlight it if it's a business expense and at the end of the month, I enter my numbers and then review the numbers.

Going back to making doing your numbers fun... I started working with a friend of mine to do recordkeeping meetings where we would enter in our numbers on our own computers. We make lunch for each other depending on whose house we go to and we rotate every other month. So we spend about an hour having lunch, reconnecting in person. And then we do our numbers for an hour and a half or two hours.

What a concept! To have time with a friend and then spend time entering our numbers and doing any accounting work that we need to do. It really works for both of us. I've found that doing that with my friend really makes it an enjoyable experience because as a solopreneur, a lot of us spend time alone and to be able to marry those typical solo activities with connection can be wonderful. Especially when it comes to something as potentially dry and boring as numbers can be. But it doesn't have to be. We can really get creative about these so-called "boring tasks." I love your idea of going out on a date with yourself to a coffee shop when you have your monthly meeting with yourself.

I love the idea of having lunch with your friend, so I'm going to add that to my repertoire of ways to make it fun because it breaks my heart that business owners get scared and intimidated by the numbers. So they just ignore the numbers and go on hoping they get done at some point.

Whatever the bank balance says I have, that's just what my business gives me. There's so many little things that they can do that can change that and I'm a big believer that everybody can learn the financials.

A lot of people are told that they're not good at math, so now they think that they're not going to be able to learn accounting and bookkeeping. I have taught basic accounting and bookkeeping to many different people for years, and everybody can learn it. It's kind of like me and marketing. I had to get over myself and quit telling myself that I couldn't do marketing because I was putting myself into that box of *"I can't."*

Once you make that decision to do something, you can get it.

I found that it starts with examining that belief. I love that, Susan. I'm kind of laughing here because in college there was a course called "Coping with Math Anxiety," and I signed up for it because I had a lot of anxiousness around math. It started with the belief I had that I wasn't good at math. I was good at English. I wasn't good at math. That's what I thought and that's what I told myself. So I signed up for this course. I got the book and never went to the class, and actually the book was in my trunk for a few months. This was years ago that I had the thought about not being good at math. As business owners, if we have that belief, we have to face that and that facing that can be a relief.

It's a big part of being a business owner, understanding your financials.

It's true, and I love math now. If somebody told me years ago, "You're going to love looking at your numbers," I would have told them they were crazy, but I do. I love it. It is data. It is information. It's like talking to a friend who has really good information for you about your business.

It's a great way to see your accomplishment and what you have done as a business owner. Small business contributes so much to our local economies as far as employment and the revenue that you bring in, so you should be proud of that. I remember the year that our pet center brought in over a million dollars in revenue.

I never would have thought that I could do that.

It's powerful.

So even though the profitability was not what I wanted it to be, still that was something where I could say, *"Okay I'm not a failure. I have a million-dollar-revenue business."*

So you can't be a failure and have that. I think everyone owes that to themselves. I think it gives you confidence in your business. When you want to give discounts, you're doing it with knowledge and not just with the idea, *"Well I hope it all works out in the end."*

Going back to entering the business numbers on a regular basis and really looking at the numbers… what happens for a lot of pet business owners at tax time is they haven't entered their numbers, so all of a sudden, they're in the midst of trying to run their business and enter in a year's worth of numbers, both income and personal, which can be so stressful.

You need timely information because if you wait until the end of the year, you have no power to change anything. It's gone. That whole year is gone and any opportunity that you had to make a change is gone. I'm a big believer that you've got to do it every month, at a minimum. The meeting that I have with myself is the second week of the month, because that gives me time to get my bank statement and get everything inputted from the prior month. I do it by the tenth or the fifteenth but no later because at that point I'm already two weeks into the next month and the month is halfway gone to make a change.

So the best thing you can do is that if you don't have time to do the number inputting yourself, then outsource to a bookkeeper to at least get your information inputted in a timely manner.

Then you need to review it as the business owner....

Right. You review the totals and compare it to last year and, hopefully, your budget. I know everybody is going to have fun and do a big budget party for themselves because that really is the best thing you can do! It's setting out your plan for the year of your business.

Yes, it is, and to really make it as fun as possible. It doesn't have to be this dry, boring experience. Looking at the numbers is so revealing. It's intimacy. It cultivates intimacy with your business. It's really looking at who is this business, what makes up this business? The numbers are very good communicators.

They are. They tell you exactly where you are and they can give you clues as to what you can do to be even better and to be more efficient, and I think that's what we deserve for the clients that we're serving is to have that confidence and ability. I remember one time, and this was a moment I was sitting at my hairdresser years ago, and she was apologizing that she needed to raise the fee that she charged to cut my hair. It was like how I used to be too, and I remember it just came out and I said, *"No, you need to charge what you are worth because I need you there to cut my hair. I don't want you to go out of business!"*

So charge what you need to charge. I think we forget about that. We have a lot of trust with our clients, so the clients want us to stay in business. You have to run your business so that you're there for them on an ongoing basis.

Again, pet care is not nonprofit business. This is a profit business.

Yes. It is okay to make money. I think that's the other thing we hear: *"You don't make money in the pet industry,"* so we think we do it just for the love and need to suffer and be in lack.

Yes, a lot of pet business owners believe that.

That is not at all true. Pet business should be a profitable business. That way you're going to enjoy it and bring more of yourself to the clients and the dogs, and everybody wins. You've got to have that energy exchange of providing a service and getting back the value for it.

As you were talking, Susan, I was reflecting on how a lot of us have this belief that we can't have it all. Perhaps we could have work we love but we can't make money from it. I want to let everybody know you can have it all. You can have work that causes you to rocket out of bed in the morning and get so excited and also make a large profit... and it's okay to have work you love and make a lot of money doing that work. It really is.

It is. That is such a good point, and if you have financial stress because you're not paying yourself, then you're not going to have that joy to get out of bed. It's going to really weigh you down and be a negative force for your business and for you personally, so no one wins in that situation.

It's true.

You can have it all.

Going back to what you said a while ago about paying yourself first. A lot of business owners that I work with don't pay themselves. They have one checking account that's both personal and business, and they are taking money out as they need from their one account. So having a separate business account, having a separate personal account and then writing yourself a check from your business is very honoring.

It's very powerful.

It's so honoring of yourself as the business owner.

You need to definitely separate accounts. It's going to make taxes easier. It's going to make actually understanding what your business is contributing to your personal and family income much clearer when you separate them and have different books for business and personal.

Yes, absolutely. Well thank you so much Susan. It's been such a wonderful pleasure having you here. I'm feeling excited to go do my numbers!

Oh, yeah!

Right now. I just feel I want to jump in.

A small victory. I'm excited, too.

Wonderful. Thank you so much, Susan. I really appreciate you sharing all of this, making yourself available and helping us lighten up around money and have it be a more fun, enjoyable experience. Have a great day. Thanks.

You too. My pleasure.

FIFTEEN

Navigating Pet Business Challenges with Ease and Grace

Interview with Dee Hoult, MBA, CDBC, CPDT, CTDI

There are some actions that, when they are done, can profoundly change the way business owners run their businesses. Dee shares some of these actions in this interview. If you are feeling a bit overwhelmed in your life and your business and need a shot of mojo to keep you going, you came to the right place.

In this chapter, you will learn:

- Five tips for new dog trainers (and any pet business owner)

- The secret for success that is often overlooked in pet business

- The #1 marketing strategy that every pet business owner needs to do

- How to practice self-care – even when you have no time

- The art of navigating business challenges with ease and grace

- And more!

Kristin's Musings:

Dee has a lot of balls in the air and still manages to seem cool, calm, and collected. This makes her the perfect person for this particular interview!

Dee Hoult's Bio:

Applause Your Paws, Inc., was founded in 2006 by Dee Hoult. She always had dogs in her life and realized at an early age that she could train dogs for basic obedience and manners. It wasn't until after she started her master's degree, however, that she realized the opportunity to create a dog training company for those dog owners in Miami who wanted an alternative to "traditional" dog training. Today, her company generates $1M in annual revenue and sees approximately 50 dogs a day between the dogs in programs at the facility and her team of in-home private lesson instructors who spend their day on the road making house calls. To find out more visit *www.ApplauseYourPaws.com.*

Interview with Dee Hoult, MBA, CDBC, CPDT, CTDI
Founder, Applause Your Paws, Inc.

Kristin Morrison: *Hi Dee. It's so wonderful to have you here. Yay!*

Dee Hoult: Yay!

I'm excited to interview the wonderful Dee Hoult, who is a very successful dog trainer. She is the owner of Applause Your Paws in Florida, and it is such a delight to have you here. Thank you so much.

Thank you so much for the invitation. I'm excited to chat with you.

So tell me, how did you get into dog training?

Do you want the long version or the short version?

How about the medium version?

How about the medium version... okay. The slightly edited version. I started my journey when I was five years old without even realizing that I was starting my journey, and it's kind of neat to look back on it, but I won my first pet tricks contest in 1987 with my first Border Collie mix. Her name was Babe.

That started a lifelong passion for animal training, and it's a hobby that I always did, always loved. I grew up volunteering with shelters, fostering dogs, rescuing dogs, training, helping friends with their dogs that were maybe a little problematic, and then I went on to school to the University of Miami.

I'm originally from Austin, Texas, and ended up in Miami, Florida, to do my undergraduate degree in marine science. My undergraduate experience actually took me down a different path which was more community involvement and leadership, so when I finished my undergraduate degree, I really didn't know what I wanted to do at that point, so I took a job in development and fundraising with my alma mater, University of Miami, and I had the most amazing woman as my boss who wasn't really a boss. She was a mentor. I have her to thank because she really encouraged me to earn an MBA, and that is what turned my hobby into a career.

I say it's half accident and then half "knowing the right people to guide me down the right path," because they sometimes know what's better for you than you can clearly see yourself. I remember sitting in one of those marketing classes doing my master's and all of a sudden I thought to myself, *"I have a skill that I adore, that I love, and I have a really great opportunity to make this a career."* So that's how I went from hobby dog trainer to professional dog trainer.

That's wonderful. How did you grow your dog training business when you first started out?

I had already been very involved in the animal rescue community here in Miami for several years before starting my business, and because of that I already had a network in place that maybe others don't have when they first start out. I definitely don't take that for granted. I know that was a huge part of my success, but I definitely didn't quit my day job when I decided that I wanted to go off on my own. It definitely took me somewhere between two and three years to really feel comfortable in my business, like I was in a happy place.

But it was off to a slow start. I would go work my nine-to-five desk job, doing fundraising and development at UM, and then maybe if I was lucky I'd have one client in the evening that I could go train, so it was definitely slow at first. It was slow and steady, and I kept up the relationships that I had with the people who were already in my network, letting them know that that was what I was trying to do.

That's great. I heard you say, Dee, that you didn't quit your day job, and it's interesting because when I'm working with pet business owners a lot of times they'll ask me if they should quit their day job and I say absolutely not.

I don't know if you experience this in your business, but when we first start a business, it's like a little baby and we wouldn't ask our infant to take care of us.

Right.

We wouldn't ask our baby to support us, so I think it's really wonderful that you were able to keep your job and start your business because it didn't put too much pressure on your new business to be a success right away.

I think looking back on the experience that you're right. It doesn't put pressure on the business because you're not financially dependent on it at that point, and you can really be passionate about it without having to worry that you're not going to make ends meet that month. I think what's hard for a lot of people is that they're just tired. When you go to work nine-to-five and then to work again six-to-ten… that's a long day.

That's a sacrifice because you're either going to make the financial sacrifice to say, *"I'm going to go from being stuble with benefits and not having to stress about money if I quit my day job or I'm going to man up and say I don't care what it takes, I'm going to work 14, 15 hours a day, every day, seven days a week, for as long as it takes."*

I think a lot of new business owners have to do that in the beginning because they do need to financially support themselves, but they also want to go after their dream and their vision, whatever that may be, so being able to juggle both in the beginning is really important and can be necessary.

Self-care is really important when people are doing that juggling act too. A lot of things go out the window. I don't know if you experienced that when you were juggling a lot?

I actually am experiencing it again right now.

Growing pains, right?

Yes, with the expansion of my business. I think it's really humbling because I look back and it's so far in the past now, Kristin, that I sometimes don't remember how tired I was or how often I have to tell my friends that I can't do something with them. I lost a lot of the other parts of my life that I enjoyed in order to start my business.

And it's my husband who reminds me that I've been through this before and I survived the first time, I will survive the second time.

I'm thinking about self-care, Dee, and how I'm experiencing it... a lack of self-care right now a bit too because a lot of new things are opening up for me which can create this idea that there's not enough time. It's not true, but that comes up, and when it does, it's even more important that I find time for me. I find that when we think we're too busy to exercise or to meditate or to practice self-care – whatever that looks like for us – that we most need to do it.

Mine sometimes is having a glass of wine with a girlfriend.

Absolutely. Whatever we do to recharge. I have a friend who meditates every day and she says that if you think you're too busy to meditate then you're too busy. Self-care is really important. So how would you... and I know you're experiencing a lack of self-care right now in your own life and maybe we can both kind of explore it as we're talking about it... but how do you incorporate self-care into your really busy schedule? What does that look like for you?

How do I incorporate it? I plan for it.

Yes. That's crucial.

I think that's the reality of running a very busy business and being blessed in that way. I think if you're spontaneous about taking a break, it may not happen. You have to recognize that and you have to be willing to schedule it in. I like that term, "self-care." I never really thought of it that way, but you have to be willing to plan the time for yourself in whatever way that means for you. That's different for a lot of people. For me, I don't necessarily need two days at home to do nothing. That's not my idea of self-care.

That's me personally. I need one day where I can be outside. I can listen to birds singing or maybe I can go kayaking and exploring down here in the Everglades, and that's different for everyone. I think you first need to recognize what it is that recharges your personal battery. What is it for you and make the time to do it; no exceptions.

It is. Putting it in the schedule where it is a nonnegotiable can make it actually happen.

It's important and it's usually one of the first things to go when people start to become successful and then it becomes all about success rather than enjoying running the business and enjoying life.

SELF-CARE IS A CRITICAL COMPONENT TO ANY SUCCESSFUL BUSINESS. IF YOU DON'T SCHEDULE TIME TO TAKE CARE OF YOURSELF, IT WON'T HAPPEN. WHEN IT DOESN'T HAPPEN, STRESS BEGINS AND YOU'LL START RESENTING YOUR BUSINESS RATHER THAN LOVING IT.

Because you love the business... but then it becomes this kind of a vicious cycle rather than running the business being a wonderful thing, like perhaps it was in the beginning when you first started.

It is. You know, I could talk about my husband forever and ever because he's wonderful, and he's a big part of why I feel like I'm successful, because I have someone in my life who unconditionally supports me and is there for me at the end of the day, but I have to remember that, yes, he's there for me and I have to be there for him too. That's one thing that I really struggled with initially as I got busier and busier and people demanded my time… I realize that I was sacrificing time that I'd spend with somebody who's the most important person to me and that's something that also is really hard to tell those customers or other people who are demanding your time. The word "no" can be hard to say.

You have to remember who in your life is most important to you too because they're the ones who keep you sane while you're crazy.

That's so true. I just love that you're talking about this because, in my own journey of becoming more successful, whatever that looks like for me, and again success can be so many different things, but what I found is that it's really about the people in my life. That to me is success: having the time to be able to spend with the people who I love. Their time is really what I equate with success. Do I have enough time in my life to spend with those who I love and who love me? If I do, I'm successful.

I work with a lot of pet business owners who are solopreneurs, so they're on their own, they're sole proprietors, and they perhaps don't have their tribe… like you have your husband and I imagine you probably have some really wonderful friends. I also have a wonderful man in my life; he's such a loving and wonderful partner. I have great people in my life and they really support me when things are really crazy.

And fellow business owners or fellow sole entrepreneurs – they can do that for you too. There were a lot of people also in my life when I first started my business who actually helped launch my business for me because they understood and they were right there; you know, people who I networked with in the community, but again I had to schedule the time for networking.

Making those new friends is important because – it's so cliché, but – they say you are who you hang out with. I strategically made the decision to hang out with people who were going to inspire me, people who I thought were successful, people who had a Rolodex that they were willing to share with me. And those people became my best friends.

They became, like you said, my tribe. They were my cheerleaders too, and we could all support each other; whereas my husband, he's not a business owner. You know he provides a certain level of emotional support, but then I found that I also needed the support that only a fellow entrepreneur could provide for me.

Especially in the pet business realm where people really get what you are going through. It's so important to have people who get what it's like to deal with the clients, to deal with the pets, all the different issues that come up. Having those resources and that tribe is so powerful. It's just incredible.

It's funny because I was talking earlier to another woman who I'm interviewing, and we were both talking about how it can be dog-eat-dog sometimes in the pet business world. There can be a lot of competition, and it's so important to realize that it's not about scarcity. It's an abundant universe. It's about exploring how we can join our resources to become even more successful than we are.

And not looking at fellow pet business owners as competition but rather exploring collaboration.

Exactly.

It sounds like you're doing that and that's so great. So, when you were starting your business and you were kind of struggling in your business, what do you think were the most important tasks that you did that really got you to where you are today? You have so many clients, you have a staff of dog trainers, you've created a really successful enterprise here. So think back to the early days when you were struggling. What did you do to get from there to here?

Networking. You're not going to get anywhere by sitting in your office or sitting at home and asking yourself how to make success happen. I spend an incredible amount of time meeting people, new people, talking to people, and maybe I learned that skill from my job in development, so I digress a little bit to talk about fundraising at the University of Miami. We're talking about fundraising for someone who is potentially going to name a building at the university, so it's not like you're asking someone for ten bucks.

How do you ask someone for ten million dollars? Well, you don't. You become their friend and you "friend-raise," not fundraise. When you develop that deep meaningful relationship with someone and they believe in you, they will take out their checkbook and they will write you a check… and I would have never believed that in many years if I hadn't experienced it.

So, I think coming into my business I already had that unique perspective that if I wanted people to buy what I was selling, then they really needed to get to know me so that they would support me and they would talk to their friends about me and they would think of me when they heard of someone who needed my services. I joined chambers. I joined professional networking organizations. I would go to any kind of community event that I could find.

Another huge thing that I did when I was first, first starting out, even before networking, is I volunteered a lot of my time to rescue community. I volunteered at our local animal shelter… wherever I could volunteer just so I could be there and my face could become known and people could get to know me and my passion. I did it because that kind of stuff will pay you back tenfold. It doesn't cost anything. It costs what to go to a networking event? Maybe ten dollars at the door?

And essentially, you could book a huge dog training package out of that if someone refers you to a client, so it's a very minimal investment other than time.

That's so true. I'm thinking about a lot of pet business owners who are shy and they're introverts and they feel more comfortable with pets versus people, what would you say to them?

I have two things to say to them. The first thing is, if you are going to run a successful business, you can't just like working with the pets. You have to be able to love interacting with people. If you don't love interacting with people, I would challenge you to really look into yourself as to why you want to own a business as opposed to working for someone who maybe wants to hire you to just train dogs full time.

Several of my in-house trainers don't have to deal with the customer. They just get to train the dogs for eight hours out of the day, every day, here at my facility, and they love that. They let me run the business because that's what I love and they get to train the dog. That's my first comment to those people who are shy or who don't like people.

My second comment is that being shy or introverted does not hold you back from learning how to network because I think it's a misconception that you have to be fake or put up some sort of weird front to attract business or be someone that you're not, but the whole concept of networking is that you want people to really get to know you.

So that you're selling yourself as a product and then letting people get to know your business. So whether you're shy or not...everyone has at least one person who loves them or friends to support them. Making professional relationships like that is no different, and you do have to get yourself there. That's probably the hardest part. Just get up off your butt and go to the event.

I promise you that if you're shy and you go to professionally network or something similar, someone else will approach you, and just be yourself. That's what I tell people. It doesn't matter that you're shy. Be yourself. You don't have to fake anything and I think when people think they have to be different than they are when they are networking, that's the part that's intimidating. But it's not true.

You don't have to fake being outgoing, just be your shy self.

I think just saying the word "Hi" can lead to so many great interactions. Be bold. Make the first move. Surprise yourself. Just say, "Hi, I'm so and so."

That's it.

Just "Hi" can move mountains. It can be very powerful. People who are introverted who own pet businesses may read this and think, "Oh my God but I don't like people, does that mean I can't run a pet business?," and I would say, "Hire a manager who does like people."

THERE'S A RECURRING THEME THROUGHOUT THESE INTERVIEWS. YOU CAN'T SIMPLY LIKE PETS AND NOT LIKE PEOPLE. PET BUSINESSES ARE INHERENTLY PEOPLE BUSINESSES, SO IF YOU'RE NOT A PEOPLE PERSON, HIRE SOMEONE WHO IS.

Hire someone who is the front-line person, who is the sales person, who is also the customer service person, who really loves people and then you go do what you need to do with the pets. You go work with the pets if that's what you really love.

Right. If you keep your day job while you are starting your

268

business, you'll have the resources to do that initially. If you quit your day job, you may not have the income to do that off the bat. And you would be the only person running your business.

So you have to identify what it is that you really want to do. I tell people all the time too, "Just because you own a company doesn't mean that you're the manager. It doesn't mean that you're the customer service expert. You just own the business."

You can hire people who are the experts if there is an area in which you don't feel comfortable or you don't know how to do something. That's what I often say to my clients who are struggling with managing all the different facets of their businesses. We can create a team and, again, a tribe of people, who can support us to go where we need to go. When you're first starting, it really is you doing everything and that can be really overwhelming for people but also really enlivening. You'll be learning new skills quickly and you're forced to do that when you start a business.

People would be surprised. If you join a local chamber or professional networking group in your area, a lot of these groups will teach you how to network. Just take that first step and get there and let the business owners who are more experienced show you how to do it. I've always been bubbly and outgoing, but being around that caliber of professionals definitely honed me.

I love that and I also think being shy can simply be a belief that we have about ourselves but maybe it's not true, or it used to be true years ago but it's not true today, so explore what's it like to be outgoing and act as if you are outgoing. Have fun playing around with being outgoing. Put yourself out there.

This might be helpful for those shy people who need to get over the hump who are thinking, "Oh my God, networking!," and the terror that might come with that. I think there are a lot of pet business owners who sometimes don't consider themselves as even able to talk to people. I have worked with a lot of them in my coaching practice, so I've seen it first-hand. It can be transformational to put your focus on what you've done right in your life and your business to give you more confidence. You can ask yourself, "What has been a challenge in your business and how did you overcome it?"

I'd like to answer that. Do you want a list or do you want me to pick one?

Pick one that you think the audience could relate to.

The biggest challenge in growing my business has been finding the right people to be on my team.

Let's say that I'm hiring for a dog training position. The best dog trainer in the world is not always the best fit for my company because even though I promised my customers that I'm going to provide excellent dog training service, every company's culture is different in what they promise their customers. I think it's so important to find that certain type of person who can reflect me and reflect my company culture, that's a very special person, and I've had several dog trainers who have come in and they just haven't worked out, but it wasn't because of their dog training skills.

So it's been difficult to find that perfect fit for my company in terms of someone who is perhaps a more novice trainer, but their personality in how they engage with their customers makes up for that, and then it doesn't matter as much. I think building a really cohesive team has been the hardest part, and I guess the first employee that you fire is always the hardest.

Maybe I'm too good at it now! I'm just kidding, but I've definitely learned the hard way when I've hired someone who perhaps instinctually I knew wasn't a good fit but, for whatever reason, I did it anyway. I don't make that mistake anymore.

If they don't feel just right, then they're not a good fit for me. So building a cohesive team is definitely the hardest challenge because the more your company grows, the more successful it is, and the more people who you have on your team, the more cohesiveness matters. I mean, you spend just as much time with those people if not more than you do with your real family. So they've got to be like your family. In a professional way, but they are your family.

Your work family. Yes, it's true. I love what you said about culture. So how would you describe the culture of your company?

The culture of my company is this: Our biggest priority is making sure that people really enjoy their experience in dog training and we want to make that customer or that dog owner feel... and not even make them feel... I genuinely want them to know how much we care and that we're there to support them in all aspects of their relationship with their dog and their life with their dog. So I would say the culture here at Applause Your Paws is one that is very sincere and very caring.

That trumps everything. Like I said, I could have the best freaking dog trainers ever, but if they don't really care about what they're doing, it doesn't matter.

I agree. It's interesting, Dee, because I was training the new owner that I sold my business to and passing the leash on to her, so to speak, and I was telling her about the company and how we've created this culture of love.

That's what most of our clients would say about the company. They say they feel really seen and cared about and loved, and I think it's really important for business owners to look at what kind of culture they are creating. Listen to your clients because they will reflect back what kind of culture it is. Creating a culture is a powerful energy and it is the personality of your business.

The culture you have internally spreads out into the culture that you have externally with your clients. Because the way that my staff treats each other, the way that I treat my employees, the way that we all interact, that's the same way that we interact with our customers and you have to practice that. It's kind of like raising kids, I guess. You have to practice that at home if you want it to stick when everybody is not at home.

That's right. You put that so beautifully. It's great to really make it a practice.

I don't know if it's just Miami because everyone likes to tease that Miami is not a nice city and there are no nice people here, so it's not very hard to win customers in Miami because all you have to do is answer the phone and be polite. I respond by saying, *"Oh come on, you don't give Miami business owners enough credit."*

Who are these people who want to talk crap about my city?

I have to say that perhaps to a certain extent people are somewhat correct because it's not that hard to treat people nicely and care. I love it when people call my business and say that my business was the third business they've called and they decided to choose us. I will ask them why they chose my company, and they will often say that everyone that they spoke to just didn't seem to really care.

That's sweet about your company. They felt your caring right away.

And I like that.

Caring matters, especially in this day and age where everything is automated and people get voicemail all the time. When you get a friendly person on the other end of the line, it's powerful. Kind of sad but true, as that used to be a given years ago.

So what advice do you give to brand new dog trainers? Maybe five tips. Something like, "I recommend that you do this, this, and this when you start a dog training business?"

Let's see… five tips. The first thing that pops into my head is brand new dog trainers or brand new business owners for that matter, please, please… in whatever marketing materials that you decide to create, have a brand cohesion.

Because it doesn't matter that you're small and no one knows who you are. Perception is everything, and when you show up with your Vistaprint® business card that has the Vistaprint logo on the back because you got it for free and your business email is at Yahoo.com, I won't take you seriously. You have to be very aware of what that first impression is even when you just start. It's an investment that you cannot afford not to make.

Get that professional image on paper. So your business card, your first brochure, whatever. It all needs to look nice and it needs to match.

Because that is your first impression. Secondly is to get yourself a separate business phone number because that way you can keep your business separate from your personal cell phone.

I recommend that all the time. That's so important.

Please get yourself a different phone number that's dedicated only to your business. Let's see what other tips can I give for brand new professional dog trainers? I guess my third tip goes again with brand cohesion.

You've got to look nice. Take an extra few minutes, and I don't care if you're a dog trainer and you get sweaty, you get hot and sometimes muddy. Taking care of your appearance makes a huge difference; your professional, personal appearance is so important when you enter a customer's home. That's different for everybody, but I think having a nice professional uniform goes a long way to make people really buy that product and believe in you. Let's see. So I'm up to three. Tip number four... I'm looking up at the sky right now, Kristin.

I'm thinking about how I want to phrase this. I think you have to have a really clear picture when you start going into a customer's home of what your intention is in helping them because the trap that I see new dog trainers fall into is that they go in and they give away so much of their time

FIVE TIPS FOR SUCCESS: MAKE SURE MARKETING MATERIALS LOOK PROFESSIONAL AND PRESENT A COHESIVE BRAND; HAVE A DEDICATED BUSINESS PHONE NUMBER; LOOK PROFESSIONAL; BE CLEAR ON YOUR INTENT; AND HAVE FUN!

and they charge the customer minimally. Then they wonder why they never see that customer again.

I think you need to have a really clear picture of what your dog training program is going to look like, how much you're going to charge for it, and the road map or game plan for that first session so that you leave the customer wanting to hire you back for lesson two, three, four, five, twenty, whatever it is.

You're not going to solve all their problems in the first session, so don't try. I think that's the rookie move. You just want to help. You feel like an eager beaver, and you get in there and you want to give them all the information, and before you know it, it's been two and a half hours and everyone's exhausted. So have a clear plan on that front.

Tip number five? Have fun. Just don't worry about it too much.

Business owners can be so serious; lighten up people!

Just love it. If you love it, your customers will love it.

They feel that. It's contagious. Well thank you so much Dee, I really appreciate you being here.

You're welcome. Thanks so much, Kristin.

SIXTEEN

Running Your Pet Business Remotely: How to Set Up Your Pet Business in Multiple Locations

Interview with Rita Reimers and Tiffany Reynolds

Do you have dreams of having multiple branches of your pet businesses on opposite ends of the country or even in nearby towns or different parts of your state? Rita and Tiffany are two pet sitters who have done it! They each have two business branches based on two different coasts... the East Coast and the West Coast. And you can too. If your vision is to have your pet business set up in two or more locations, you'll want to read this as Tiffany and Rita share their challenges and delights about having a pet business in multiple locations. Hint: It's not for sissies and it's very rewarding!

In this chapter, you will learn:

- The facts about running your business on opposite ends of the country, from pet sitters who have successfully done it

- Why re-creating what you've already done in one location might not be enough

- How to handle crises that arise in other locations far from where you are physically located

- What technology is needed if you want to expand to locations far from your current business location

- The challenges and gifts of having multiple locations

- And more!

Kristin's Musings:

Oh these wonderful ladies! They were both in the midst of very intense workweeks, yet they graciously made themselves available for you, and for me to interview them. Having worked with many pet business owners who wanted to (and did) set up their businesses in multiple locations, I knew that this was an important topic and an interview that needed to happen. I'm very grateful to both Rita and Tiffany for giving of their time and energy to make this interview happen even in the midst of their busy lives. (And each of them is an incredible and generous soul, which I imagine you will get from reading this chapter.)

Rita Reimers's Bio:

Rita Reimers is a well-known cat behaviorist, offering nationwide cat behavior counseling services through her company, The Cat Analyst. She is Founding CEO of Just for Cats Pet Sitting, with locations in Beverly Hills, CA, and in Charlotte, NC.

After the sudden death of her beloved cat, Sadie, Rita shared her grief in her book, *Sadie's Heart, Loving & Losing Our Cat Companions: A Story of Pet Love, Loss, & Grief Recovery*. Rita has been featured in *CAT FANCY, CATS USA ANNUAL,* and *KITTENS USA ANNUAL*. To find out more visit *www.JustForCatsPetSitting.com*.

Tiffany Reynolds's Bio:

Always having a love of animals and wanting to provide the best care for them, Tiffany established Pet and Home Care, LLC in 1999, starting out on her own with only one client. Now, over 15 years later, she has grown her clientele to over 2,500 and has over 30 employees and two locations. Pet and Home Care's main branch is in Potomac, MD and they have also launched the Los Angeles location. Tiffany takes great pride in offering the best pet and home care services available. Tiffany has also expanded the services that Pet and Home Care, LLC, provides to include not only walks and in-home visits, overnight care, doggy daycare, and cage-less boarding, but to offer full-service home care in Maryland as well. To find out more visit *www.PetandHomeCare.com*.

Interview with Rita Reimers and Tiffany Reynolds
Multi-Area Pet Sitting Service Owners

Kristin Morrison: *I'm very happy to welcome Rita and Tiffany here. Thank you so much for being a part of this, you two!*

Rita and Tiffany both have businesses that are located in two different states that they operate remotely, and they're going to talk to us about how they created that vision and what it's like to actually have businesses that are in two different states. So I want to start with you, Rita. What brought you to the world of pet sitting? How did that happen for you?

Rita Reimers: Many years ago when I was married, I worked as a computer consultant, as did my husband. We both traveled a lot. We had two kitties, and I was fortunate to meet a very nice lady who had a pet sitting business. I had never heard of that kind of business before.

I thought it was such a nice business that when I decided that I wanted to take a step back from the corporate world, I always remembered that business. I'm also a big animal lover, so my friends were always asking me to watch their pets for them, walk their dogs, and take care of their kitties, so I was already doing it for free anyway. So I decided to start up pet sitting.

At first, I was doing dogs and cats, but as I got bigger, I found that I have more of an affinity toward kitty cats. There really wasn't a niche for that, so I decided to make my business cats only, and as we grew, I became more well known as being the cat specialist. So that's really how it all started.

So it was through meeting another pet sitter and experiencing it that way?

Right, way back in the late 80s, early 90s, when pet sitting was really brand new. It wasn't something that a lot of people even knew existed.

I can relate because I started my pet business in 1995 and there wasn't a lot of information at that point. There weren't a lot of pet sitters out there then. There definitely wasn't a lot of competition. And for you Tiffany, what brought you to the world of pet sitting?

Tiffany Reynolds: Well, as a teenager, I was babysitting and doing all kinds of odd jobs to earn money, and some of the clients who I was babysitting for started asking me to watch their dogs, and I did a great job. They loved it, and they told their friends, and their friends told their friends and I started picking up a bunch of clients. I started putting out fliers, and the next thing you know, it turned into a full-time job in high school, and it just kept growing and growing.

That's great. How long have you had your business, Tiffany?

Fifteen years.

And Rita, how many years have you had yours?

Fourteen.

Great. And in which states do you have your businesses, Tiffany?

I started my business in Potomac, Maryland and we also service northwest D.C. A year ago, I moved to Los Angeles, and we've opened a service here as well.

That's great. So your business is on two separate coasts.

Yes.

And what about you, Rita? Where are your businesses located?

I started in Los Angeles, California, where you are now, Tiffany, that's so funny! And I relocated to Charlotte, North Carolina. So now we're opening a branch here in Charlotte as well.

That's great. Tiffany, what were some of the motivating factors for you to start your business?

To start it originally or in California?

To start a second branch of your business in another state. You said you had it in Maryland and then you moved it to L.A. What was the motivating factor for you to create a second branch in Los Angeles?

The sunshine. Mainly the weather and my sister who moved here. My business was at the point at which I had most of the hands-on work taken care of by my staff and all of our software was digital, so I was able to work anywhere. I thought it would be a good opportunity to expand and live in a new area and get the business going here as well.

That's great. And what about for you Rita, what was the motivating factor to create a second branch of your business in North Carolina?

I had lived here previously and my parents located here just as I left. We actually haven't lived in the same city for about 25 years. I built my Los Angeles business to a point at which it was very successful, but I was also the primary pet sitter there. I wanted to be back near my parents, but I also wanted to take a step back from doing the actual pet sitting and the easiest way to do that was to not be there, so clients couldn't whine and say, *"Oh, but I want you to be my sitter."*

It's amazing isn't it? When I lived in Bali and India, there was something so powerful about being absolutely away from where the business was located because there's an inability to service the clients! There is just no way you can do it. It's powerful and I know for me, that experience of being very far away from my business helped me cultivate a different relationship with my business: one that allowed it to really become an "adult" and shine and be able to stand on its own two feet, so to speak, without me in the picture at all. Have you two experienced that? Where stepping away has helped your first location of your business grow in new ways? What's that been like for you, Rita?

Definitely because if you're working in your business and servicing clients as the pet sitter, there's no way you can keep your eye on the bigger vision and really take care of the things that retain clients and that maintain good staff members. Being away from it has helped me to able to see the big picture, to manage it better and be more attentive to my clients' other needs, and be able to be more responsive to their inquiries because I'm not out doing ten pet sits and then getting back around to returning my calls and emails. So they are able to access me better and quicker, and I think they feel serviced a little bit better because they get almost instantaneous responses from me when they request something.

That's great. And what about for you, Tiffany? Has it been a similar experience?

Absolutely. I also find that it's harder for me to delegate things when I'm there because I feel the need to do it myself, but not being there, I'm forced to delegate and to train further and to let my staff have more control and help with different tasks. So it has been very beneficial, and I'm looking forward to seeing how the new branch will develop too.

> GAINING SOME DISTANCE FROM YOUR BUSINESS, EITHER LITERALLY OR FIGURATIVELY, ALLOWS YOU TIME TO KEEP YOUR EYE ON THE BIGGER VISION FOR THE BUSINESS AND FORCES YOU TO DELEGATE.

That's great. What has been one of the biggest challenges about leaving your main branch and moving to a new location? What have been some of the biggest challenges? Rita, why don't you start?

For me there were a couple challenges. For one, I'm very lucky that I have a wonderful assistant manager, Melanie, in the Los Angeles area because I needed someone else to hold the main key box. So the logistics of those types of things and somebody to run keys between the sitters if one sitter is away has been crucial. Usually it was me to hold onto all of their keys so that I could have substitute sitters take their jobs. Now it has to be Melanie. So, like Tiffany said, I had to learn to delegate because I was forced to by not physically being there. That was a big challenge for me. It's not easy for me to delegate responsibility and ask somebody else to take on a big responsibility like that.

It requires a lot of surrender to let go of our business in that way. We often decide to own a business because we want to be the leader and in control, and I totally get it, Rita. It's so challenging to let go of that control and to delegate. I really experienced that also as my company got bigger and bigger, and I began to let more and more of my personal pet care jobs go. And began to delegate more.

It was scary at first but very empowering too.

Rita: Exactly. By delegating, I was able to let Melanie shine. She didn't even know she wanted that type of involvement in the business until I asked her to and got her more involved, and now she feels just as responsible for everything that happens in the business as I do, so I really have somebody who is more of a partner in the business.

That's great. I experienced that too in my business where I had two main managers who were helping me run it, and I have to say I couldn't have done it without them. They were really invested in the business with their heart, and it sounds like Melanie is as well.

She definitely is.

That's sweet. What about for you, Tiffany? What have been some of the challenges for you of having your business there and being in Los Angeles?

Well, it's gone pretty smoothly. I'm very blessed as well to have a wonderful manager on hand who deals with all the day-to-day tasks. The biggest challenge that I have found is picking up more clients in California. I took for granted how easy it was to get the business rolling in Maryland because there wasn't a lot of competition there, but here there is a lot of competition. Los Angeles is very saturated with pet sitters. So the biggest thing right now is getting more clients.

I experienced that when I went from one county to another. It wasn't another state, but it was still challenging. I had two counties, two very large counties, and I had taken for granted how easy it was in some ways to start my business in the first county. It's like relearning and redoing it. You think it's going to go like it was with the first location, but starting a business in a second location is like starting a new business in a way, isn't it, Tiffany?

It really is. We have all the framework in place in the second location, so now it's just a matter of getting out there and getting known in the community.

Exactly. And what have been some of the logistical items that you've had to have in place? Like Rita, you talked about the keys and how Melanie holds on to the keys. What have been some other logistical and technical items that you've had to have in place, Rita?

Well logistic-wise, the time difference is a big factor for me because sometimes I'm up at 11 or 12 o'clock at night here talking to potential new clients because they can't talk to me until after work, which for them is seven or eight o'clock. So I'm working pretty late into the night here.

So that's one challenge that I hadn't anticipated, and another is the fact that if we have an emergency, it can be hard to deal with being so far away; we had one a couple weekends ago where a cat had to be taken to the vet and I wasn't there to do it. The sitter had to do it by herself, and I was there to support her emotionally, but I really felt my absence when that emergency happened. I really wanted to be there and that's the old, *"I want to take over and do it thing,"* but that's another challenge!

Technically, we put a new system in place about a month ago that I think has really helped. Our old scheduler system wasn't great, and now the sitters have it right in the palm of their hand. They can see exactly where they need to be. It's great. So I don't have to micromanage as much or make sure that they know their schedules and where they have to go. So that new scheduling software helps a lot.

Software is so crucial, isn't it? If you want to run a pet sitting business or any pet business, you really need an administration software system to enable you to run it more easily and effectively. And if you're thinking about creating business locations in two different states, it's crucial.

Rita: You have to have the right one too.

It's really true. We're not going to mention the name of the software system that you used that just wasn't right, but I do want to mention that you figured out that there is another one that really works much better for you. When I'm coaching pet business owners, I really encourage them to try a few different software systems, so they can see which one really works the way that their brain

SOFTWARE IS A CRUCIAL PIECE OF RUNNING AND ADMINISTERING ANY TYPE OF PET BUSINESS; HOWEVER, BE CERTAIN YOU TRY A FEW TO DETERMINE WHICH ONE IS BEST FOR YOU.

works. When I was starting out years ago and I know when you both were starting out too, there weren't a lot of software systems available. Now there are so many to choose from. It's great, it's such a gift that there are so many to choose from.

And what about for you, Tiffany? What have been some technical things that you've had to have in place?

A few years ago, we rebranded our business. We changed our company name and got a toll-free 800 number and a great domain name. Once those items were in place, that's when I started thinking about branching to other areas. Once we had the branding covered, it was much easier to open up somewhere else.

People can't really tell where we're based since we have the 800 number, and once again, the software was key to having the flexibility to be able to run the business from anywhere. We are hoping to expand to even more cities in the future.

That's great. Are you thinking about opening your business in more cities, Rita? Have you thought about that?

I have thought about that. My hometown is actually Buffalo, New York. I've thought about maybe going that way, but like Tiffany was saying earlier, I'm kind of doing the same thing here trying to start up in Charlotte. It's just like starting a brand new business, and I sort of took for granted that I did it before, so I thought it was going to be easy here and it's not so easy. It's very saturated with pet sitters here in Charlotte as well, but the one plus or niche that I have is there are no other "cats only" pet sitting services here. So I have a little easier time than I might if we catered to dogs and cats. We do have some clients here, but it's slow and I did what you did, Tiffany. I've got the 800 number. We rebranded with a name that's not regionally specific like our old name was. It can be tough. I would love to go to other cities, but I have to make sure I can get Charlotte off the ground first.

I have to say, Rita, I have no doubt that you will be able to. Just watching you and your business grow throughout the years has been incredibly wonderful. I would imagine that you are an inspiration for a lot of pet sitters and probably your friends and family too. Is that true? Have they told you that what you've done with your business has been inspiring to them?

They don't understand. My friends think I'm crazy. They'll ask me when I'm going to get a real job. They really don't understand this profession.

That's too bad because it's more real than a "real job," in my opinion. Where else do you get to create your own hours and be with the furry critters? There are so many benefits to owning this type of business.

And, Tiffany, I'm thinking about you and if you had to do over again as far as the move and starting two branches, what would you have done differently? Is there anything that you would have done differently?

Yes, there are a few things. I would have definitely made a switch to the new software prior to the move because it's been a little bit difficult getting that up and running and trying to grow here in Los Angeles and at the same time manage Maryland. It's definitely been a bit of a challenge. I also would have been more competitive with my rates.

I was set in my ways by keeping my Potomac, Maryland, rates, and when I came here there was definitely a significant drop in prices. I was really trying to hold on to my rates and keep them the same in Los Angeles as they were in Maryland, but I finally realized that I have to be more competitive. So I wish I had lowered my rates sooner. I wish I had done more SEO and PPC on my website right away.

I'm glad we are talking about rates because that's a great point: a lot of pet sitters put their rates on their website. Have you done that, Tiffany, and do you have two different rates for the different areas?

I haven't updated them on our business website yet. I am on several different websites where people find pet sitters in the area, and on those websites, I have reduced the rates and it's worked. I've picked up a lot of new clients. That's been really helpful, and I'm trying to decide about setting some firm rates on our company website. I'm still playing around with those numbers, seeing what will work best.

What do you think you'll end up doing? Do you think you'll end up having a different webpage for the different rates in Los Angeles?

Tiffany: Absolutely. I'm going to have to have a different landing page for Los Angeles because not only will the rates be different, we also offer different services here. For example, in Los Angeles, I can offer group dog hikes and I do home dog boarding in my home, but in Maryland we don't do the group hikes and we have a dog facility for all the boarding. I do not have a facility here and I don't plan to open one. So we are slightly different with our services, so yes, different web pages to come.

What about for you Rita, what would you have done differently if you had to do it over again? Or is there anything that you would have done differently?

I think I would have stopped being the primary sitter about five years sooner than I did. That's one thing. I think that the other is that I would have rebranded. This is the third time I've rebranded. I would not have done regionally specific company names that second time we've branded because now I'm having to put another name on top of that, so it confuses some of our former or current clients who have been with us for a long time. So I think I would have put more thought into our business name.

I can understand how that would be confusing and also necessary for you to create a more generic name, so you can really reach more people in the different areas.

I'm thinking about technology here, and I want to go back to technology because you were both saying how important that was for creating your second branch of the business. Is there anything else besides the software system as far as technology goes that has been really helpful for you to have your business in two different states? What about you, Tiffany?

Other than our company software? That's the main technology that we actually have in place. Otherwise just utilizing a different website for people to do searches for pet sitters and trying to have our company and myself as an individual listed as many places as possible. There are more avenues for people to find us that way. Otherwise, we still use a payroll company and I have an accountant who handles my QuickBooks.

Email is huge for us. I have to always make sure I have Internet access everywhere I go. And that hasn't been an issue. I'm really grateful for the software. It's really bringing us in a new direction.

That's great. What about you, Rita? Anything else in addition to the software that you would recommend technology-wise?

I recently went to direct deposit for payroll instead of writing out checks manually like I did for years, and it's so much better. It's quicker and the sitters get paid faster, and I feel like we're a grown-up company now.

That's great. It's powerful to take that step and have somebody do it for you. The delegation of those administrative tasks is so crucial in order to be able to expand the way you two have.

CONSIDER OUTSOURCING TASKS LIKE PAYROLL, AND USE DIRECT DEPOSIT. THAT FREES YOUR TIME TO CONCENTRATE ON GROWING AND IMPROVING YOUR BUSINESS RATHER THAN WRITING CHECKS.

And so what about the biggest gifts? We've talked a lot about challenges that you've had, but what have been some of the biggest gifts that you've experienced in having your business be in two different locations? What about you, Tiffany?

The biggest gift is being so close to my little sister. It's the first time that we've ever lived in the same city together, so we've spent a lot of time together and I'm really blessed to be able to have the opportunity to do that. It's also been great meeting lots of new people, new friends, new clients, and just being able to get back to being hands-on with the pet care.

I stopped doing the pet sitting about five years ago because I was overseeing the majority of the operations in Maryland, but now being here in Los Angeles, I'm able to be hands-on and enjoying meeting new clients and taking care of all kinds of animals. I didn't realize how much I was missing that. I feel very blessed to be back with the animals and also to be in a state that never rains!

It really doesn't, does it? Los Angeles is sunny, sunny, sunny.

What about you, Rita? What have been some of the biggest gifts for you in making this choice to move?

First I have to say, Tiffany, that you're making me homesick for Los Angeles. The biggest gift is my parents. I'm an only child, and my parents and I haven't lived in the same city since 1985, so being able to be back in Charlotte has been a gift. We're not from here, but they relocated here about 15 years ago. I live about 30 miles from them now as opposed to 2,500 miles, so I enjoy being able to meet my mom for lunch like we did a couple weeks ago just because we can. That was nice.

That's so sweet. It seems like both of you moved to be near family, which is so wonderful, especially in this day and age where people are so disconnected from their families. I find that incredibly heartwarming, and it's such a big decision to make a big move like that. It's very courageous of you. Wow.

Rita: Big decisions don't scare me. It's the little ones!

You're so funny, Rita. So, going back to logistical things around having two different businesses in two different states, do you have separate emails that you use for each location or do you use one email? How does that work? Rita, why don't you start?

I do have two different email addresses because we have a different website for each business.

I'm preparing for the day when I can have a manager at each location, so I can be a little bit more removed again and that would enable me to open that Buffalo location. I am also thinking that maybe in the future when I want to retire, I may want to sell off the business's separate pieces. So while I want them joined together under an umbrella, I also want the ability to easily separate them out if I need to.

I love that. I love the visioning that's happening for you and the thinking ahead into the future. It's so great. And what about for you Tiffany, do you just have one email address for your businesses?

We have the main office email address where our clients use to communicate. So everything comes into there. My manager handles the emails in Maryland and anything from California she forwards on to me and I personally reach out to the client and get them set up and meet with them.

Going back to handling things that happen that are challenging; like Rita, you were talking about your staff member having to take a cat to the vet. Tiffany, how have you dealt with things that have happened where ordinarily you'd be there but you're not able to be there. Can you describe a situation and how you handled it?

Well, it's the same way I would if I were there. I take the appropriate steps and actions needed to resolve the situation and get whoever needs to be involved involved... if it's clients or an employee or maybe a family member. I haven't had any problems. My staff is very hands-on. We did have an animal that had to go to the vet recently as well and the pet sitter was at the house and it was his duty to get that dog to the vet quickly because the dog was failing fast. So he put him in his car, took him to the vet, and everything was fine. The client was very appreciative.

The dog got into medication that he wasn't supposed to get into, and the dog then became very ill. Handling problems, even though I'm far away, has been fairly easy. The only big challenge that I've found is the time difference, like Rita mentioned. When I'm waking up in California, part of the day is already done in Maryland, so I might miss something in the morning, but my managers start early so that really hasn't been a problem.

I love how you said you know your staff members will be able to take care of important things. I also trained mine to self-manage because I think it's so important for them to be able to do what they need to do. I think they also appreciate that: having that autonomy to be able to take care of things and handle things as they arise feels good to them and gives them the control and allows me more freedom. Any final tips that you have for those who are thinking about starting a pet business in another state? Any advice for them, Rita?

I would just make sure that you have someone in place who you can trust to be your right-hand person and that when you delegate something to them, you have to trust that they're going to get it done.

They may do it a little differently than you might have done it, but as long as they're getting it done and everything is okay and they're getting a cat or dog to the vet the way they should, there's nothing bad happening. You have to trust that how they're going to get things accomplished is okay and you really have to learn to let go.

You really do have to learn to let go. It's so true. It's a great lesson in surrender. What about for you, Tiffany? Any final words that you have for people who are thinking about starting another branch of their business?

Well, like I said before, I think that one of the most important things is having your branding accessible for multiple areas, having staff that's ready to take over your original location, and just be ready to roll with the punches.

One of the things that I also think is really important is having a thorough employee handbook, so your employees at your original location have guidelines on what to do, and then you can replicate that in your new location as well. There's no reason to reinvent the wheel. You know you can learn from your past locations and brand it into your next one and really get the word out.

Another technology thing that I missed before was social media. We're big on Facebook and Twitter, and it's really important to keep people involved with your company, keep reminding them that you're there. I love sharing pictures of the animals that we're taking care of and a lot of the clients really appreciate that too. Just staying digital and ahead of the curve is really important and staying competitive with your prices and services is important too.

Thank you so much, both of you, for taking the time out of your busy schedules to be here and to share your experience. It means so much to me. I know it means a lot to those who are reading this right now too. So thank you so much.

Tiffany: You're welcome. It was fun.

Rita: Thanks for having me.

Thank you, Rita. Thank you, Tiffany. I wish you all the best as you expand even more.

SEVENTEEN

Using Yoga and Mindfulness to Relieve Stress in Your Pet Business

Interview with Lisa Maria

Feeling stressed? There may be some very simple actions you can do now to relieve that stress. And (ahem!) we need to say this: Please consult your doctor before beginning an exercise program. Om!

In this chapter, you will learn:

- The hidden benefits of yoga to create ease in business and your life

- How to increase a sense of health and well-being with this simple pose

- To create confidence easily and quickly

- The #1 habit that creates focused intention in business and life

- Yoga poses that are especially beneficial for pet business owners

- And much more!

Kristin's Musings:

I've known Lisa for years. She is one of those rare souls who inspires those around her to take a deep breath of relaxation because her energy is so calming. If you are going a million miles an hour these days, I really encourage you to STOP and soak up some of her good energy in this chapter!

Lisa Maria's Bio:

Lisa Maria is a yoga teacher and author committed to sharing yoga as a guide to a fulfilling life of clarity, connection, and contentment. A recurring guest on ABC TV's "View from the Bay," Lisa's journalism background includes co-producing and co-hosting weekly talk radio shows, which featured numerous cultural visionaries including Deepak Chopra, Wayne Dyer, and Marianne Williamson. Her articles have appeared in *Yoga Journal, Fit Yoga, YogiTimes, Common Ground, Yoga Magazine UK,* and others. As the Northern California Workshop Manager for YogaWorks and Yoga Tree, Lisa curates workshops and trainings for one of the largest yoga education centers in the world. Lisa leads weekly yoga classes, workshops, and retreats. To find out more visit *www.Lisa-Maria.com.*

Interview with Lisa Maria
Author and Yoga Teacher

Kristin Morrison: *Welcome, Lisa Maria! Lisa is an author and a yoga teacher, and we are going to talk about healthy living, about yoga and how that can help you in your business and your life, and I'm so happy to have you here Lisa, thank you.*

Lisa Maria: Thank you, Kristin. It's a pleasure to be here.

It's so great to have your energy... your good energy, your sweet spirit, and your knowledge too. I really am curious: Is there something that happened in your life that caused you or inspired you to want to take yoga classes and then later teach yoga?

Absolutely. I, like many people, had heard of yoga but didn't have any concept of what it was about, and I prejudged it before I knew what it was about. So I didn't really open up to trying yoga for quite some time, and when I finally did, I started to get an inkling of what it was about. I had it in my life in bits and pieces.

I was pregnant. I was becoming a mom. I wanted to really create a healthy lifestyle and make sure that I was at my peak for that experience. I found I was really challenged with many parts of the experience of becoming a new mom and the challenges that go along with that. Yoga became a necessity instead of just an activity.

It became an integral part of my life where I was able to go to a yoga class and breathe deeply. I had a lot of really strong emotions coming up, and my panic attacks would go away. My grief would go away.

I had financial fear. I had relationship fear. I was far away from my family, and my sister was pregnant at the same time. So it really helped me transition through a very difficult part of my life, and then at that point, it just became a part of me.

Wow. I really appreciate you sharing all that, Lisa. I know for me, yoga has been incredibly helpful during those really stressful times in my life. Having that practice, that place to go to let out the stress has been such a gift. When you were talking, I really got on a deeper level how our bodies carry so much tension and stress.

If we're not releasing it in some way, it can get really stuck, and for me, I've noticed yoga has helped to move that stress and tension out. Have you felt that as well?

Oh, absolutely. The body holds onto everything. The body remembers everything. If we don't move through those difficult emotions, they get locked in the body. Stress is one of the biggest killers in this country; it leads to heart disease, cancer, strokes. So by taking on a yoga practice – it can be as simple as you need it to be or as complicated as you want it to be – you're changing your health and your life in a powerful way.

So true. I love that we're talking about stress because a lot of pet business owners experience a lot of stress. They're working with the animals. They're also running their businesses. So they're out there in the "field," but then they're also in the office. If they are pet sitters and dog walkers, they are driving around a lot, there's traffic, and having the experience of having that place to go to whether it be a yoga studio or their living room where they can just let go can be so helpful. Also, I've found the breathing aspect of yoga to be really helpful to me as well as to some of my clients who practice yoga because when we're living our busy lives, we often forget to breathe or we're taking really shallow breaths. Have you noticed that as well?

Absolutely. I'm smiling because it's really nice to be able to find some ease and comfort simply by breathing consciously if you're driving, if you're at a desk, if you're out walking the dogs, and it's also really possible with a little bit of yoga to make your body a comfortable place to be, to feel comfortable in your own skin. So no matter where you are, by tuning into your breath, you'll be able to access some calm.

I'm thinking that we spend so much money and energy and time to make our houses and cars comfortable and we sometimes forget about the body. That's truly our home! So that brings me to the question of how can really busy pet business owners make time for yoga? A lot of them might be thinking they have no time, yet if we don't make time for these important self-care activities, it can affect every area of our lives. So what would you say to pet business owners who tell you that they'd love to do yoga, but they don't have any time?

There are a lot of excuses for not doing yoga. There's the "I'm not flexible" excuse which I love because rarely is someone flexible when they begin yoga. We are in a certain pattern, and that's what we're used to. So we can begin breaking that pattern a little bit, by taking one deeper breath. Taking two deeper breaths, three deeper breaths... maybe your yoga practice is when you walk from the refrigerator to the sink, you walk really mindfully. Maybe when you're in your car, you do a little twist in your car seat... it's finding ways to weave the yoga into what you're already doing, so it doesn't become something that feels stressful. The last thing I want people to feel is that not doing yoga is another stress.

I know that sometimes when I'm driving to go get a massage, I've gotten stuck in traffic, and then I'm so stressed out as I'm driving to a massage and I'm thinking how ridiculous that is. It's a good reminder to remember that my massage begins when I get in the car driving to the massage therapist's office. I try to remember that when I'm driving to yoga class too. I think it really starts when we get into the car.

Absolutely. Another thing that's really important to remember is that even though someone might get into yoga because it helps to bring in a sense of health, it really affects all the layers of our being. So think about yoga as a way to clean your inner body, the emotions, and the intellect… just like you would brush your teeth, take a shower, and feed yourself. The yoga is another part of your self-care, and by practicing yoga, you're going to be able to be comfortable in your skin, and you're going to have the experience of feeling calm, and you're going to have an experience of feeling your intuition really coming alive. Life starts to become a lot clearer.

Your priorities order themselves, and situations that used to trigger you, people who used to trigger you, or maybe there's an animal that's a trigger (maybe there's an animal that you're nervous about walking, maybe the dog is new to you or maybe the dog has some behavioral issues) may begin to shift. You'll begin to remember that taking a deep breath wherever you are is going to give you an instant freshness like a shower.

As you're talking, I am feeling that freshness within myself. I'm taking these wonderfully deep breaths right now. I really want to encourage anyone who's reading this right now to take some deep breaths and to allow this time to come back to yourself, to your body, to your breath, and allow yourself to get back in your body instead of being only in your mind.

There's one thing I want to point out about the breath. Because we are so habituated to stress, particularly in western cultures, we end up doing oppositional breathing, so instead of the lungs and belly expanding, we contract because the nervous system is compromised. The breath starts to shield the body to the outside world because it's trying to protect the body.

Sometimes when you're feeling stressed, your breath gets shallow and when you inhale you feel your belly draw in instead of expand. Take your hands, place one on your belly and one on your chest. Take a breath in and a deep breath out and notice if you are breathing properly. On the inhale does your belly rise, does your chest rise, do you feel a sense of expansion and filling through the torso, through the lungs? That's really important to make sure you have that deep inhale, and a deep exhale when you are breathing.

So, when you're inhaling, the belly should come out, is that correct?

Yes. Think of it like you want to fill up a balloon, like your lungs are balloons. You want to fill them up. So as you're inhaling, you should be filling up your balloons, which are your lungs, and as you're exhaling the balloons are getting smaller, right?

Yes. This is so good, Lisa. I had been doing "reverse breathing" for years, and it was only when I took a yoga class that I realized I had been breathing incorrectly for many years. The yoga teacher pointed out the correct way to breathe. I was shocked to noticed how habituated I was in the reverse action of breathing. I really thought my belly was supposed to go in when I inhaled.

> PROPER BREATHING, FILLING YOUR LUNGS LIKE THEY ARE BALLOONS, IS THE PERFECT STRESS RELIEVER: IT'S FREE AND YOU CAN DO IT ANYWHERE, ANYTIME.

I had that experience too.

I think a lot of us do and I'm also thinking just how stress relieving breathing is. I experience this a lot with my coaching clients when they're really amped up about something. They don't want to take a deep breath because they have to feel whatever is freaking them out. But feeling it is often the first step to moving through it, so if they are willing, we'll stop for a moment and breathe together for a minute or two.

If you could put breathing in a pill, it would be the best selling drug on the market because the benefits are enormous.

It's true. I know I'm enjoying being conscious of my breath right now and am grateful for this conversation with you to have that experience. I'm usually pretty aware of my breathing, but there's even more consciousness right now.

Another layer is that breathing consciously brings us into the present. We become really grounded in where we are right now, and that gives us the ability to live our lives from a place of power because all of our attention is in the present moment.

When you are consciously breathing, you're not in the future. You're not in the past. You're here, right now. You have all of your faculties, all of your energies available to work with for whatever task you have at hand. Plus, our lives are made up of a series of moments. If we're not living in these moments, we're not living our lives.

It's true. I want to be awake for all of it.

It's a good goal.

Awake for every last bit.

We have to remind each other.

It's true. As you were talking, I was reflecting on how things in my life may be challenging and it's almost like my holding in the breath is a way not to feel. Yet as we talked about earlier, feeling the feeling really moves it out. So just trusting that we can handle the feelings that arise and knowing that the breathing will really move them through and out.

Absolutely. Strong feelings, strong emotions are not something that we're taught to deal with in a skillful way. We're usually taught to suppress, repress, contain stuff, pretend, or deny.

If you're not expressing your emotions in a healthy way or

processing them through physical activity, breathing, meditation, journaling – if you are not expressing them and moving through them, the emotions come out sideways. They come out as stress. You snap at your coworker, you're impatient with the dog, you're angry in traffic.

It's important as we tend to these different parts of our lives that there is no such thing as repressing or denying. These emotions have a huge impact, not just on our lives, but on the people around us and the animals that are around us. Animals even more so because they are really sensitive beings and they are tuned into energy in a way that most human beings aren't.

So whatever you're carrying with you, the animals are going to pick up on that and it's really important to clean yourself with the breathing, with a little stretching so you can feel present, available, and you can step into your best self when you are with them.

When you were talking, I was reflecting about my own life. When I first made the decision a number of years ago to really begin to move through painful feelings instead of avoiding them, whatever they were, I discovered that when I consciously feel painful feelings, it's like I take more rocks out of the river to allow the flow of life and joy. So much joy is available.

If we're holding on and afraid to feel whatever we're feeling – fear or anger, or whatever that might be – then we're also inhibiting our capacity to experience joy. Life is a series of feelings. It's all about feelings. It's so important for us to really be able to step fully into our joy, and it's I think impossible to do that if we're not feeling the painful feelings in an honest and open way with ourselves and then letting them go.

> NEGATIVE EMOTIONS ARE GOING TO COME OUT ONE WAY OR ANOTHER. CONSCIOUSLY FEEL PAINFUL FEELINGS TO GET THEM OUT OF THE WAY TO ALLOW MORE JOY TO FLOW IN.

I absolutely agree with you 100 percent!

I know a lot of pet business owners are working with the animals and a lot of them are also working at their desk or at the computer a lot. What's a good yoga pose for that? Can you talk about a good yoga pose for pet business owners who are on their computer a lot?

If you're on a computer a lot, the one thing that's really great to do is take care of your hands and your wrists. Make little gentle fists, not hard fists but gentle fists and rotate your wrist one direction, and then change direction and go the other direction, and that begins right away to open up the muscles and get more energy to flow through there. You can also take your hands and stretch one hand into the other to get the wrists even more open. Then you can also do it the other way.

That's great. A lot of business owners want more confidence in running their business. What would you say is a good pose for confidence?

Well, first of all, we've touched on the breath. The breath is going to immediately get you connected to yourself. It's going to help you to get more present, and when you're in that present moment, you'll have access to more of yourself, so the breath will help with confidence.

In terms of physically what to do with the body, notice when you are hunching over at your desk and sit up nice and straight instead. That allows the energy to move really smoothly through the body. Scientific studies show that how we hold our bodies has a powerful influence on our emotional state.

It's true. I recently saw a TED Talk about this very subject. About people who wanted more confidence, and there was this "confidence pose." The TED Talk speaker jokingly called it the Wonder Woman pose. You put your hands on your hips, stand up straight and tall, and spread your legs just a little bit. If you stand there for a minute or two, you'll begin to gain more confidence and a sense of feeling empowered. I really recommend that pose before a client meeting. Maybe you're feeling a little nervous, and if you do the Wonder Woman pose, it can shift things, even if you're a guy!

Yes, before you have your meeting, you can stand in the bathroom stall in your power pose!

Exactly. Just do it for a minute or two and see what happens. You'll have a different experience when you do. So one final pose that I'd love to ask you about is what can pet business owners do to increase a sense of well-being and happiness? What do you recommend?

> SIMPLE YOGA STEPS TO TAKE NOW AND EVERY DAY: BREATHE, SIT UP STRAIGHT AND TALL WHEN AT YOUR DESK, SMILE, AND PRACTICE THE WONDER WOMAN POSE. YOU'LL BE AMAZED AT THE DIFFERENCE THOSE THINGS MAKE IN YOUR BUSINESS AND YOUR LIFE.

Continuing on this same theme, the breath is immediately going to make the body happier biologically. You're going to take in more oxygen, which adds to a feeling of well-being. The body is going to feel lighter. And smiling! I really believe that smiling, even if you are having the most miserable day, will dramatically transform how you feel because when you have a smile on your face, it automatically uplifts you, automatically changes how you feel. It automatically changes how you speak, the quality of your voice, how you interact with people around you. I'm sure that you have heard the suggestion to smile when you pick up the phone. When you pick up the phone, always put a smile on your face because that comes through the phone.

It really does. Such a pleasure to talk to you, Lisa. Thank you so much for your time and your beautiful energy and spirit. I just adore you and you're wonderful.

Oh, Kristin, thank you so much. I really believe in what you're doing. I believe in what all of these pet business owners are doing around the world with animals. I believe that we have a sacred contract with animals, and it truly is sacred work. It's special work to be able to interact with animals, to be a steward of these beings who are here at the mercy of humans and who aren't always well taken care of.

Pet business owners are a special part of a movement that is really growing to take good care of these animals. It literally gives me chills because there didn't used to be pet sitting services and other pet services on the scale that's there now. Years ago, people didn't care about their animals. They'd leave them in the yard tied up or they'd leave them in the garage. It wasn't something that people had consciousness about, but now people are getting that consciousness and it is a beautiful thing. I'm so grateful for you and what you do and for what all of the people are doing in the pet business world. It's really powerful.

Thank you so much. I have chills hearing you say that. I feel the same way about us being stewards for these incredible creatures that are here to bless our lives. And in blessing the animals' lives, we're also blessing their owners' lives. Pet business owners are creating more peace on the planet as a result of the loving care that they are giving to the pets and their people. So thank you so much, Lisa. I wish you all the best. Thank you.

Thanks again. Take care and remember to breathe and smile.

EIGHTEEN

How to Make Your Business Blog Profitable, Easy, and Fun to Write

Interview with Lisa Taron

Do you have a blog, but it's been weeks since you've written anything in it? Or do you know you "should" have a blog but you don't know why? Or (let me guess), you don't see the point of adding blogging to your business to-do list? Ta-da! She's here! Lisa to the rescue! In her witty and wise way, she talks about the why, when, and how of blogging. You'll come away inspired and ready to blog. (I know I did!)

In this chapter, you will learn:

- Why, as a pet business owner, it's so important that you have a blog
- What makes a blog successful
- How to create time to blog (even if you think you don't have time)
- How to make blogging fun (yes, you read that right)
- How to make money from your blog
- And much more!

Kristin's Musings:

I was not prepared for this woman. (No one probably is!) Wow, what a fun person. I love her silliness and humor. That's Lisa. You never know what you are going to get from her, and that's one of her gifts. She's one in a million. She's also built a blogging empire, and I declare her the Pet Blog Queen (although she might still prefer to call herself The Pet Blog Lady). Enjoy.

Lisa Taron's Bio:

The Pet Blog Lady (aka Lisa Taron) has followed her blogging passion for over six years. Her blog celebrates "all things pets," from heartwarming stories of the incredible human/animal bond and product reviews, to helpful tips for pet parents and silly musings about her life. Her past work experiences include radio broadcasting and managing seniors' homes. She is an entrepreneur and was a very, very proud dog mom to her 13-year-old Bichon Frise, Oscar (aka Sir Fetch-a-lot) who passed on in 2015. She lives in the Okanagan Valley in British Columbia and her popular blog gets thousands of viewers each day! Visit her website at *www.PetBlogLady.com*.

Interview with Lisa Taron
Founder, The Pet Blog Lady

Kristin Morrison: *I am so delighted to welcome Lisa Taron here. Thank you Lisa, for being here.*

Lisa Taron: Thank you for asking me. I'm delighted.

Lisa Taron is known as The Pet Blog Lady. She is also an illustrator. She is passionate about celebrating the love that we have for our pets. She is also very passionate about helping entrepreneurs step powerfully into their business and their lives, and I just want to welcome you here, Lisa. So let's dive right in. How did you get started in blogging?

I had an online printing business, and it was a company in which you can make books, cards, and calendars about any subject, but I was really passionate about helping people and inspiring people to write books and do projects about their pets. I decided to start a blog and I called it "The Pet Book Lady." It was about creating books and cards about your pets and pet topics. In the process, I really fell in love with blogging, and I was so drawn to blogging about all things pets.

I changed my business name from The Pet Book Lady to The Pet Blog Lady. That came to me at a conference a couple years ago when, for the hundredth time, someone wanted me to explain what The Pet Book Lady was about. I had this moment; I realized I needed to change my name. I went online to see if The Pet Blog Lady was available and it was. So hence, I became The Pet Blog Lady.

That's great. And what do you like about blogging?

It's a form of expression for me. It's an avenue in which I can be creative. I love how I can connect pet-loving people with businesses. I know when you're in business, you can panic, like how are you going to reach people who could buy your products? Well, it's twofold. I love celebrating pets through my articles and reviews and connecting pet parents with the products out there.

That's wonderful! So going back to blogging, what do you think is most important for pet business owners when they're blogging? What do they really need to know?

Well, there are a few things. One thing is don't blog if you don't want to. If you're about to write a blog post and you're just not feeling it, don't bother because a blog post should really be very genuine and heartfelt. What I'm saying is, if it's not fun, don't do it.

Personally, I like to post almost every day, but there might be a day where I'm just stuck and I can't, so I'm not going to force it when that's happening for me. So that's one thing I would recommend.

As far as what to blog about: tap into your passions. For me, I'm very passionate about that bond that people have with their pets, not just dogs and cats. I just did an article on hamsters and how – to me – having a pet is a rite of passage. I think every kid should have a hamster, gerbil, or some little creature in their life.

So look at the passions in your life and draw from that. If you're online or in your community and you see something going on that just piques your interest, explore it and blog about it. There's a reason why our brains are drawn to certain things and our hearts are too. Follow that urge to learn more about a topic because by wanting to learn more, you're more apt to express that to your blog readers and your followers.

> THEY SAY, "WRITE WHAT YOU KNOW." WHEN IT COMES TO BLOGGING, WRITE ABOUT THE THINGS YOU ARE MOST PASSIONATE ABOUT.

I really believe that. When I'm blogging, I try to do it when I'm feeling inspired, rather than feeling that I "have to."

What I've told some of my clients who are having a challenge with blogging is for them to "interview" a pet that they care for and to write a blog post interview where the pet "talks."

I love that. It's creative and pet owners would love it too.

They absolutely love it.

It's fun and light. And you can do some serious pet interviews too. You can interview a dog that's been through a really rough road and tap into some resources about how to start your own pet food bank or how to get involved in rescue or fostering.

I agree. And also, you can blog about pet food recalls. You can also highlight rescue pets that need homes. That's a really wonderful way to do service with your blog.

It gives you the warm fuzzies.

It really does. I know you've done some rescue work, which is just fabulous.

I love doing rescue work. There are a couple of rescue groups that I'm involved with. One is Hope for Paws in Los Angeles. I like to get the word out about what they're doing, and another one is a rescue group in Mexico. I'm going to go there in a couple weeks actually. The SPCA in Puerto Vallarta.

I really love it. If I can help them reach people out there for either donations or to foster or to adopt, it's such a win-win for everybody.

I agree. So speaking of reaching people…. You have quite a number of followers and people who read your blog all the time. How did you get such a big following for your blog?

How I describe it is that you really can't be your own little island. You need to connect with other groups of people out there. Reading other similar blogs and reaching out to the blog authors can be helpful too.

It builds a relationship, because in essence it's all about relationships. One thing that I have come across is that some bloggers are in a scarcity mindset, thinking that there are only so many readers out there or there aren't many companies that will sponsor blogs. You really have to have an attitude of abundance. There is so much to go around. Find your niche and tap into that. You'll be amazed.

I love that you mentioned scarcity versus abundance. I deal with that again a lot with my coaching clients where they're experiencing a dog-eat-dog world. Years ago, I experienced that sense of competition when I first started my pet care company. I would put up fliers on bulletin boards, and folks would tell me they would see my competitor removing them and putting her own there. It fueled this sense for me that there is not enough and that other business owners are not safe. I had to really tap into that place of the abundance mindset... that there are plenty of pets for everyone.

Absolutely.

I believe now, and it took some inner and outer work to get to this place, is that it is an abundant universe. If we're tapping into our passion and stepping fully into what we're here to do, I feel like the abundance just naturally flows to us.

It is a mindset that's positive and it draws good energy to you. If you're thinking of scarcity, it makes you panic. Scarcity gives you feelings of stress and the feeling of, *"Oh no, I'm not going to get my share."* That's just an awful place to be.

It really is. It's awful in both business and in life. I think about scarcity being like holding our hands closed instead of opening them and receiving.

That's a good one, and you can add "jazz hands."

I like that. That works too. So speaking of abundance, how would you recommend that people create money from their blog? I know you've been able to do that. How can pet business owners do that too?

There are different ways. When you're just starting off, you may be hesitant to take on a blog post for free, but when you're starting off and building up readership, it's good practice, definitely, or if you're doing a product review.

When I first started, it was and still is like a pet store in my office. I have more products than I know what to do with. But take on these things and build up your readership, and when you're starting to become recognized out there, you can have sponsor posts. That's one thing I do a lot and am very clear at the beginning. There is a disclosure made with FTC regulations. I need to be transparent. And that way, a company can have photos and information about their product and services. So that's a way to make money.

You can put ad space on your blog. A lot of bloggers are moving away from that because you don't want your blog looking like one big ad. Right now, I'm pretty well at my max when it comes to ads. I might even taper it down a bit, but these are companies and people who I really believe in. And companies that I am in a relationship with and I like having them on my blog.

Another thing you can offer are affiliate programs. For example, let's say you are a doggy blogger and you may get involved with a company that sells high-end dog beds. You may have a local ad on your side bar and do a posting about it.

You will have to have a disclosure that you are an affiliate of this particular company, and by affiliate, I mean they will create a special link that you're sending your readers. If that reader purchases something or even sometimes if they just go in and enter a contest, you can get paid per entry or a percentage of that product purchase. There is a whole world out there. I'm just starting to get into it, but there are lots of affiliate companies. If you're a business that sells pet food and you get an affiliate with another company and they represent a certain product, make sure they're not also selling pet food too because it just makes you look silly. It's just not good business.

I agree. I really liked how you said that you work with companies that you believe in because I think that's so important. That you have ads from companies that you really believe in and you have sponsored blog posts from companies that you feel good about. You are not selling out for money. It's not worth it when you do that.

I have turned products and offers away that were just not the right fit.

I have too. It's so important to stand behind what you believe in.

You might think, *"I could really use these few hundred dollars,"* but then you don't really believe in this product, or it was sent to you and it doesn't work, it's made poorly. At the end of the day, you need to answer to yourself and that's really important as a blogger.

I agree. I only refer to products and services that I totally believe in. I want to fully stand behind whatever I'm referring, and people know that about me and I want them to have a great experience with the products and services that I'm referring them to.

IF YOU'RE BLOGGING ABOUT A PRODUCT OR WORKING WITH AN AFFILIATE, YOU MUST ABSOLUTELY, POSITIVELY STAND BEHIND IT 100 PERCENT. IF NOT, YOUR READERS WILL SEE YOU AS A PHONY.

I appreciate that people know that about me. That I only refer what I believe in 100 percent.

I think if we're advertising lots of different products and services on our blog, it can get a little hard for our audience to determine if we truly believe in what is being offered or referred to.

The message gets really diluted, and you want to have that integrity and keep tabs on it all the time. Because it's a social media world. If you're taking on a product just because you could use the money or you want the free product and it turns out to be a really lousy product and you've been referring it to your clients or readers, then people aren't going to believe your recommendations. You will suffer in the end.

I agree. It affects the reputation of whoever is talking about the product and highlighting it on their site.

Absolutely. It's especially important as you get bigger and more well known as a blogger. The founder of Triberr is named Dino Dogan. He is a fantastic entrepreneur and he is a believer in bloggers becoming "brand ambassadors." This might take the form of a company you are endorsing having a very prominent banner on your website. They believe in you and you believe in them, and together you're growing. Some of the big bloggers become blog ambassadors for companies. So that's something to aspire to.

That's wonderful. I work with a lot of pet business owners who rarely write on their blog. Perhaps they started a blog, they wrote a couple of posts, but they haven't been inspired to continue writing blog posts. How can they get their mojo back when it comes to writing, and what if they think that they're not writers? How can they go about creating more blog posts?

I love that word, "mojo." I use that all the time. Writing is a skill, but again, people put too much worry on writing. They might say, *"I can't write a blog because I've never written an article. I've never gone to graduate school,"* or whatever.

Again, writing a blog should come from the heart. There are tools out there to help you with your grammar if you're struggling with actually putting sentences together. It comes back to writing about what you're passionate about, and if you are passionate, that will help with the frequency too. So many businesses that I've talked to think they have to blog every day. It doesn't have to be every day, but if you can make an effort to blog even just once a week that can be fine.

Mix up things. See what piques your interest and have it be a mixture. So if you're a company that sells... I always use this example: high-end dog collars. Do a post about your company and what you do in your company. The next post write about the safety of collars and hazards of watching your dog getting their collar caught in the rail. Look at what your readers have said about your product and success stories. There is so much information out there that it's about taking the blinders off that prevent you from seeing the options. I think the blinders are fear.

I think it's wonderful, and often for the clients I work with, it's more important to write a blog post and actually be okay with making a mistake than it is to not write a blog post. Just play around with it and see. I've worked with a lot of people who have found that they have a love for writing that they had forgotten about or that they never knew existed.

That happened for me. I mean, I did writing in school, at university, and it was so boring. The papers are boring, and the footnotes and all that... you just want to hang yourself.

But I didn't really know that I had a creative side. I am an artist, so I knew that I had that creative part, but to play around with words is so fun. And if you feel like you need some education about writing, look into your local college or distance ed program for writing programs, and then have fun with it. It doesn't all have to be blog posts. I mean there could be videos. Videos are really hot right now. So if you have little YouTube clips, post them. Post pictures on Facebook. You know… a real mix. Mixture is the best variety. I'll sometimes post a serious blog segment about a rescue and include a call to action for my readers. Other times I'll have a very silly, amusing one. I tend to use a lot of silly ones actually. Then I'll have a blog post that's sponsored, it talks about a product, and then a blog post about something I think readers might be interested in. I was at a pet first-aid course this week and I fell in love with the whole idea of pet first aid. Now I want to become a pet first-aid instructor. So if I hadn't taken that course, that light bulb would have never gone off and I'm going to have so much fun blogging about that process.

I know! Pet first aid is a whole other world for pet business owners to be able to dive into.

It is and it's being recognized, and it's being validated by vets too. This is first-responder stuff. We're not learning to become vet techs or veterinarians. We're just learning how to save lives. That course was so interesting. I just loved it.

I've talked to a lot of pet sitters and dog walkers who have taken it, and they have been really blown away by the information. It only takes a day or so to learn it.

The class I took was ten hours, and there are some courses they offer that are taught over two days, but it's doable in terms of time. And you're left with materials. And information. I lost my dog, Oscar, but if he were to stop breathing and I knew this information, I would have known what to do.

Exactly. I'd like to talk a little about posting on a blog. One of the things that comes up when I'm talking to pet business owners is that they feel like they have to write a long blog post. My advice to them is less is more, because people really don't want to read a huge, long blog post.

We're such a busy society right now. Our attention spans are really short. Look how long we search the web. If something doesn't come up right away, we're clicking and we're looking for something else.

Definitely have substance to your blog posts but don't feel like you have to write a manifesto. I should probably look at my blog

BLOGS AREN'T LIMITED TO WORDS. MIX UP YOUR BLOG WITH PHOTOS AND VIDEOS.

posts and see how many words my posts generally are. I know they really range. For days when you don't feel like posting, you can do "Wordless Wednesday," which is a great thing for pet bloggers. You're basically just posting a photo.

Oh, that's neat.

Yes, more tools. You can use photos and videos in your blog. Your readers may be more likely to share your blog post if you have pictures and videos.

Blogging comes up so high on the search engines too. That's another reason why it's so important for pet business owners to do it.

Years ago when I started blogging, people really were seeing blogs as a self-amusing online journals. There are still self-amusing blogs out there, but blogging has come such a long way. One thing I'd like to mention to readers is to not jump in to blogging without knowing what you want it to look like. You need a design that looks nice. There are a lot of blog templates out there. It becomes your baby, for sure.

Our creative spirit can come through. Your blog is there and it's viewable online, so you really want it to be something that you feel good about but, again, don't be a perfectionist trying to make it perfect.

No, it'll keep you up at night.

I would say spell check is very important because it's important to have good grammar and spelling.

Yes. I cringe when I see grammatical errors. I think you know what I mean. You don't have to be Mark Twain, but put some effort in, and yes, use spell check. Formatting is important too. Nothing worse than seeing a blog that's all in caps and bold. It's like someone is yelling at you.

Or it's like Goldilocks and the three fonts. You don't want something so big or something so small. You want it just right. Simple is good. Blogs can be pliable and flexible. I don't know anything about designing websites. They scare me with all the code involved and it's very finicky to change something on a website; whereas, a blog is so instant and you get to know the tools that you're working with; it's come a long way.

And don't be afraid to get your hands dirty, get in there, and play around. You can do a lot of things in draft mode without publishing it to the public before you are ready.

Blogging is a great tool.

It really is and it's a great way to connect with your audience, whatever that audience is, and for them to get to know you and to see your personality come through in your blog.

I had this discussion with someone the other day who didn't want her readers to know anything about her. She just wanted them to know about her product, and even on the contact form there's nothing about her. That's kind of sad. And the opposite isn't good either. You don't have to be telling your deepest, darkest secrets.

But your readers do want to know who you are, and I'm a believer that not only are you branding your product but you're branding yourself. Nothing brings me greater joy than when I get phone calls asking if I'm The Pet Blog Lady or when I'm at a conference and someone wants to know my real name because they only know me as my brand. To brand yourself is a positive thing. Again, it's a trusting relationship. We're all human. I want to know who's behind the pictures and the articles.

I agree. I think it's important to reveal some of our personality, and it can sometimes be tricky to figure out how much to reveal.

Yes, it can. I had some struggles back in the spring and I was honest with my readers. I took some time off and I was open about it. I didn't go into great detail, but I tell you, I had so many hits and shares on that post. Because I was being real. We're not some "super person" because we know how to type and put photos in.

I think more and more people really want authenticity. Brené Brown has a beautiful TED Talk about vulnerability and how powerful vulnerability is. I think vulnerability creates the sense of people being able to relate to the person behind the blog.

That's how I think blogs actually got started. Certainly now it's an excellent business tool and a marketing tool, but years ago it was simply a form of expression out there to the world and for those who wanted to reach out, share themselves, and connect. It's a beautiful thing.

It's kind of like journaling. And revealing that inner self to our readers to a certain degree.

As a pet blogger, we have a bond. It's that bond of that love that we have for our pets. That's what I like to convey through my blog. Your readers might become instant friends who you might not have met in another way, but it's that attraction that we have to being pet parents that can bring us together.

It really is about a common bond between people who love pets. It's gorgeous.

It is. I love it. I just felt I was born to do this. I wouldn't be doing this if I didn't have fun. If it starts to become a chore then you revisit that. Even if I weren't making any money or being sent products to review, I would still just love it.

I have three mottos around work and I really try to make sure that each project, whatever that may be, whether it's writing a book, whether it's starting a new business, really fits under all three. The motto is: Have fun. Do good. Make money.

I love that.

I think it's one thing to have fun and do good, but I don't really want to start a nonprofit unless I'm really intentional about it.

I love that. If you do what you love and it's something that fuels your day every day, you're more apt to connect with your real self and a living is more likely to come from it. I'm involved in a few other online things and I have a couple little odd jobs. I've actually worked part time in a funeral home. I love it. It's that I love being around families and helping out. My dream someday is to blog for a living and with these other online businesses to be able to live anywhere. I'm heading to Mexico in a couple of weeks to work at the sanctuary that I'm in love with and to bring back five dogs from Mexico to find loving families. My dream is to live here part time and there part time. To have a very simple life and then off I go to Mexico for five or six months a year and still make a living as a blogger and help down there with the dogs, and fish. I love fishing.

I've done that and I can say that it's wonderful to live part time in another country. I lived in Bali for six months in 2011, and I was there for two months in 2010. I also was in India part time during that period as well. I sold my pet sitting company that

I had for 18 years. I sold it last December, but I had managers running it while I was gone. I didn't do any coaching while I was away. I had just finished writing my book and it was this great experience of being able to enjoy life. It was great.

It's living the dream. Maybe because of my experience living with seniors and also being in the funeral business too. You've got to live your life to the fullest.

Exactly. If not now, when? That was kind of the epiphany I had. I went to a meditation retreat a few years ago, and they had us imagine if we had six months to live what we would do. I went into this meditation and I saw myself with my travel backpack and a big smile. I was so shocked that came up. I would travel if I knew I was going to die? It just seemed so odd to me. Before the meditation started, I thought I would want to be with friends and family, but seeing myself with that travel backpack on and smiling woke me up to the fact that my time on this planet is limited and something in me, my soul, was really saying, "You need to get out there and travel."

Yes, and people who are looking at starting pet businesses, too, I hear this so many times: *"Oh, I would love to work with animals, but I don't have any business background,"* or, *"I don't know…I'd love to be a cat sitter, but who wants a cat sitter?"* They set up these blocks for themselves before they've even started. It's sad, because when they do step out and make things happen for themselves, they marvel and say, *"Oh, I wish I would have done this a long time ago."*

We're all capable of doing whatever that it is that we want to do. Whatever is our dream. We're the ones who hold ourselves back. We may think it's out there. But it's an inside job.

We are our own worst critics.

We really can be. And going back to the blog, when we can really bring self-love into our writing and the way that we run our business and also the way that we live our lives, that's powerful.

For anyone who's on the fence about blogging, is fearful that they can't write, or think it's going to be a complicated process in itself, or wonder, *"Who's going to read my blog?"* … just let those go.

If you need more support, look for the resources out there. I even have the *Blogging for Dummies* book. I have a *Dummies* book for everything.

But do take the first step because the last thing you want to do is to miss out on the experience. Be patient with yourself, especially if you are starting a blog. Let's say you have a doggy daycare and you want to build up more business or sell more products, either being online or at your doggy daycare, don't expect incredible results right away. Everything takes time, but if you're willing to put the effort in and build on that, it is a great way to connect with people and build those relationships. Far more than a website or Facebook. Facebook is very limited. It's great, but a blog will get you into the conversation.

It really will, and it is a conversation with the comments and feedback. It can be very fun and interactive.

And contests are great. They are fabulous. I've got some contests going on all the time. Right now, I have a big gift basket for a dog owner from Bayer. I did a project with Bayer with the tick medication.

You can use RaffleCopter. They will ship the prize to that person. Readers love giveaways.

I do a hashtag on Twitter, something like #GiveawaysOnNow. All these people come out of nowhere when I do that. If you're looking at giving some of your products away, it's a very small investment on your end. Or get involved with other companies, and they do the shipping. It's marvelous.

That's fantastic. Thank you so much, Lisa. I really appreciate you being here. This was really incredible.

It's been an honor.

Any last thoughts that you have?

You know, enjoy yourself. Go out there, start cruising around with the blogs, and have fun.

Wonderful. Thank you so much, Lisa.

You're welcome.

NINETEEN

Secrets for
Pet Business Success

Interview with Andrea Arden

Are you feeling challenged by the big and little details in your pet business? Want to discover some tools for making your business (and your life) run more smoothly? If so, this is the chapter to read. Andrea also shares her top three secrets for pet business success, so you and your business can hit the ground running!

In this chapter, you will learn:

- How Andrea was "discovered" by TV producers and what might help you get discovered too (and you probably rarely do it!)

- The best business advice she ever received and how it changed her business

- How to emotionally deal with negative Yelp and other online reviews

- Andrea's top three secrets for pet business success

- What to do to keep your business running smoothly

- And much more!

Kristin's Musings:

I felt more than a bit giddy after this interview with Andrea. Her playful energy is so infectious and fun. She also has over two decades of pet business wisdom to share. Definitely some good juju coming out of this woman! Read and you'll see what I mean.

Andrea Arden's Bio:

Andrea Arden is an Animal Planet pet expert and cast member on *Dogs101, Cats101, America's Cutest Pet*, and *Underdog to Wonderdog*. Her extensive media experience also includes the *Today Show, Live with Kelly & Michael, 20/20, Dateline NBC, Nightline, The View*, and the Emmy Award-winning *Pet Department* on FX. Andrea is also a professional speaker, and author of *Dog-Friendly Dog Training, Barron's Dog Training Bible, Train Your Dog the Lazy Way*, and *The Little Book of Dog Tricks*. With over 20 years as the director of Andrea Arden Dog Training, New York City's leader in the field of animal behavior, Andrea's team has helped hundreds of thousands of families and their companion animals live cohesive and enriched lives together. In addition, she is an active supporter of numerous animal-related organizations, including the Animal Legal Defense Fund, which has been fighting to protect the lives and advance the interests of animals through the legal system for three decades; Pets for Patriots, which advocates for the permanent placement of adult dogs and cats with military families; and Dogs for the Deaf, which rescues and trains dogs for those with hearing impairments. Visit her website at *www.AndreaArden.com*.

Interview with Andrea Arden
Dog Trainer and Animal Behavior Expert

Kristin Morrison: *It's great to welcome Andrea Arden here. Andrea is a dog trainer. She is an Animal Planet pet expert. She is the author of many books. She is also a professional speaker, and it's wonderful to have you here, Andrea. Thank you.*

Andrea Arden: Thank you for having me.

So, let's dive in. How did you get started in the dog training business?

I got started all the way back when I was a child. My dad was so passionate about animals. We had no fewer than seven or eight dogs as part of our family at any one time. We had cats. We had pigs and goats.

So I was an animal lover, a person who's really passionate about animals. I went to college for the riding team. Then once I left college, I had a number of different jobs, but I started apprenticing at a dog training school.

That came about because I got a dog. And before I got the dog, I had found a dog training school and I contacted them about getting some training for my dog. I think contacting them before I got the dog gave them the indication that I was really serious about dog training, and they offered me an apprentice position. So it was great.

So then you got to work with your dog and you learned how to become a dog trainer through that dog. That's great.

Yes, we learned together. His name was Oliver. Yes, it was great.

What kind of dog was he?

He was a Gordon setter. And he went on to be a dog that accompanied me on TV shows for many years and was my buddy in life and was a wonderful, wonderful dog. I still miss him.

I bet you do. It's hard when they depart.

It's tough.

So, what were some of the challenges that you experienced when you were first starting your dog training business?

I would say once I went off on my own and started my own dog training school, which was probably the biggest challenge. I found that it was a constant juggling act. So I was working during the day doing private lessons. I was teaching group classes at night. Then in between all of that, I had to figure out a way to not only market my business to other pet professionals, like veterinarians and pet groomers, but I also had to spend time on the phone returning client calls. It really felt like I was working almost 24 hours a day. Even in my sleep, I felt like I was focused on my business. It was a good thing that I was so young when I started because it took a lot of energy!

The other thing that I found really challenging was that 20 years ago when I started, there really weren't a lot of resources like you're offering to help people in regard to starting in the pet industry — to really give them a sense of what it's about, what it takes to be in the pet industry, and what the potential challenges are and how to overcome those challenges.

It's true. I started almost two decades ago, and there was hardly anything to help me grow my pet business and solve the challenges that can arise when you have a pet business.

So if you look back to when you were struggling with working so much, how were you able to carve out time for yourself? How did you make that happen?

I don't know if I really did carve out a lot of time for myself. I think the time I carved out was spent with my dog, and then I got another dog. On the weekends if I had a few hours free, I would go to dog training seminars. I would take my dogs for hikes. I mean really, my life was dogs 24/7, which it still kind of is now actually, truth be told. Not so bad.

But it took about ten years until I was able to be in a position in which I could actually take chunks of time off, which may sound a little intimidating to people, but it's a job that I love so much that looking back, I don't resent it at all. I think that it was wonderful.

It's wonderful to be in a profession that you just love, isn't it?

It's amazing. A lot of people approach me on a regular basis (whether it be calling me, email, in person) asking how they can get involved in this industry, and often times they say that the reason that they want to get involved is because they love animals and they don't like people.

That would be the one time when I would say, *"This is probably not the right industry for you because animals that you're working with tend to come attached with a human being, so you're going to have to work with both. But if you love animals and you at least like people, you don't have to love them but if you at least like them, then it's a great industry to be in."*

It's funny. I was talking about that with Ian Dunbar and that was definitely something that came up in our conversation: the need for pet professionals to at least like people.

It's true. The minute that somebody says to me, *"I'm leaving my career because I don't want to work with people,"* I hesitate to encourage them to go into this field because often times I feel like calling myself a dog trainer doesn't really do justice to what it is I and other trainers do. We're educators and I would say the primary focus is actually educating people on how to educate their dogs.

The super fun part is educating the dogs, having the training session in which you have the dog that has that light bulb moment and you say, *"This is why I really love what I'm doing."* But a lot of the time, it's about dealing with people and people's frustrations and helping them overcome their emotions that they're feeling if their dog is having a behavior issue or if it's something as simple as a new puppy owner who is frustrated because they got in over their head.

> HAVE YOU NOTICED THE RECURRING THEME FROM SEVERAL OF THESE EXPERTS: THE PET BUSINESS IS ULTIMATELY A PEOPLE BUSINESS. YOU MUST AT LEAST LIKE PEOPLE IN ORDER TO SUCCEED.

It's true. And I'm thinking that here you've become this pet behavior expert and dog expert on Animal Planet. How did you get that big break? I mean that's incredible.

It was a cool break. I was apprenticing at a dog training school and I was there when I could be. I was there at least five days a week for a few hours and what that meant was that I was cleaning, I was answering the phones, I was obsessed.

One day the phone rang and it was a guy. I thought it was a prank caller who said they were looking for a trainer for a TV show. So I immediately sent the call on to one of the trainers at the school because I have a phobia of having my picture taken. So I thought if I'm not comfortable having a picture taken with a still camera, how am I ever going to be on TV?

A few days went by and my boyfriend at the time said that I was crazy. He told me I needed to audition for the show, so I did. I got the job on a show called the *Pet Department* on a brand new network called FX. It ended up being five years of hanging out with some amazing people who were so incredibly supportive.

I've remained friends with a bunch of them. We actually just had our twentieth reunion a few months ago and Tom Bergeron was there. He's on *Dancing with the Stars* and a bunch of other people who may not have necessarily got their big break in TV, but it really gave some of them a jumping off point to become even bigger celebrities.

So I feel really, really grateful. From there, I just kept doing more shows until eventually I developed a relationship with Animal Planet.

Just answering the phone. That's all it took.

There you go. So, pet business owners, if you want to get on Animal Planet, just answer your phone, which a lot of business owners don't do these days. It goes into voice mail.

It's true. I think I'm guilty of that.

Exactly. So what do you think is really essential for new dog trainers who are just starting out? What do you think is really important for them if they want to create a successful business?

Well, the first thing that I would say – and it's a hard one – is that I think people need to be willing to commit a good chunk of time to their education before they can charge people for their expertise. I know that people are gung ho. I was too. I know that they want to get out there and start working with pets.

They want to make a living doing what they love, but I think ethically you really do need to have a solid foundation of understanding about what it is that you're trying to teach before you charge somebody for it. I worry sometimes when people take an eight-week program in which they become certified and then they feel they're ready to handle a lot of behavior issues, which I don't think is realistic.

So the first challenge is your education, taking it seriously, recognizing that this is a profession. You should treat your business professionally. You really should put in the time and effort. That means going to seminars, maybe apprenticing which is what I did, reading as many good books as you can get your hands on, and basically immersing yourself in the type of training that you want to do.

That's great. I love that. What is some of the best business advice that you've ever heard or that you've received?

I'm going to say that the best advice that I have ever received was from Dr. Ian Dunbar. When I tell you what it is, it's going to sound strange, and it took me ten years to adhere to his advice, but I finally did it and it's changed my life. His advice was, "Don't answer your own phone. Hire a phone person." That was it.

I know years ago when he told me this, I thought I couldn't afford a phone person. I realized I spent ten years in the juggling act and spending so much time playing phone tag with people and spending expansive amounts of time on the phone with potential clients. This caused me to really start to get burned out.

I was having a hard time giving my best to the clients who would actually schedule time with me or in my group classes. Eventually, I was able to afford to have somebody answer the phone and it really has been life changing.

I get it. I did that in my business too, and it was transformational. It was about eight years into my pet sitting company when I did it. I hired a couple managers to help me, and it was so transformative for me. It gave me the breathing room that I needed. It was incredible.

I do think that if I had to say what the one thing is that can be most challenging about any aspect of the pet business, whether it's pet sitting, dog training, grooming, even if you're a veterinarian, it's burnout.

We're so emotionally invested in the animals that we work with and trying to help, and we're also emotionally invested in the families and they're so emotional with us around their pets that often you end up spending enormous amounts of time and energy with one client or two clients a week. You get to the point where you just don't have any more to give, and that's not a good thing.

You think you're doing your best for that client by constantly being available, constantly talking to them on the phone even outside of the lessons or group class, but sometimes what happens is you're not really being fair to yourself or your other clients. So you really do need to take care of yourself in that regard.

For me, getting somebody to answer my phones and manage my business in general really allowed me to breathe.

BEST BUSINESS ADVICE? GET SOMEONE TO ANSWER YOUR PHONE! PHONE TIME CAN DRAIN YOUR TIME AND ENERGY FROM THE CORE VALUE YOU OFFER CLIENTS.

True, and I think also we teach people how to treat us. If we're constantly talking to our clients and returning calls at all hours of the day and night, that can really impact our lives because we teach them that we're available all the time.

Yes, and it's a hard one because I would have to say, especially at the point in my business, I'm lucky enough to have clients who really respect our training school. They recognize that we're professionals. They treat us with respect, and that's wonderful.

That's a very good feeling, but there are times when you get people who don't. I think that treating somebody with respect is also respecting their time and the value of their time and their energy. So I've had to learn. It's been really hard to have ways to explain to people why I can't talk to them at ten o'clock at night even though they're very frustrated and nervous about their puppy not being on a housetraining schedule.

That can be hard, because if you are good at what you do in the pet industry, it means that you're a caring person, at least to some degree, so it can be hard to set boundaries.

It can be, especially for caretaker personalities. And generally, people who are drawn to the pet professions are caretakers by nature. So it can be hard to say no. I've told a lot of my clients that "no" is not a four-letter word. Just say it.

That's good. I'm going to remember that line. I try to explain to clients and to young trainers that you wouldn't expect to be able to call your doctor unless it was a real emergency at ten o'clock at night and get them on the phone. They need breathing room and we do too. Maybe dog training is not as lofty a career as a doctor, but it's still a career. It's a profession, and I think we need to treat ourselves professionally, so we are treated professionally by others.

I love that. On another note, a lot of pet business owners are having this sort of love/hate relationship with Yelp. It's a totally different subject, but I'd love to talk with you about it.

I just got chills when you said Yelp.

I know. You think of the word "yelp" like the sound a dog makes when it's in pain, right? So how do pet business owners deal with a bad Yelp review? I've been talking to so many pet business owners about this, and it can cause them so much angst.

It's a tough one. I've been lucky, knock wood, that I think I only have a couple negative reviews, but I will tell you I'm extremely sensitive, and when I saw those reviews, it really jarred me.

There was one in particular that really jarred me because it was a very severe aggression case. They'd only had the dog for four days. When I walked in, I was told it was basic manners. The dog had punctured both of the owner's hands multiple times. It had attacked a child. It was a very, very bad case. I spent about two hours with them, which is longer than my normal lesson.

It was a very emotional experience for all of us, but it was also rewarding because we had made some progress with the dog. He was actually able to show some impulse control. He was responsive to exercises like hand targeting. So I felt that there was potentially some hope for this dog and this family being able to be as one.

When the woman asked me if I thought that she should not keep the dog, I said, *"I don't really feel comfortable answering that question, and to be honest with you, part of it is because I feel like as trainers, when we're asked that, there is no win. If I tell you maybe you shouldn't keep the dog and you do and the dog turns out to be part of your family and you love the dog, you're going to think I'm a bad person. And if I tell you to keep the dog and something bad happens, you're going to say that I wasn't responsible."* But she promised me that she wouldn't be upset either way, and I actually explained to her that since they wanted to have children soon, I thought that this was not a good situation.

Lo and behold a few days later, I got a horrible review. It basically said that I made the dog out of control. I was trying to sell her more business, which was not true. In fact, that is one place in which I am not a good businessperson. I am not good at a sales pitch. I figure if you want to work with us you will, if not you won't. That's the one time I actually responded to a Yelp review. The reason was because I felt that it was so far away from what had actually happened that I wanted to clarify that.

The one thing that she said which was spot on was that she thought I spoke very quickly, so I apologized for that. I do. I'm a native New Yorker. I speak quickly, and I also am really enthusiastic, so I try to get a lot into each lesson. Other than that, I think she was expressing her own frustration. So my advice to pet business owners in a situation like that is the title of that famous song: "Let It Go." You have to let it go because Yelp is powerful, but there's something way more powerful which is in-person referrals.

If you develop a good reputation, if you do your job well and you make friends with vets and groomers, and if other people in your profession respect you, word of mouth will carry you a lot further than even 20 or 30 great reviews on Yelp. So don't worry about it too much. Don't do what I did.

REGARDING YELP… LET IT GO WHEN IT COMES TO NEGATIVE REVIEWS. FOCUS YOUR TIME AND ENERGY ON BEING THE BEST YOU CAN BE AND YOUR REPUTATION WILL CREATE THE BEST REFERRALS.

I have had so many pet business owners calling me in tears. They feel really upset about it, and it can be very challenging.

On another topic, how do pet business owners make themselves visible and seen in a sea of other pet business owners who are doing the same thing? What would you recommend?

I was lucky because when I started I don't feel like there were quite so many people out there, at least in my neck of the woods in New York City. Now I feel like the industry is pretty flooded, which is great. There are lots of people wanting to get into the field and they are. I think one of the best ways that you can make yourself visible is to specialize. I think that people in the dog training industry are so quick to think that they have to offer everything.

They might list all these different services on their website. They deal with aggression, offer agility, obedience training, basic manners. We do this, we do that. That's great if you can offer all of that, but that's a lot to offer. Maybe you really love working with puppies and you become the puppy expert in your area. Maybe you really like working with separation anxiety and you focus your educational energy on learning the ins and outs of that so that local vets know you're the go-to person for that behavior issue. I think that specializing is a great way to make yourself stand out from the crowd. Once you decide you want to expand a little bit more of what you offer, then so be it.

What would be your top three tips for business success? I know you talked about getting a phone person, which I completely agree with. What are three other tips that are really important for business success?

I'm going to say that no woman or man should stand alone. Probably one of the most important things is to create a supportive team around you. Now that team could be something like I have where it's people who actually work with me on my training team. If you are not at that point, you could reach out to other professionals and develop professional and also potentially personal relationships, becoming friends. Pet professionals can offer you a lot of support.

It can be a lonely thing to start a small business on your own, and it can be challenging because there are so many things that you have to learn. And to not have people who you can reach out to for help is hard. You can ask those you are connected to about resources: *"I don't know a good printer, do you?,"* or, *"I don't have a lot of money to spend and you're a well-respected groomer in an area, can you give me some tips on referrals?"*

Another tip is make time for yourself. I didn't follow that advice because I didn't get it back then, but I do know that I did experience a period of burnout. There were a number of years in which I found it very hard to teach group classes because I was so burned out. I'm back to it now. A lot of the trainers I've known for the last 25 years have become burned out.

Some have left the profession altogether. I think you need to pick at least one day a week in which you do not answer the phone.

You don't check your emails and you're gone, because it can really wear on you. When you tell yourself that you are taking the day off but then check your email and get an email from a client who is frustrated about something… you've ruined your day off. And the final tip is getting a phone person as soon as you can; that's a big one.

That's so important. So what else do you do to take care of yourself in your busy life? I heard you say that you take one day off a week. What else would you recommend?

I spent so many years not doing anything that was fun for me outside of the animal world that last year I finally started taking classes in different things. I started taking a class in Italian. I started taking photography class. I started taking Pilates classes. I don't do them all now. I don't have that much time, but I do try at least once a week to do something like that's not dog related for a couple of reasons.

One is, it's fun. The other is that I found it really gave me a good refresher. It's like a computer when you refresh it. And it's also about being a student. Sometimes you forget what it's like to be on the other side of the learning experience, and I've gotten a lot of giggles out of it. I laugh when I look up in the mirror at Pilates class and I see myself being goofy and the instructor sort of looking at me like I'm not doing it right. I get frustrated but I also laugh at myself when I can't figure out what it means to adjust the f-stop on my camera, but it's fun. It makes me laugh.

A side benefit to the photography classes is I've now become addicted to taking pictures of animals. So I not only spend my time teaching classes, doing private lessons, but in my free time, you are pretty likely to see me walking around with a big camera around my neck.

I always love seeing people with big cameras around their necks. I'm not a photographer, but I am tempted to just get one to wear around my neck because it looks cool, but especially in Manhattan where you are. That's super cool.

I think people will think you're a tourist.

Exactly. They don't ask you directions. That's nice. Any final words of advice that you have for pet business owners?

It sounds so simple, but I would say have fun. I tend to be giggly and goofy anyway, but having fun is not only contagious to your clients, dogs like it when you giggle and have fun. It also is a really, really good way to de-stress when you are dealing with some of the challenges of being a small business owner. Be light hearted about your business and your life and allow yourself an opportunity to just look at the funny side of whatever it is that is happening and move on.

That's important. A sense of humor. We often forget it as business owners. It's funny, Andrea, one of the speakers that I interviewed recently is an improv teacher, and she talks about infusing humor into your business. It was such a fun interview to do because she had me laughing all the time. She was making all these faces and she was goofy. It was so fun.

I had a client, Robert De Niro. I was so nervous on my way to the first lesson with him. I don't usually get nervous around celebrities because I live in New York City, and I've been around them so long and we have lots of celebrity clients. If you're in Los Angeles or New York, you typically do have some celebrity clients. So I was excited to go see him. The first couple of lessons, he was so deadpan and so serious. I think it was the fourth or fifth lesson and I said to his assistant, *"I don't know if he likes me. I don't know if this is going to work out."* She said, *"No, no… he saves a lot of his energy for on camera. He's working on a film right now. He likes you. Don't worry about it."*

I think it was the fourth or fifth lesson when I got him to laugh and I was like, "*Yes! I can do it. I can make Robert De Niro laugh.*"

Even when he's in character. That's pretty good.

It's a badge of honor for me.

Absolutely. That's fantastic.

I do want to say that I love the two pictures that are on each side of you. Living in Gratitude and Occupy Your Heart. Two thumbs up. Great.

Thank you. Those are two of my mottos. They bring me a lot of joy.

Well, they brought me joy now. That's a nice reminder. I feel like I'm going to figure out a way to print those out and put them on my desk.

If I see the Occupy Your Heart one, I'll get you one and send it to you. I got it at a grocery store a few weeks ago. It's actually a greeting card. I'll keep a lookout and I'll be happy to mail it to you. The Living in Gratitude card was a postcard from a business, so I don't think I can get that one, but I'll keep my eye open for the other one.

Thank you.

You're welcome. Have a great day, Andrea. Thank you so much for your great tips.

You're welcome. Take care.

PROSPEROUS PET BUSINESS
MORE MONEY. MORE EASE. MORE FREEDOM!

www.ProsperousPetBusiness.com

BUSINESS START UP • HIRING • RAPID GROWTH HELP • BURN-OUT CURES
Business Coaching - Online Success Groups for Pet Business Owners - Start Up Kits

Programs to Help You Achieve Pet Business Success...Now!

Having read these interviews and now knowing that it is possible to achieve success in your business, you've set your sights on creating a business and life that align with what you value and cherish.

To help speed your process, here are some programs that provide greater support than you might get from a book alone.

Pet Business Coaching with Kristin Morrison

Are you ready to take your business to the next level but need support to help you do that? I can help you take your business where you want it to go, quickly and easily. I've helped thousands of pet business owners from around the country, and I can definitely help you with whatever challenges you face in your pet business.

Visit my business coaching page for testimonials and to sign up for business coaching with me:

www.prosperouspetbusiness.com/pet-business-coaching

4-Week Pet Business Online Group Programs

Need support to create a profitable and easy-to-run business *and* a great life?

I offer group pet business programs throughout the year, and you are welcome to join me and other pet business owners who are excited to support each other to create a most successful business and fulfilling life. Each program has a private Facebook group to keep you connected and feeling supported long after the program is over.

This is a virtual program, and it's designed so you can participate from anywhere in the world. You can even attend from your pet sitting, dog training, or doggy daycare office. And if you miss a class, no problem – the recording will be available for you.

The 4-Week **Jumpstart Pet Business Program** is a recovery program for those pet business owners suffering from pet business burnout (you know who you are).

The 4-Week **Catapult Pet Business Program** is for those who want to create more success in their business with ease (and you also know who you are).

You can learn more, read testimonials from past graduates, and sign up now by visiting **www.ProsperousPetBusiness.com** or by visiting the web pages below:

**Catapult Pet Business Program:
www.prosperouspetbusiness.com/
catapult**

**Jumpstart Pet Business Program:
www.prosperouspetbusiness.com/
jumpstart**

Prosperous Pet Business Podcast

Did you know that Prosperous Pet Business has a podcast? Each month, I release audio episodes to keep you listening and learning in your pet business (and in your life). There are a lot of episodes already available and waiting for you, and they are all free. Check them out!

You can listen by subscribing on iTunes or you can go to the Prosperous Pet Business podcast page:

www.prosperouspetbusiness.com/pet-business-podcast

Enjoy, and happy listening!

Want to watch, listen, and learn from the conference speakers?

We each learn best through different methods. For some of us, we learn most easily through watching and listening, and for others, we learn best from reading the material.

If you'd like to bring these interviews to life by watching, listening, and learning from the conference videos, you can right now. (Yes, right now. The videos are available for immediate download with lifetime access.)

The Prosperous Pet Business Online Conference videos are available for purchase, and you can *see* and *hear* all of the information that you've been reading.

You can find the conference videos, pet business eBooks, and many other pet business success recordings and business tools at:

**www.prosperouspetbusiness.com/
pet_business_products_and_ebooks**

Best Year Yet! Coaching

Are you ready to create the most incredible pet business and life possible? Need help creating a business and life plan for the next 12 months? I can help you create a solid business and life plan to help you have your best year yet—starting any time of the year.

Best Year Yet! coaching includes a powerful online software system that will help you create your goals as well as score them, so you stay on track to achieve them. You get your own Best Year Yet! plan to use as your guide for the entire year.

I will help you set ten business/life goals, and we will review those goals and evaluate them to make sure they are in alignment with what you most value and cherish. I offer weekly, monthly, and/or quarterly coaching sessions to keep you on track. It's a powerful system to organize your goals, visions, and desires (both business and personal).

Visit my Best Year Yet! Coach website to find out more about my Best Year Yet! Coaching Service:

www.BestYearCoaching.com

PROSPEROUS PET BUSINESS

MORE MONEY. MORE EASE. MORE FREEDOM!

Pet Sitting ❧ Dog Training ❧ Pet Grooming ❧ Dog Walking ❧ Doggy Day Care

I would love to hear how this book has helped you succeed in business!

Email: admin@ProsperousPetBusiness.com

Connect with Prosperous Pet Business on these social media sites:

Facebook: www.Facebook.com/ SixFigurePetBusinessAcademy

Twitter: www.Twitter.com/PetBizCoach

LinkedIn: www.linkedin.com/in/sixfigurepetsitting

Instagram: www.instagram.com/petbizcoach

Pinterest: www.pinterest.com/sixfigurepetbiz

Prosperous Pet Business Recommended Reading

Want to read more on how to create prosperity in your business? Below are some of the books that are on my bookshelf and that have been crucial to my business success.

Dog Training and Behavior:

How to Teach an Old Dog New Tricks
by Dr. Ian Dunbar

> *This book contains easy and effective methods to train your dog (or your client's dog). It's comprehensive and thorough for the motivated dog owner or pet business owner who wants to use positive methods to train dogs.*

Doctor Dunbar's Good Little Dog Book
by Dr. Ian Dunbar

> *This is a brief yet thorough puppy training guide that can also be used on adult dogs. You'll find information on socialization as well as basic manner training.*

After You Get Your Puppy by Dr. Ian Dunbar

> *There are crucial guidelines to follow if you want a well-behaved and well-adjusted pup, and this book outlines them. Effective methods for socialization with people and other dogs, as well as bite inhibition. A must read for new pup parents!*

Barron's Dog Training Bible by Andrea Arden

> *A complete dog training guide for dog owners. Need a holiday gift for your clients? This makes a great gift for new puppy parents and old-dog parents alike.*

Dog-Friendly Dog Training by Andrea Arden

Complete with illustrations, this book is simple yet profound when it comes to learning about dog training. It's a fun read that uses positive-based training methods. Yay!

Parenting Your Dog by Trish King

Have you often thought of your clients (and perhaps even yourself) as a dog mom or dad? This book applies effective human parenting methods to dogs. Includes an easy reference format, which makes training your dog simple and easy. Uses reward-based training methods.

Creating an Optimum Lifestyle and Business Building:

Sabbath: Finding Rest, Renewal and Delight in Our Busy Lives by Wayne Mueller

Oh, I adore this book. When I'm feeling frazzled and need to relax, this book instantly calms me down with its short, soothing chapters. It's a great book to read before bed.

It also offers gentle reminders of what really matters most in this life and helps get me back on my right life track when I've slipped off.

Let Your Life Speak: Listening for the Voice of Vocation by Parker Palmer

Anything by Parker Palmer rocks my world. He's a profound thinker, speaker, and writer. I heard him speak at a local university a few years ago and his soulfulness was intoxicating. I immediately got all his books and each one is a gem. This one addresses the peaks and valleys of finding our true vocation. He also writes frankly about his battle with depression when he was in the not knowing "hallway" of life. A beautiful read by a beautiful man.

Overcoming Undereaming by Barbara Stanny

If you find yourself having a hard time asking clients for a raise or are consistently offering discounts, this book is for you.

Earn What You Deserve by Jerrold Mundis

This book is an easy, quick read and contains powerful information about how to thrive financially.

Pet Sitting for Profit by Patti Moran

Awww, nostalgia! This was the first business book I read when I started my pet business many years ago (and it was the only book for pet business owners out there at that time). Even though it was written years ago, it's a timeless classic that has been updated throughout the years to be relevant for today's pet sitter. It's filled with powerful tips for pet sitters and dog walkers.

Six-Figure Pet Sitting by Kristin Morrison

I wrote this book for pet sitters and dog walkers. A book reviewer for the National Association of Professional Pet Sitters (NAPPS) wrote: "Run–don't walk–to the nearest computer to order this book... and to have a business and a life–both! –that match your dreams." You can find the print version on Amazon and the eBook version on the Prosperous Pet Business website.

Six-Figure Pet Business by Kristin Morrison

This is basically the same information I wrote for pet sitters in Six-Figure Pet Sitting *(so if you have that book, don't get Six-Figure Pet Business, and vice versa). This book has a lot of the concepts of* Six-Figure Pet Sitting *and was written especially for dog trainers, pet groomers, and doggy day care owners. Steve Appellbaum from Animal Behavioral College (ABC) reviewed it and wrote, "As someone who started training dogs professionally in the late 70s, I remember a time when books on dog training were rare and those published were mostly* about breeds and/or dog shows. One area that has always been underrepresented is the subject of business. This lack of information creates a real challenge for the typical dog trainer. Not only does Six-Figure Pet Business *explain important business principles in an understandable fashion, it is replete with up-to-date tips designed to help dog trainers in the real world."* You can find the print version on Amazon and the eBook version on the Prosperous Pet Business website.

Sadie's Heart, Loving & Losing Our Cat Companions: A Story of Pet Love, Loss, & Grief Recovery
by Rita Reimers and Iris Goldman

Rita is a long-time pet sitting business owner with a deep affinity for cats. In this book, she describes her journey of losing a pet in a way that only someone who has been there can share. Makes a great gift for cat lovers and clients who have recently lost a cherished feline.

The Diamond Cutter: The Buddha on Managing Your Business and Your Life
by Geshe Michael Roach

If you want to incorporate spirituality into your finances, this book is for you. Here's what one Amazon reviewer had to say about this book: "A cross between the Dalai Lama's Ethics *and Stephen Covey's* 7 Habits *book,* The Diamond Cutter *will have you gardening a path to the bank."*

The Artist's Way by Julia Cameron

This is a book written for creatives, but I found it to also be a powerful book for cultivating creativity in business. This powerful book has been influential in cultivating my creative side (an often overlooked skill in business) as well as helping me get to the heart of why I want money (freedom to be with the people I love and to have plenty of time to do the things I love to do including travel for extended periods of time).

Busting Loose from the Money Game
by Robert Scheinfeld

Get ready for your mind to be blown. This book is a fascinating read. That's all I'm going to say about it. I don't want to give anything away! He's also written Busting Loose from the Business Game, *but start with this book first.*

About the Author:

Kristin Morrison started her pet care company in 1995 and it grew to be one of the largest pet care companies in California before she sold it eighteen years later. Kristin has provided pet business and life coaching for thousands of pet sitters, dog walkers, dog train-  ers, and other service-based pet business owners from across the United States, Canada, the UK, and Australia. In 2008 she founded Six-Figure Pet Sitting Academy™, which provides coaching, webinars, and business products for pet sitters and dog walkers. She also created Six-Figure Pet Business Academy™, for all service-based pet business owners including dog trainers, pet groomers, and dog daycare owners.

Kristin is a nationally recognized speaker at pet business conferences around the country. She hosts the annual Prosperous Pet Business Online Conference in addition to hosting the podcast Prosperous Pet Business, which can found on iTunes. Kristin wrote the books *Six-Figure Pet Sitting* and *Six-Figure Pet Business* in addition to the *Prosperous Pet Business: Interviews with the Experts* series.